AF443527

TENTH SCANDINAVIAN CONFERENCE
ON ARTIFICIAL INTELLIGENCE

Frontiers in Artificial Intelligence and Applications

FAIA covers all aspects of theoretical and applied artificial intelligence research in the form of monographs, doctoral dissertations, textbooks, handbooks and proceedings volumes. The FAIA series contains several sub-series, including "Information Modelling and Knowledge Bases" and "Knowledge-Based Intelligent Engineering Systems". It also includes the biennial ECAI, the European Conference on Artificial Intelligence, proceedings volumes, and other ECCAI – the European Coordinating Committee on Artificial Intelligence – sponsored publications. An editorial panel of internationally well-known scholars is appointed to provide a high quality selection.

Series Editors:
J. Breuker, R. Dieng-Kuntz, N. Guarino, J.N. Kok, J. Liu, R. López de Mántaras,
R. Mizoguchi, M. Musen, S.K. Pal and N. Zhong

Volume 173

Recently published in this series

ISSN 0922-6389

Tenth Scandinavian Conference on Artificial Intelligence

SCAI 2008

Edited by

Anders Holst

Swedish Institute of Computer Science, Sweden

Per Kreuger

Swedish Institute of Computer Science, Sweden

and

Peter Funk

Mälardalen University, Sweden

IOS

Press

Amsterdam • Berlin • Oxford • Tokyo • Washington, DC

ISBN 978-1-58603-867-0
Library of Congress Control Number: 2008926620

Publisher
IOS Press
Nieuwe Hemweg 6B
1013 BG Amsterdam
Netherlands
fax: +31 20 687 0019
e-mail: order@iospress.nl

Distributor in the UK and Ireland
Gazelle Books Services Ltd.
White Cross Mills
Hightown
Lancaster LA1 4XS
United Kingdom
fax: +44 1524 63232
e-mail: sales@gazellebooks.co.uk

Distributor in the USA and Canada
IOS Press, Inc.
4502 Rachael Manor Drive
Fairfax, VA 22032
USA
fax: +1 703 323 3668
e-mail: iosbooks@iospress.com

Tenth Scandinavian Conference on Artificial Intelligence
A. Holst et al. (Eds.)
IOS Press, 2008

v

Preface

The Tenth Scandinavian Conference on Artificial Intelligence continues a tradition of being one of the most important regional AI conferences in Europe.

This year's conference is organised by SICS, the Swedish Institute of Computer Science together with SAIS, the Swedish Artificial Intelligence Society. It is not only the tenth SCAI conference and 20th year SCAI anniversary but also the 25th anniversary for SAIS, and we are proud to celebrate this jubilee year with six special guest speakers and a three day conference. 51% of the papers submitted to the conference where accepted for oral presentation and 17% for poster presentation.

The topics of this years contributions have a broad range, from Machine Learning, Knowledge Representation, Robotics, Planning and Scheduling, Natural Language, Computer Vision, Search Algorithms, Industrial Applications, to Philosophical Foundations. These contributions exemplify the diversity of research in artificial intelligence today and confirm the achievement and magnitude of 25 years AI research in Scandinavia. It has also lead to a strong research community that is well integrated and multidisciplinary. We continue to cover a balance between theoretical research and valuable application results for use in business, medicine and industry and AI is an increasingly dynamic and interesting research area than ever before.

We are honoured to present invited speakers Kathleen A. McCormick, Ph.D., F.A.C.M.I, Chief Scientist/Vice President of SAIC in Health Solutions, USA; Manfred Jaeger, Associate Professor at Aalborg University, Denmark; Agnar Aamodt, Professor at Norwegian University of Science and Technology, Trondheim, Norway; Erik Sandewall, Professor at Linköping University, Sweden; Patrick Doherty, Professor at Linköping University, Sweden and Carl Gustaf Jansson, Professor at Stockholm University, Sweden.

The editors of this volume would like to thank the members of the Program Committee for their competent assessment of the contributed papers. We also like to thank the members of the Organising Committee, the SAIS Jubilee Committee and the SAIS Master's Thesis Award Committee. We are happy to also be able to introduce the winner of the SAIS Master's Thesis Award 2008, Malin Aktius from the University of Skövde.

We acknowledge the generous support of our industrial sponsors Google, Minst, Robotdalen, Volve AS and also the Swedish Institute of Computer Science whose support and economic warranty made this conference possible.

Stockholm, May 2008
Anders Holst
Per Kreuger
Peter Funk

Invited Speakers

Agnar Aamodt	Norwegian University of Science and Technology
Malin Aktius	University of Skövde, Sweden
Patrick Doherty	Linköping University, Sweden
Manfred Jaeger	Aalborg University, Denmark
Carl Gustaf Jansson	Stockholm University, Sweden
Kathleen A. McCormick	SAIC in Health Solutions, USA
Erik Sandewall	Linköping University, Sweden

Organising Committee

Anders Holst (Chair)	SICS
Peter Funk	Mälardalen University
Kersti Hedman	SICS
Per Kreuger (Program Chair)	SICS
Lars Mollberg (Jubilee Chair)	Ericsson
Vivian Vimarlund	Linköping University

Program Committee

Per Kreuger (Program Chair)	SICS, Sweden
Pekka Ala-Siuru	University of Oulu, Finland
Jarmo Alander	University of Vaasa, Finland
Jens Arnspang	Aalborg University Esbjerg, Denmark
Christian Balkenius	Lund University, Sweden
Henrik Boström	University of Skövde, Sweden
Torben Brauner	Roskilde University, Denmark
Joerg Cassens	Norwegian University of Science and Technology
Weiqin Chen	University of Bergen, Norway
Henning Christiansen	Roskilde University, Denmark
Paul Davidsson	Blekinge Institute of Technology, Sweden
Patrick Doherty	Linköping University, Sweden
Göran Falkman	University of Skövde, Sweden
Roar Fjellheim	University of Oslo, Norway
Peter Funk	Mälardalen University, Sweden
John Gallagher	Roskilde University, Denmark
John Hallam	University of Southern Denmark
Fredrik Heintz	Linköping University, Sweden
Timo Honkela	Helsinki University of Technology, Finland
Anders Holst	SICS
Eero Hyvönen	Helsinki University of Technology, Finland
Stefan Johansson	Blekinge Institute of Technology, Sweden
Lars Karlsson	Örebro University, Sweden
Terje Kristensen	Bergen University College, Norway
Ville Kyrki	Lappeenranta University of Technology, Finland

Anders Lansner	Royal Institute of Technology, Sweden
Jan Eric Larsson	Lund University, Sweden
Helge Langseth	Norwegian University of Science and Technology
Magnus Lie Hetland	Norwegian University of Science and Technology
Brian Mayoh	University of Aarhus, Denmark
Lars Mollberg	Ericsson, Sweden
Lars Niklasson	University of Skövde, Sweden
Djamila Ouelhadj	University of Nottingham, UK
Tomi A. Pasanen	University of Helsinki, Finland
Tapani Raiko	Helsinki University of Technology, Finland
Thorsteinn Rögnvaldsson	Halmstad University, Sweden
Juha Röning	University of Oulu, Finland
Lambert Spaanenburg	Lund University, Sweden
Kasper Stoy	University of Southern Denmark
Bjørnar Tessem	University of Bergen, Norway
Vivian Vimarlund	Linköping University, Sweden
Tom Ziemke	University of Skövde, Sweden

SAIS Jubilee Committee

Lars Mollberg (Chair)	Ericsson
Sture Hägglund	Linköping University
Fredrik Heintz	Linköping University

SAIS Master's Thesis Award Committee

Fredrik Heintz (Chair)	Linköping University Sweden
Henrik Boström	University of Skövde
Lars Karlsson	Örebro University

Sponsoring Institutions

This conference is supported by Google, Minst, Robotdalen, Volve AS, Ericsson, the Swedish Institute of Computer Science (SICS), Linköping University and Mälardalen University.

Contents

2. Poster Presentations

3. Invited Talks

1. Presented Papers

Tenth Scandinavian Conference on Artificial Intelligence
A. Holst et al. (Eds.)
IOS Press, 2008

The Observer Algorithm for Visibility Approximation

Per-Magnus OLSSON [a] and Patrick DOHERTY [a]

[a] *Department of Computer and Information Science. Linköping University*
{perol, patdo}@ida.liu.se

Abstract. We present a novel algorithm for visibility approximation that is substantially faster than ray casting based algorithms. The algorithm does not require extensive preprocessing or specialized hardware as most other algorithms do. We test this algorithm in several settings: rural, mountainous and urban areas, with different view ranges and grid cell sizes. By changing the size of the grid cells that the algorithm uses, it is possible to tailor the algorithm between speed and accuracy.

Keywords. Visibility, occlusion calculation, unmanned aerial vehicles, constrained path planning.

Introduction

We wish to perform visibility calculations as a part of a larger framework used for planning and simulating missions for unmanned aerial vehicles (UAVs). One part of the planning process is path planning where we search for a path between two positions. As the search is done in a graph which can cover large areas with arbitrary granularity, a large number of nodes might be used. We wish to calculate whether the nodes are visible from some positions, which can be the locations of our own personnel that the UAV should be visible to at all times or the locations of potential adversaries that we wish to stay out of sight from. When the node visibility has been calculated, it can be used when doing the path planning. This makes it possible to force a UAV to use a path that fulfills certain visibility constraints. The requirements make it difficult to use existing algorithms to determine visibility and this is the reason for developing an algorithm for visibility approximation.

1. Previous Work

In computer graphics, visibility calculations are used to determine what objects are visible and should be rendered on the screen. Frustum culling is used to remove (cull) the objects that are outside the viewer's field of view (frustum), from the rendering queue. Occlusion culling is used to remove the objects that are occluded by other objects and thus not visible. An example is the occlusion culling of a small object that is occluded by a larger object. A lot of research in computer graphics has been based on hierarchical spatial partitioning methods such as quadtrees, as well as potentially visible sets (PVS) and portals [1]. It is also common to use specialized graphics hardware to improve the performance of culling algorithms. Earlier work has mainly dealt with indoor environments due to the computational complexity of outdoor environments. Occluders and occluder shadows has previously been used in an algorithm to determine visibility [2]. Good results were achieved for urban environments if the occluders could be determined in advance. The requirements on the occluder makes it is difficult to use the algorithm in a non urban environment. A survey of different visibility algorithms in computer graphics is provided in [3]. Most of these require either extensive preprocessing and/or specialized graphics hardware.

In the area of robotics, visibility is often used as a means to calculate areas that have low visibility. Several algorithms for visibility calculations in 2D environments have been devised [4]. These have been used in settings where a robot tries to avoid being seen by one or more sentries while moving to a goal position. Algorithms for finding a covert paths in the presence of stationary and moving sentries has been devised by [5] [6]. An approximate visibility algorithm was devised and used in a simulated environment [6]. That algorithm requires means of finding the visibility in some different directions, and uses that data to get an approximate visibility measure in all other directions.

A ray casting algorithm shoots an infinitely thin ray from the start position to the goal position. As the ray is moved towards the goal, it is checked for intersection with objects in the environment [1]. Ray casting algorithms are often used in Geographic Information Systems (GIS). GIS are performing visibility calculations to determine what is visible from a certain location. Few companies are willing to disclose information about how this is done, but it is believed that these calculations are performed with massive amounts of ray casting [7]. Often a ray for every 0.1 degrees is used, which often results in poor performance due to the amount of calculations that have to be performed. GIS systems normally calculate visibility to certain positions in a horizontal plane and positions outside the plane are omitted. Ray casting algorithms work directly on the polygons that model the world and the objects. In games and simulators, the amount of polygons used to model the environment has increased steadily for several years and the increase is expected to continue in the future. Consequently the time spent ray casting is also expected to increase as environments get more complex and detailed. As the ray casting algorithm is exact, it will give the correct answer as long as all objects are included in the intersection checking. An often neglected implication of using a fixed number of ray casts to calculate visibility in circles is that as the distance from the originating point increases, the distance between the individual rays also increase and the resemblance between the visibility calculated by the rays and the actual visibility decreases.

2. The Observer Visibility Algorithm

In this section we present a new approximating visibility algorithm called the Observer algorithm.

2.1. Motivation

In our research laboratory we have several applications that are used in our research in the area of unmanned aerial vehicles [8]. One of these applications is used for mission planning. In this application we visualize the environment including terrain, buildings and other objects. The terrain consists of a height field with superimposed meshes for buildings and other objects. A grid with square grid cells is placed in a top down view of the world. The grid cell is considered to have the same elevation value in the whole cell, and this value is determined by sampling the height field in the middle of the cell. As grid cells are considered atomic and are the smallest entities used in calculations, we consider grid cells as either visible or not visible.

In this setting we want to determine the visibility from some position in all directions on the ground as well as in the air. Due to the large amount of ray casts that are necessary to determine visibility in all directions, and the potentially very large number of polygons used in modeling the environment, it is not always feasible to use ray casting methods. The algorithm must be able to handle both rural and urban terrain in different scales without time consuming precalculations or dependence on specialized hardware. Even at low resolution, the amount of memory required to store preprocessed data would be prohibitively large, and thus we can not depend on preprocessing. As most existing algorithms can not be used and we can accept the use of an approximate algorithm, we set out to formulate a new algorithm.

2.2. Algorithm Formulation

To represent what is visible from a certain position, we introduce the concept of an *observer* . The observer is an abstract entity that can represent a human, or any other entity for which we can measure the field of view (FOV). The observer has a position, heading and pitch. Other parameters are maximum view range as well as horizontal and vertical FOV. The horizontal FOV is centered around the heading, and similarly the vertical FOV is centered around the pitch. If there are no intersecting objects and the horizontal field of view is 360 degrees and the vertical field of view is 180 degrees, a sphere is formed around the viewer's position. As the observer is positioned in the middle of the sphere, all calculations should start in the middle and continue outwards toward the circumference. As a sphere forms a circle when viewed in two dimensions, we can calculate the grid cells in a horizontal plane, and then calculate the values for top and bottom of the FOV each cell.

This also allows us to take advantage of the fact that the terrain generally is 2.5D, i.e. a height field where each (x, z) coordinate pair corresponds to a single y-value. We rely on the fact that buildings and other objects can be seen as being a part of the height field when using an orthonormal projection. We wish to use a higher level representation of the world, so we use grid cells and store the elevation for each cell in a tessellated height field.

With the intuition in mind about an observer's FOV being a sphere, an algorithm was devised to work accordingly. The algorithm consists of three parts. The first part calculates the set of grid cells that make up the circumference of the observer's view range, adjusted for the edges of the simulated world and the observer's horizontal FOV. This can be done for example using Bresenham's circle algorithm [9] which is used here. The circle algorithm calculates the coordinates for points along the circle's circumference. The points are checked to determine if they are inside the grid as well as inside the observer's horizontal FOV. If a point is not inside the observer's FOV, it is discarded. If a point is not inside the grid, it replaced by the closest point that is inside the grid in the direction towards the observer.

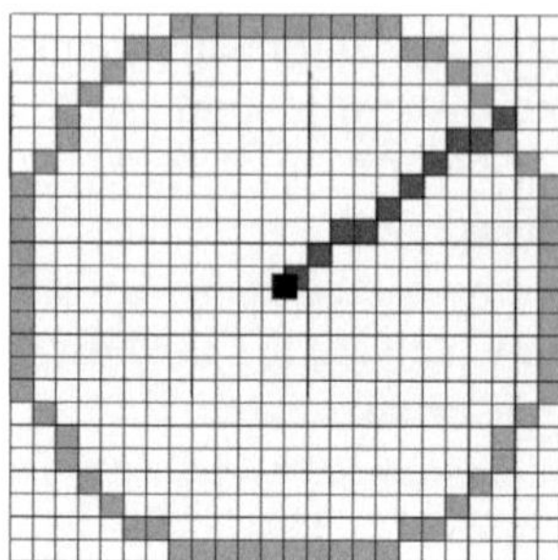

Figure 1. Schematic view of the circumference cells and traversal along a line, starting from the observer in the middle, marked as a black square.

The second part of the algorithm determines which grid cells are visible along a straight line from the observer to a grid cell located at the circumference of the view field. The grid cells from the first part of the algorithm are used here, as they represent the edge of view field. A general line drawing algorithm is used here, to determine which cells are covered, and we use a modified version of the Bresenham line algorithm [9]. The grid cells are traversed from the observer's position and outward towards the edge of the view field circumference along the grid cells determined by the line algorithm. As the line drawing algorithm is discrete, it will go through a number of grid cells along the traversal. These potentially visible cells are further analyzed in the final part of the algorithm. An overview of the first two parts of the algorithm is shown in figure 1.

The third part is performed for each potentially visible grid cell, where the values for the top and bottom of the view field are calculated for each cell. Depending on the terrain height and the values of the FOV, three possible cases exist:

- If the top of the FOV is less or equal to the grid cell's height, the grid cell is set to be blocked, as the object in the grid cell is higher than the FOV. Thus the grid cell is not visible and the analysis along this line is terminated.
- If the bottom of the FOV is above the grid cell height, the grid cell is marked as not visible, as the FOV is entirely above the height in the grid cell.
- If the bottom of the FOV is equal to or below the grid cell height, the grid cell is marked visible and the equation for the bottom of the FOV is set to match the height in the grid cell.

A schematic picture of the three cases is shown in figure 2. If the grid cell is either not visible as the height in the grid cell is below the view field or the grid cell is visible, the analysis continues along the line. When the visibility for all grid cells along a line has been calculated, the process is repeated along the next line. As this is done, the new line will sometimes go through grid cells that have their visibility already calculated. In that case, the old values are copied and the analysis continues. The output of the algorithm is a matrix showing the visibility for all grid cells within view range at ground level, as well as the maximum and minimum height values for the field of view in all non blocked grid cells.

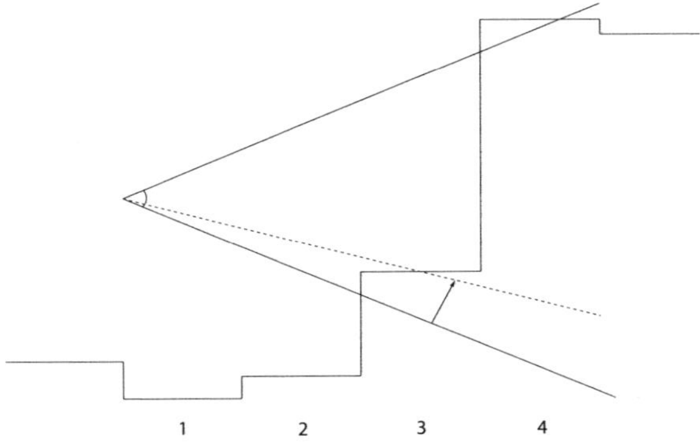

Figure 2. View of the third part of the visibility calculations, depicting the three cases. The first two cells are not visible, the third one is visible and the bottom of the field of view is adjusted to match the height of the third cell. The fourth cell is blocked as the object in the cell is higher than the top of the field of view.

2.3. Algorithm Pseudo Code

Line (1) makes up the first part and lines (2) - (3) are the second part. The third part consists of lines (4) - (14).

```
(1)   circumferenceCells = GetCircumferenceCells(observer pos, observer FOV);
(2)   for all circumferenceCells
(3)      lineCells = GetLineCells(observer pos, circumferenceCell);
(4)      for all lineCells
(5)         CalculateFOV(lineCell pos);
(6)         if FOV top <= lineCell height
(7)            lineCell visibility := blocked;
(8)            break for loop;
(9)         else if FOV bottom > lineCell height
(10)           lineCell visibility := not visible;
(11)        else if FOV bottom <= lineCell height
(12)           lineCell visibility := visible;
(13)           AdjustFOV(lineCell pos);
(14)        endif
(15)     endfor
(16) endfor
```

2.4. Theoretical Properties

For an observer with a 360 degree horizontal and 180 degree vertical FOV, where the FOV forms a sphere around the observer, the time complexity is $O(n^2)$, where n is the number of grid cells along an observer's view range. At each step, positions for top and bottom of the view field are calculated, which is $O(1)$. A ray casting algorithm needs to perform $O(n^3)$ ray casts to determine the visibility of the volumes in a sphere. Also, the operations performed are different for the two algorithms, which make a large difference in practice.

3. Results

A series of tests were run to determine the performance of the algorithm. As the algorithm is approximate, we investigated how accurate it was compared to a ray casting algorithm and the time it took to perform the calculations.

3.1. Test Setup

For testing in a rural area, we used height data measuring 1100*900 meters in which the height data was used to create a height field. The elevations from buildings and other objects in the area were included in the height field. A tessellated height field was created, with square grid cells, whose cell sizes are shown in the tables 1 - 6. The grid cells form the base for cubic grid volumes, with all sides of equal length. A mountainous area was created by scaling the elevation of the rural terrain by a factor of 15, yielding elevations up to 600 m. For testing in an urban setting, we used a 1000*1000 m urban area with several large buildings, up to 300 m high. In all cases, the visibility was restricted to a maximum height of 500 m above the lowest point in the height field.

Within the volume 100 random positions were generated. All positions were required to be at least 40 m away from each other, and an observer was placed at each position. All observers had a 360 degree horizontal and 180 degree vertical FOV. The view range was changed between the tests, 100 m and 200 m were used. When all positions had been generated, the visibility algorithm was executed including creating all observers and calculating the visible grid cells.

For comparison, a ray casting method was used. The ray casting algorithm was taken from the Open Dynamics Engine [10] which is a high performance physics engine. From each position, the set of potentially visible grid volumes was determined, using position and view range. A ray cast was made from the observer's position to an end position in the middle of each grid volume. If no object was intersected between the starting position and the end position, the grid cell was judged to be visible. The set of visible volumes calculated by the ray casting algorithm was compared to the set of visible volumes calculated using the observer visibility algorithm. All tests were run on an Intel Core2Duo 2.4GHz processor running Debian Linux. The calculations were performed once and the results are shown in tables 1-6.

3.2. Quality Measure

As the observer algorithm is approximate, we compare the result of the calculated visibility with the exact ray casting method. For each position, the sets of visible grid volumes are calculated using both methods and compared. If a grid volume is visible to both methods, it is judged "Correct". If it is only visible to the observer algorithm, it is judged "False Positive" and if it is only visible to the ray casting algorithm it is "False Negative". The tables show the fractions of grid volumes in each category.

3.3. Test Results

The difference between doing intersection test on triangles versus the tessellated height field becomes more apparent with the longer view range and smaller grid size, and the difference in time is expected to continue to increase as view ranges are further increased

Table 1. Measures for algorithms in a rural setting using 100 m view range.

Cell size [m]	Time [s]		Quality		
	Observer	Ray casting	Correct	False Positive	False Negative
5	0.66	246.93	0.8915	1.8E-4	0.1084
10	0.09	32.84	0.8111	2.9E-4	0.1886
15	0.03	12.19	0.7439	5.3E-4	0.2555
20	0.02	5.78	0.7390	2.8E-4	0.2608
30	< 0.01	2.06	0.6897	0	0.3103
40	< 0.01	0.88	0.5922	0.0011	0.4067

Table 2. Measures for algorithms in a rural setting using 200 m view range.

Cell size [m]	Time [s]		Quality		
	Observer	Ray casting	Correct	False Positive	False Negative
5	6.43	7547	0.9290	4.1E-4	0.0706
10	0.58	953.4	0.8989	6.4E-4	0.1005
15	0.16	335.81	0.8702	0.0012	0.1286
20	0.07	151.15	0.8245	8.5E-4	0.1746
30	0.02	50.36	0.7629	2.3E-4	0.2369
40	0.02	18.43	0.7543	0.022	0.2435

Table 3. Measures for algorithms in a mountain setting using 100 m view range.

Cell size [m]	Time [s]		Quality		
	Observer	Ray casting	Correct	False Positive	False Negative
5	0.62	2859	0.8804	0.0165	0.1032
10	0.09	402.42	0.7991	0.0236	0.1773
15	0.03	132.73	0.7366	0.0241	0.2393
20	0.02	62.86	0.7251	0.0283	0.2466
30	< 0.01	21.94	0.6768	0.0335	0.2897
40	< 0.01	11.53	0.5898	0.0284	0.3817

and grid cell sizes are decreased. From tables 1, 3 and 5 we can see that execution time for the Observer algorithm is very similar despite very different kinds of terrain. The same applies for tables 2, 4 and 6. The correspondence with the ray casting algorithm improves as grid cell sizes decrease, which is to be expected as the grid cells used for storing the height values is smaller and more information is stored. Although the algorithm here is approximate, it yields good results quickly when the grid cells are small. The algorithm is approximately correct and is used to calculate visibility constrained paths, and we can rely on a priori collision detection calculations and on board proximity sensors to avoid any potential obstacles that might have been neglected by the algorithm.

Both the quality and the performance with respect to time is good when used with grid cells that are among the smaller of the grid cell sizes tested here, and it is feasible to use the observer algorithm for real time visibility calculations in our application area where the view ranges used sometimes are longer than tested here. We consider this algorithm an alternative to existing ray casting based algorithms, especially since it is possible for a user to choose between speed and accuracy by changing the cell size.

Table 4. Measures for algorithms in a mountain setting using 200 m view range.

Cell size [m]	Time [s]		Quality		
	Observer	Ray casting	Correct	False Positive	False Negative
5	5.77	71274	0.9053	0.0295	0.0653
10	0.52	9413	0.8617	0.0451	0.0932
15	0.14	2927	0.8296	0.0545	0.1159
20	0.06	1325.66	0.7838	0.0585	0.1577
30	0.02	427.27	0.7253	0.0695	0.2052
40	0.02	198.32	0.7132	0.0748	0.2120

Table 5. Measures for algorithms in an urban setting using 100 m view range.

Cell size [m]	Time [s]		Quality		
	Observer	Ray casting	Correct	False Positive	False Negative
5	0.66	1646.82	0.8434	9.3E-4	0.1556
10	0.09	235.19	0.7661	0.0018	0.2321
15	0.03	75.09	0.7001	0.0027	0.2972
20	0.02	35.85	0.6916	0.0035	0.3048
30	<0.01	12.83	0.6332	0.0073	0.3595
40	<0.01	7.22	0.5504	0.0089	0.4407

Table 6. Measures for algorithms in an urban setting using 200 m view range.

Cell size [m]	Time [s]		Quality		
	Observer	Ray casting	Correct	False Positive	False Negative
5	6.61	44377	0.8757	0.0016	0.1227
10	0.59	5960	0.8453	0.0034	0.1513
15	0.15	1826	0.8140	0.0054	0.1806
20	0.07	822	0.7714	0.0063	0.2223
30	0.02	271.59	0.7008	0.0091	0.2901
40	0.02	131.36	0.6960	0.0160	0.2880

4. Future Work

If the grid cells are too large to handle small objects, or these objects are not located where the ground is sampled, these are not taken into consideration by the algorithm. This is because they are not large enough to make an impression when sampling the height field, and they are thus not included in the visibility calculations. If the small objects are not included in the calculations this leads to overestimation of visibility and this can be decreased by sampling the height values in several positions in each grid cell, and using the highest found value for the whole cell. This will decrease the amount of "False Positive" but can also increase the "False Negatives".

Occasionally the visibility for some cell may not be calculated because no line will go through that cell, depending on which line traversal algorithm is used. This will leave gaps in the calculations which can be remedied by adding extra cells along the circumference and calculate visibility along lines ending with these cells as normal.

As described here, the algorithm can not handle a terrain that is three dimensional. This can be improved by storing all occurring height values for the cells. When the observer's FOV intersects such cell with several height values, it would be split into several FOVs and each one would have to be handled separately.

5. Conclusion

We have presented a algorithm for visibility approximation that is a substantial speed up compared to ray casting based algorithms. It differs from many other visibility algorithms as it does not require extensive preprocessing or specialized hardware. As the algorithm does not depend on the polygons that model the world, the performance can be expected to be good even when used in complex and detailed environments. Despite the simplicity of the algorithm it yields good results in different terrains as well as with different grid resolutions. It differs from other algorithms as it is possible to choose between speed and accuracy. Testing has been performed in a framework for UAV mission planning, where it enables real time visibility calculations from several positions and with varying parameters. In our application, the resulting visibility data is used as input to a path planning algorithm, enabling real time calculation of paths that fulfill certain visibility constraints.

Acknowledgements

We wish to thank Kaj Holmberg, Department of Mathematics, Linköping University for the environment used for testing in the urban setting. This work is supported in part by the National Aeronautics Research Program NFFP04 S4203 and the Strategic Research Center MOVIII, founded by the Swedish Foundation for Strategic Research, SSF.

References

[1]　D. Hearn and P. Baker, *Computer Graphics with OpenGL*, Prentice-Hall, 2003.

[2]　P. Wonka, Occlusion Culling for Real-Time Rendering of Urban Environments, *Institute of Computer Graphics, Vienna University of Technology*, 2001.

[3]　D. Cohen-Or and Y. Chrysanthou and C.T. Silva and F. Durand, A Survey of Visibility for Walkthrough Algorithms, *Transactions on Visualization and Computer Graphics* **9(3)** (2003), 412-431.

[4]　M. Marzouqi and R. A. Jarvis, *Covert Robotics: Covert Path Planning for Autonomous Robot Navigation in Known Environments*, Proceedings of the Australasian Conference on Robotics and Automation, 2003.

[5]　A.Y. Teng and D. DeMenthon and L.S. Davis, Stealth Terrain Navigation, *IEEE Transactions on Systems, Man and Cybernetics* **23(1)** (1993), 96-110.

[6]　M. Marzouqi and R. A. Jarvis, *Fast Visibility Evaluation for Covert Robotics Path Planning*, Proceedings of the IEEE International Workshop in Safety, Security and Rescue Robotics, 2005.

[7]　S. Rana, *Development of ray tracing algorithms in GIS for urban visibility analysis*, presented at the 2006 Meeting of the Association of American Geographers, 7-11 March 2006.

[8]　P. Doherty and P. Haslum and F. Heintz and T. Merz and P. Nyblom and T. Persson and B. Wingman, *A Distributed Architecture for Autonomous Unmanned Aerial Vehicle Experimentation*, Proceedings of the 7th International Symposium on Distributed Autonomous Systems, 2004.

[9]　J. Bresenham, Algorithm for computer control of a digital plotter, *IBM Systems journal* **4(1)** (1965), 25-30.

[10]　Open Dynamics Engine, http://www.ode.org.

Tenth Scandinavian Conference on Artificial Intelligence
A. Holst et al. (Eds.)
IOS Press, 2008

Efficient AUC Maximization with Regularized Least-Squares

Tapio PAHIKKALA [a], Antti AIROLA [a], Hanna SUOMINEN [a], Jorma BOBERG [a], and Tapio SALAKOSKI [a]

[a] *Turku Centre for Computer Science (TUCS), Department of Information Technology, University of Turku, Turku, Finland, firstname.lastname@utu.fi*

Abstract.
Area under the receiver operating characteristics curve (AUC) is a popular measure for evaluating the quality of binary classifiers, and intuitively, machine learning algorithms that maximize an approximation of AUC should have a good AUC performance when classifying new examples. However, designing such algorithms in the framework of kernel methods has proven to be challenging. In this paper, we address AUC maximization with the regularized least-squares (RLS) algorithm also known as the least-squares support vector machine. First, we introduce RLS-type binary classifier that maximizes an approximation of AUC and has a closed-form solution. Second, we show that this AUC-RLS algorithm is computationally as efficient as the standard RLS algorithm that maximizes an approximation of the accuracy. Third, we compare the performance of these two algorithms in the task of assigning topic labels for newswire articles in terms of AUC. Our algorithm outperforms the standard RLS in every classification experiment conducted. The performance gains are most substantial when the distribution of the class labels is unbalanced. In conclusion, modifying the RLS algorithm to maximize the approximation of AUC does not increase the computational complexity, and this alteration enhances the quality of the classifier.

1. Introduction

Classification problems constitute a typical supervised machine learning task domain, where the aim is to construct algorithms which predict for each input instance the class or classes to which it belongs. In binary classification, the task is to judge for every input instance whether it has a certain property (a positive example) or not (a negative example), and assign exactly one of two possible class labels accordingly. The task is often solved by mapping the input instances on a real-valued scale; the larger (smaller) the image is, the more confident the classifier is about the instance being a positive (negative) example. The binary output is then constructed by setting a threshold which divides the instances into positive and negative examples.

Evaluating the ability of the classifier to predict the class labels correctly is essential. Various criteria for this classification performance exist, and in performance evaluation, one must select a measure that reflects the chosen criterion. In binary classification, selecting the area under the receiver operating characteristics curve (AUC) measure has been recommended (see, e.g., [1,2,3]).

AUC corresponds to the probability that given a randomly chosen positive and negative example, the classifier will correctly distinguish them. Because AUC is calculated directly from the real-valued output, it has the potential to describe the classification performance in more detail than measures requiring a fixed threshold: if the performance of the classifier is measured by comparing only its binary output with the correct classification, the value of the performance evaluation measure may strongly depend on the threshold placement. Another advantage of AUC is its invariance to the distribution of class labels [4].

The desire for using AUC in performance evaluation has naturally led to the design of algorithms that aim to maximize AUC. In the framework of support vector machines, this task has proven to be challenging (see, e.g., [5,6,7]): The need to consider all positive-negative example pairs instead of individual examples easily leads to too expensive computations, and hence, approximative heuristics have had to be used to reduce the computational complexity. Moreover, the performance gains have often been modest, or not statistically significant.

In this paper, we address AUC maximization with the regularized least-squares (RLS) algorithm, also known as the least-squares support vector machine [8]. The standard RLS algorithm maximizes an approximation of the classification accuracy (ACC), that is, the proportion of correctly classified examples. It has been shown to achieve a classification performance similar to the regular support vector machines [9].

In our recent study [10], we introduced a RLS-based ranking algorithm that we call RankRLS, and applied it to the task of pairwise ranking of data points in information retrieval tasks. Although the number of possible data point pairs in such tasks grows quadratically with respect to the number of the individual data points, the computational complexity of the RankRLS algorithm was shown to be equal to the standard RLS regression. A similar algorithm was independently proposed by [11]. As the problem of AUC maximization can be naturally cast into the problem of comparing positive-negative data point pairs, RLS is a particularly suitable basis for developing an efficient AUC maximizing classifier.

Here, we introduce the AUC-RLS algorithm that maximizes regularized least-squares approximation of AUC for binary classification. It is based on the same approach as RankRLS. We show that AUC-RLS preserves the computational efficiency of the standard RLS algorithm, and outperforms RLS in maximizing AUC in testing.

2. Accuracy and Area Under ROC Curve

Let $\mathcal{X}$ be the input space that can be any set and let $\mathcal{Y} = \{1, -1\}$ be the output space. We call the set of possible input-output pairs $\mathcal{Z} = \mathcal{X} \times \mathcal{Y}$ the example space. We say that $z = (x, y) \in \mathcal{Z}$ is a positive example if $y = 1$. Otherwise z is a negative example. Further, let us denote $\mathbb{R}^{\mathcal{X}} = \{f : \mathcal{X} \to \mathbb{R}\}$, and let $\mathcal{H} \subseteq \mathbb{R}^{\mathcal{X}}$ be the hypothesis space. In supervised learning, we are given a number of training examples with known class labels that we use to select a hypothesis from $\mathcal{H}$ for prediction of the outputs of unseen examples. Formally, let $X = (x_1, \ldots, x_m) \in (\mathcal{X}^m)^{\mathrm{T}}$ to be a sequence of inputs, where $(\mathcal{X}^m)^{\mathrm{T}}$ denotes the set of row vectors of size m whose elements belong to $\mathcal{X}$. Further, we define $Y = (y_1, \ldots, y_m)^{\mathrm{T}} \in \mathcal{Y}^m$ to be a sequence of the corresponding output values. We also denote $z_i = (x_i, y_i), 1 \leq i \leq m$. Together, X and Y form a training set $S = (X, Y)$.

We now consider the performance measures that we use to evaluate how well the hypotheses perform in a prediction task. In the following measure definitions, we use the training data, but the measures can, of course, be analogously defined for any sequence of data points. The error rate indicates the proportion of correctly classified data points. Formally, the error rate of f measured with X and Y is

$$p_{\mathrm{ERR}}(Y, f(X)) = \frac{1}{m} \sum_{i=1}^{m} \frac{1}{2} |y_i - \mathrm{sign}(f(x_i))|, \tag{1}$$

where $f(X) = (f(x_1), \ldots, f(x_m))^{\mathrm{T}} \in \mathbb{R}^m$, and sign is the signum function. The constant $\frac{1}{m}$ is a normalizer ensuring that the result is always between 0 and 1. The ACC performance measure can be simply defined as $p_{\mathrm{ACC}}(Y, f(X)) = 1 - p_{\mathrm{ERR}}(Y, f(X))$.

The AUC measure, in turn, can be calculated from the following formula which is also called the Wilcoxon-Mann-Whitney statistic:

$$p_{\mathrm{AUC}}(S, f(X)) = \frac{1}{m_+ m_-} \sum_{y_i=+1, y_j=-1} \frac{1}{2}(1 + \mathrm{sign}(f(x_i) - f(x_j))),$$

where m_+ and m_- are the numbers of positive and negative examples, respectively (see [12] for a proof). Analogously, we also define a measure area over ROC curve (AOC) whose optimum is at 0 instead of 1:

$$p_{\mathrm{AOC}}(S, f(X)) = \frac{1}{m_+ m_-} \sum_{y_i=+1, y_j=-1} \frac{1}{2}(1 - \mathrm{sign}(f(x_i) - f(x_j))) \tag{2}$$

$$= \frac{1}{m_+ m_-} \sum_{y_i=+1, y_j=-1} \frac{1}{2}(\mathrm{sign}(y_i - y_j) - \mathrm{sign}(f(x_i) - f(x_j))),$$

where we have also written the expression $\mathrm{sign}(y_i - y_j)$ which is equal to 1, to emphasize that our aim is not to classify individual data points but pairs of them. Clearly, $p_{\mathrm{AOC}}(S, f(X)) = 1 - p_{\mathrm{AUC}}(S, f(X))$, and hence, when we aim to find a hypothesis that maximizes AUC, we can select the one minimizing AOC.

3. RLS and AUC-RLS Algorithms

Following [13], we consider algorithms for hypothesis selection in the framework of regularized kernel methods consisting of a cost function and a regularizer. The cost functions, that are usually approximations of the performance measures, indicate how large error a hypothesis has with respect to the training set. The purpose of the regularizer is to penalize too complex hypotheses that overfit at the training phase, and thus are not able to generalize to unseen data. In the framework, the hypothesis space $\mathcal{H}$ is so-called reproducing kernel Hilbert space determined by a positive definite kernel function k. Then, the learning algorithm that selects the hypothesis f from $\mathcal{H}$ is defined as

$$\mathcal{A}(S) = \operatorname*{argmin}_{f \in \mathcal{H}} J(f),$$

where

$$J(f) = c(f(X), Y) + \lambda\|f\|_k^2, \tag{3}$$

c is a real valued cost function, $\lambda \in \mathbb{R}_+$ is a regularization parameter, and $\| \cdot \|_k$ is the norm in $\mathcal{H}$. By the generalized representer theorem [13], the minimizer of (3) has the following form:

$$f(x) = \sum_{i=1}^{m} a_i k(x, x_i), \tag{4}$$

where $a_i \in \mathbb{R}$ and k is the kernel function associated with the reproducing kernel Hilbert space mentioned above. For the training set, we define the symmetric $m \times m$ kernel matrix K to be a matrix whose elements are $K_{i,j} = k(x_i, x_j)$. For simplicity, we also assume that K is strictly positive definite. This can be ensured, for example, by performing a small diagonal shift. Using this notation, we rewrite $f(X) = KA$ and $\|f\|_k^2 = A^\mathrm{T} K A$ where $A = (a_1, \ldots, a_m)^\mathrm{T}$.

A natural way to minimize the training error would be to directly use the error rate (1) as a cost function. Similarly, when we aim to maximize AUC, the corresponding cost function to be minimized would be AOC (2). However, it is well-known that the use of this type of cost functions leads to intractable optimization problems. Therefore, instead of using (1) and (2), we use functions approximating them. For the error rate (1), we use the following type of least-squares approximation

$$c(Y, f(X)) = \sum_{i=1}^{m} (y_i - f(x_i))^2, \tag{5}$$

that is, the sum of least-squares errors made on each training example. Analogously for AOC (2), we use the following type of least-squares approximation

$$c(Y, f(X)) = \sum_{y_i=+1, y_j=-1} (y_i - y_j - f(x_i) + f(x_j))^2. \tag{6}$$

This cost function can be interpreted as least-squares error of regressing the label differences $y_i - y_j$ with the prediction differences $f(x_i) - f(x_j)$. We used a similar approach in [10], where a least-squares based cost function that compared all the the query-document pairs related to the same query was proposed for ranking tasks in document retrieval.

By substituting (5) into (3), we get the standard RLS algorithm whose solution can be obtained from

$$A = (K + \lambda I)^{-1} Y, \tag{7}$$

where A determines (4) [9]. The solution (7) can be obtained by inverting a $m \times m$ matrix with computational complexity $O(m^3)$. On the other hand, substituting (6) into (3) provides us an AUC maximization method we call AUC-RLS whose solution is

$$A = (LK + \lambda I)^{-1} LY, \tag{8}$$

where L is a $m \times m$ matrix, whose entries are defined as

$$L_{i,j} = \begin{cases} m_- & \text{when } i = j \wedge y_i = 1 \\ m_+ & \text{when } i = j \wedge y_i = -1 \\ -1 & \text{when } y_i \neq y_j \\ 0 & \text{otherwise} \end{cases}, \tag{9}$$

where m_+ and m_- are the numbers of positive and negative examples, respectively.

The calculation of the solution (8) requires multiplications and inversions of $m \times m$ matrices. Both types of operations are usually performed with methods whose computational complexities are $O(m^3)$, and hence the complexity of AUC-RLS is equal to the complexity of the standard RLS.

4. Primal Form of AUC-RLS

For such cases where there are very large amounts of training data available, the cubic complexity of AUC-RLS training can be prohibitive. In the literature, the problem of finding a minimizer for (3) is known as the dual formulation. We next derive the primal form of the AUC-RLS algorithm that is applicable whenever the linear kernel is used. Similarly to the standard version of the RLS, the primal form is computationally more efficient than the dual form in cases where the dimensionality of the feature space is smaller than the number of training examples. This is formally shown below.

First, we assume a situation where the data points can be represented as real valued vectors whose dimension h corresponds to the dimensionality of the feature space, that is, $\mathcal{X} = \mathbb{R}^h$. Further, we assume that $h < m$. Now, the sequence of inputs can be written as a matrix $X \in \mathbb{R}^{h \times m}$. If we consider only the linear kernel, the function (4) minimizing (3) can be equivalently expressed as

$$f(x) = x^\mathrm{T} X A = x^\mathrm{T} w, \tag{10}$$

where $w = XA$ denotes the normal vector of the hyperplane that determines the RLS solution. The vector, as we have shown in [10], can be obtained from

$$w = (XLX^\mathrm{T} + \lambda I)^{-1} XLY. \tag{11}$$

Calculating (11) involves matrix multiplications of $O(hm^2)$ complexity. However, we can speed up the calculation in the following way.

Without losing generality, we can re-index the training examples so that the indices $1, \ldots, m_+$ are assigned to the positive and the indices $m_+ + 1, \ldots, m$ to the negative examples. Now the corresponding L can be decomposed into $L = D - PQ$, where D is a diagonal matrix whose diagonal elements are given as $D_{i,i} = L_{i,i}$ and P and Q are defined as

$$P = \begin{pmatrix} \mathbf{1}_{m_+ \times 1} & \mathbf{0}_{m_+ \times 1} \\ \mathbf{0}_{m_- \times 1} & \mathbf{1}_{m_- \times 1} \end{pmatrix}, Q = \begin{pmatrix} \mathbf{0}_{1 \times m_+} & \mathbf{1}_{1 \times m_-} \\ \mathbf{1}_{1 \times m_+} & \mathbf{0}_{1 \times m_-} \end{pmatrix}.$$

Now (11) can be re-written as

$$w = ((XD)X^{\mathrm{T}} - (XP)(QX^{\mathrm{T}}) + \lambda I)^{-1}(X(DY) - X(P(QY))). \qquad (12)$$

The computational complexity of the matrix inversion is $O(h^3)$. The multiplication $(XD)X^{\mathrm{T}}$ can be performed in $O(h^2 m)$ time. All other matrix operations in (12) have lower computational complexity. Thus the resulting overall complexity of primal AUC-RLS is $O(h^3 + h^2 m)$, making the method preferable to the dual version whenever m is considerably larger than h.

5. Experiments

We evaluated the capability of the AUC-RLS algorithm to maximize AUC on a real world dataset by considering a well-known text classification problem: the assignment

Table 1. Comparison of the performance of the AUC-RLS and RLS algorithms in terms of AUC on the Reuters-21578 dataset. In the first column is the name of the predicted class and in the next two are the AUC-values for the tested algorithms with 95% confidence intervals in parentheses. The last two present the numbers of positive examples in the training set of 500 documents and test set of 12397 documents.

class	AUC-RLS	RLS	pos. train set	pos. test set
acq	0.980 (0.978–0.983)	0.979 (0.977–0.982)	94	2275
bop	0.966 (0.947–0.985)	0.880 (0.843–0.917)	4	101
cocoa	0.931 (0.891–0.970)	0.837 (0.776–0.899)	2	71
coffee	0.969 (0.948–0.990)	0.962 (0.950–0.975)	5	134
corn	0.970 (0.959–0.982)	0.950 (0.936–0.964)	11	226
cpi	0.947 (0.925–0.969)	0.601 (0.555–0.648)	3	94
crude	0.976 (0.969–0.982)	0.975 (0.969–0.982)	23	555
dlr	0.971 (0.961–0.981)	0.946 (0.926–0.965)	10	165
earn	0.994 (0.993–0.995)	0.993 (0.991–0.994)	158	3806
gnp	0.987 (0.981–0.993)	0.923 (0.891–0.956)	5	131
gold	0.970 (0.953–0.986)	0.922 (0.897–0.948)	4	120
grain	0.979 (0.973–0.985)	0.974 (0.968–0.980)	23	559
interest	0.965 (0.956–0.974)	0.952 (0.941–0.962)	19	459
livestock	0.701 (0.642–0.761)	0.637 (0.578–0.696)	3	96
money-fx	0.954 (0.946–0.962)	0.947 (0.938–0.957)	28	689
money-supply	0.949 (0.930–0.968)	0.907 (0.877–0.937)	7	165
nat-gas	0.957 (0.933–0.981)	0.941 (0.920–0.962)	5	100
oilseed	0.898 (0.877–0.919)	0.816 (0.783–0.849)	6	165
reserves	0.943 (0.908–0.977)	0.511 (0.458–0.564)	2	71
ship	0.949 (0.934–0.963)	0.925 (0.907–0.942)	13	273
soybean	0.876 (0.839–0.913)	0.805 (0.757–0.853)	4	107
sugar	0.985 (0.979–0.991)	0.964 (0.952–0.976)	6	156
trade	0.978 (0.970–0.986)	0.969 (0.960–0.977)	20	466
veg-oil	0.890 (0.865–0.914)	0.697 (0.656–0.739)	4	120
wheat	0.984 (0.978–0.990)	0.976 (0.969–0.983)	12	271

of topic labels for Reuters newswire articles. Our approach was to transform the problem into a series of binary classification tasks, and to compare the AUC performance of the AUC-RLS and standard RLS algorithms on each of these sub-tasks.

Our experiments were conducted on the Reuters-21578 dataset[1]. To simulate a situation where only a very limited amount of data is available, we extracted a representative set of 500 documents for training purposes. The extraction was performed so that the class distributions in the extracted subset were guaranteed to be approximately the same as in the whole dataset. The rest of the documents were reserved for final validation.

We considered the task of predicting the 25 most numerous classes, each separately using one-vs-all approach. All of these classes had at least two positive examples in the training data. Some of the documents belonged to more than one of the considered classes and some to none of them. Thus it was possible for a document to be a positive example in more than one of the 25 classification tasks, or in none of them.

In the tests we applied the linear kernel. Ten-fold cross-validation was used on the training data to choose the values of the regularization parameter λ individually for each class. In each case the parameter that produced maximal AUC taken over all of the folds was chosen. Fold partitions were stratified separately for each classification task. The classifiers were trained on the 500 training documents using the chosen parameters, and then tested on the 12397 test documents. To evaluate the statistical significance of the results on the level of individual classes we calculated the 95% confidence intervals for the classifiers' AUC scores for each class. These intervals were obtained with SPSS 11.0.

The results are summarized in Table 1. All the AUC-values are, by definition, real numbers between 0 and 1, 0.5 being the random baseline. AUC-RLS outperformed the standard RLS on each of the 25 classification tasks. When considered together, the results clearly show the difference between the performances of AUC-RLS and RLS to be statistically significant. It should be noted that for some classes the difference is notably larger than for some others. The greatest performance differences can be found in such cases where the class distributions are most unbalanced (e.g., cocoa, cpi, reserves). For the largest classes (e.g., acq, earn, crude) these differences are much more modest, or even negligible. To summarize, AUC-RLS performed reliably, whereas the standard RLS gave in many cases much worse results.

6. Conclusion

The main outcome of this study is a computationally efficient algorithm, AUC-RLS, that outperformed the standard RLS algorithm in maximizing AUC. The performance gains achieved by using the AUC-RLS algorithm were emphasized when the distribution of the class labels was strongly unbalanced. In conclusion, AUC-RLS retains the computational efficiency of the standard RLS algorithm and clearly improves AUC performance.

Our experiments consider AUC maximization with RLS in the binary newswire article classification task. As usual, the generalizability of the results to other application domains and machine learning tasks is limited. However, the achieved performance gains encourage us to study the performance of AUC-RLS in other domains. In particular, we anticipate AUC-RLS to be an attractive method for many real-world classification problems because the class label distribution is typically strongly unbalanced in reality. In

---

[1] Available at http://www.daviddlewis.com/resources/testcollections/reuters21578

the future, we plan to design efficient cross-validation algorithms for AUC-RLS in ways similar to the ones described by us in [14,15].

Acknowledgments

This work has been supported by the Academy of Finland and Tekes, the Finnish Funding Agency for Technology and Innovation.

References

[1] Andrew P. Bradley. The use of the area under the ROC curve in the evaluation of machine learning algorithms. *Pattern Recognition*, 30(7):1145–1159, 1997.

[2] Foster J. Provost, Tom Fawcett, and Ron Kohavi. The case against accuracy estimation for comparing induction algorithms. In *Proceedings of the Fifteenth International Conference on Machine Learning*, pages 445–453. Morgan Kaufmann Publishers Inc., 1998.

[3] Jin Huang and Charles X. Ling. Using AUC and accuracy in evaluating learning algorithms. *IEEE Transactions on Knowledge and Data Engineering*, 17(3):299–310, 2005.

[4] Tom Fawcett and Peter A. Flach. A response to Webb and Ting's on the application of ROC analysis to predict classification performance under varying class distributions. *Machine Learning*, 58(1):33–38, 2005.

[5] Alain Rakotomamonjy. Optimizing area under ROC curve with SVMs. In José Hernández-Orallo, César Ferri, Nicolas Lachiche, and Peter A. Flach, editors, *Proceedings of the 1st International Workshop on ROC Analysis in Artificial Intelligence*, pages 71–80, 2004.

[6] Ulf Brefeld and Tobias Scheffer. AUC maximizing support vector learning. In *Proceedings of the ICML 2005 Workshop on ROC Analysis in Machine Learning*, 2005.

[7] Thorsten Joachims. A support vector method for multivariate performance measures. In *Proceedings of the 22nd International Conference on Machine Learning*, pages 377–384. ACM Press, 2005.

[8] Johan A. K. Suykens and Joos Vandewalle. Least squares support vector machine classifiers. *Neural Processing Letters*, 9(3):293–300, 1999.

[9] Ryan Rifkin. *Everything Old Is New Again: A Fresh Look at Historical Approaches in Machine Learning*. PhD thesis, Massachusetts Institute of Technology, 2002.

[10] Tapio Pahikkala, Evgeni Tsivtsivadze, Antti Airola, Jorma Boberg, and Tapio Salakoski. Learning to rank with pairwise regularized least-squares. In Thorsten Joachims, Hang Li, Tie-Yan Liu, and ChengXiang Zhai, editors, *SIGIR 2007 Workshop on Learning to Rank for Information Retrieval*, pages 27–33, 2007.

[11] Corinna Cortes, Mehryar Mohri, and Ashish Rastogi. Magnitude-preserving ranking algorithms. In Zoubin Ghahramani, editor, *Proceedings of the 24th Annual International Conference on Machine Learning*, pages 169–176. Omnipress, 2007.

[12] Corinna Cortes and Mehryar Mohri. AUC optimization vs. error rate minimization. In Sebastian Thrun, Lawrence Saul, and Bernhard Schölkopf, editors, *Advances in Neural Information Processing Systems 16*. MIT Press, 2004.

[13] Bernhard Schölkopf, Ralf Herbrich, and Alex J. Smola. A generalized representer theorem. In D. Helmbold and R. Williamson, editors, *Proceedings of the 14th Annual Conference on Computational Learning Theory and and 5th European Conference on Computational Learning Theory*, pages 416–426. Springer, 2001.

[14] Tapio Pahikkala, Jorma Boberg, and Tapio Salakoski. Fast n-fold cross-validation for regularized least-squares. In Timo Honkela, Tapani Raiko, Jukka Kortela, and Harri Valpola, editors, *Proceedings of the Ninth Scandinavian Conference on Artificial Intelligence*, pages 83–90. Otamedia Oy, 2006.

[15] Tapio Pahikkala, Hanna Suominen, Jorma Boberg, and Tapio Salakoski. Transductive ranking via pairwise regularized least-squares. In Paolo Frasconi, Kristian Kersting, and Koji Tsuda, editors, *Workshop on Mining and Learning with Graphs*, pages 175–178, 2007.

Tenth Scandinavian Conference on Artificial Intelligence
A. Holst et al. (Eds.)
IOS Press, 2008

Fast Learning in an Actor-Critic Architecture with Reward and Punishment

Christian Balkenius [1], Stefan Winberg
Lund University Cognitive Science, Sweden

Abstract. A reinforcement architecture is introduced that consists of three complementary learning systems with different generalization abilities. The ACTOR learns state-action associations, the CRITIC learns a goal-gradient, and the PUNISH system learns what actions to avoid. The architecture is compared to the standard actor-crititc and Q-learning models on a number of maze learning tasks. The novel architecture is shown to be superior on all the test mazes. Moreover, it shows how it is possible to combine several learning systems with different properties in a coherent reinforcement learning framework.

Keywords. Reinforcement learning, reward, punishment, generalization

Introduction

Reward and punishment are often seen as opposite values on the same dimension. This is especially true for reinforcement learning where reward is often represented by positive reinforcement values, while punishment is represented by negative values. Although such a view of reward and punishment may be useful in many cases, it ignores the fundamental difference in how it is appropriate to react to the two types of situation [1].

It is useful to distinguish between passive and active avoidance [1]. Active avoidance is the situation when it is necessary to try to escape, for example when being chased by a predator. Passive avoidance on the other hand does not necessarily require any action. All we need to do is avoid doing something dangerous, such as avoiding running over a cliff.

For appetitive learning, it is useful to be able to generalize to new similar situation. If one situation or action has proved to be rewarding, it is useful to try out similar actions in the future to explore if they too will result in a reward. The appetitive part of a learning system should thus maximally generalize previously learned behaviors to new situations. To make this possible, it is necessary that the coding of the current situation or state contains sufficient information to support generalization. However, a maximally generalizing system will obviously overextend its behavior to situations were they are not appropriate. Context provides a mean to greatly reduce the number of incorrect generalization, making it easier to separate the relevant information about a given situation. Context can be thought of as any information that can be used to characterize the situa-

---

[1]Corresponding Author: Lund University Cognitive Science, Kungshuset, Lundagård, SE-222 22 Lund, Sweden; E-mail: christian.balkenius@lucs.lu.se.

tion, such as the task, question, place or even the goal. Studies made on animals suggest that a behavior learned in one context is carried over to other contexts, but learned inhibition of a behavior will be unique to each context where the behavior was extinguished [8,10]. Most reinforcement learning algorithms learn to complete a single task in one context, but animals apply what they learn in one context to other contexts as well.

The solution we propose is to divide the input into one focal part, which can be seen as the attended part of the environment, and a contextual part, which codes for the situation [3]. The focal part is used to control actions by being directly associated with behaviors while the contextual part is used to select between different possible behaviors. Previous studies have shown that it is possible to construct a context sensitive artificial neural network that fulfills these demands [5,15], while simultaneously avoiding catastrophic forgetting [9]. It has been used to model context sensitive categorization [5], task-switching [5] and developmental disorders [6]. We recently tested this type of mechanism within a Q-learning framework [16]. Here, we develop these ideas further and implement context sensitivity in an actor-critic framework [7]. In addition, we investigate how punishment can be included to speed up learning.

1. Overview of the System

The general reinforcement learning framework illustrated in Fig. 1 was used for all the simulations and implemented in the Ikaros system [4]. A simpler version of this framework has been previously described [16], and it is here extended by the addition of an actor and critic [7] and a dedicated punishment system. The extended framework consists of the five main modules ACTOR, CRITIC, PUNISH, RL-CORE, and SELECT.

The module ACTOR is responsible for action selection in each state. It has three inputs and one output. One input-output pair is used to calculate the expected value of each possible action in the current state. The other two inputs are used to train the module on the mapping from a state delayed by two time steps to a target delayed by one time step. Any of a number of algorithms can be used as ACTOR, ranging from tables to different types of function approximators and artificial neural networks. Because of the separate input for training and testing, the module ACTOR can simultaneously work in two different time frames without the need to know about the timing of the different signals. Here we use the context sensitive function approximator we have previously developed [5,15,16].

The module CRITIC is used to estimate the expected value of an action a in each state. Learning is dependent on the current policy of the ACTOR module and the CRITIC module must learn to evaluate the actions of the ACTOR module. Just like the ACTOR module, the CRITIC module has three inputs and one output. The inputs are separate for training and testing but receive the same data. The function is similar to the ordinary implementation of actor-critic architectures [7].

The purpose of the module PUNISH is to learn weather or not any of the surrounding states of the current state is inaccessible. That is, if action a in state s will lead to the return to the same state or not. How this is done is often rather specific to the task at hand but can usually be done by analyzing the state and action vectors of previous time steps to see if the selected action caused a state change or not. If not, a negative association is formed between state and action which will greatly reduce the risk of repeating this

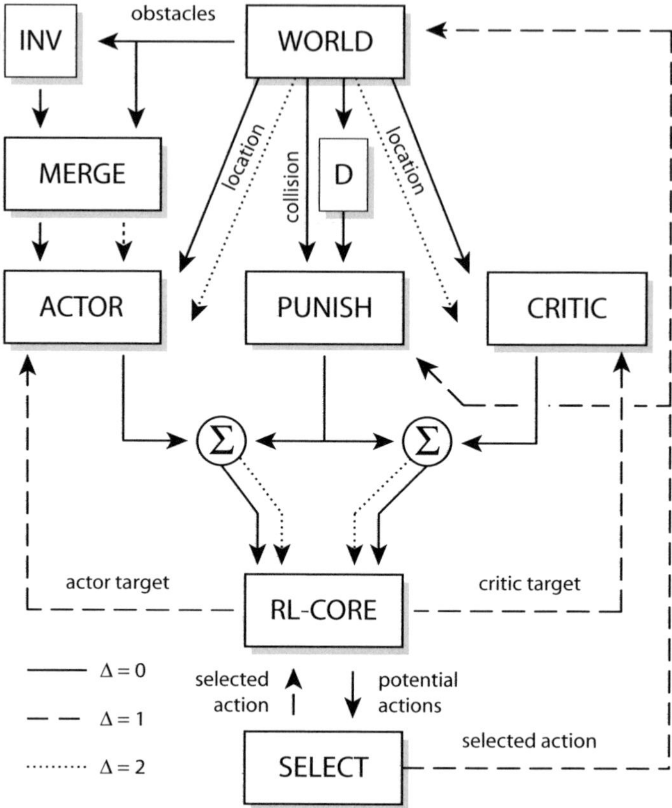

Figure 1. Overview of the general reinforcement learning framework. The different lines indicate different delays (Δ) on the connections. See text for further explanation.

behavior. The learning in the PUNISH module is driven by the collision signal from the environment. This signal is active each time the agent tries to move into a wall. When the PUNISH module receives a collision signal, it will learn to associate the attempted action in the current situation with punishment, which reduces its likelihood in the future. Since the state is coded in a way that allows generalization of punishment to other identical situations (see below), the agent will rapidly learn to not try to move into obstacles.

The module RL-CORE is the reinforcement learning specific component of the system. This module receives information about the current state in the world, the current reinforcement, the action selected at the previous time step and data from both the AC-TOR and CRITIC module in the current state. This is used to calculate the training target for the ACTOR and CRITIC modules. The target vectors are both equal to the input vector of the CRITIC from the last time step, but for the ACTOR module's target vector, the value of the action selected the last time step is replaced with the maximum discounted action value received from the CRITIC in the current time step. For the target vector of the CRITIC module, the incoming reinforcement signal is used.

The module SELECT performs action selection based on its input from RL-CORE. It may also potentially have other inputs that determine what action is selected. This module may for example implement Boltzmann selection or ϵ-greedy selection [13]. It may also use different forms of heuristics to select an action. It is even possible that the action selected is entirely independent of the inputs from RL-CORE. In this case, RL-CORE will learn the actions performed by some other subsystem.

All communication between the different modules consists of numerical matrices. The connections may optionally delay the signal by one or several time steps (Fig. 1). One advantage of this framework is that the different modules can be exchanged to build different forms of reinforcement learning systems. Another advantage is that all timing is taken care of by the delays on the connections between the different modules. If the world is slower at producing the reward, the only things that need to be changed are the different delays in the system.

An important part of the architecture is its ability to handle generalization in different ways in different parts of the system. The ACTOR, CRITIC and PUNISH modules all receive input about the current state of the world, but they are coded in different ways to support different forms of generalizations.

The information about obstacles around the current location in the world consists of a binary matrix with 1 for obstacles and 0 for open space. This matrix is inverted (INV) and merged (MERGE) with the original representation to form vector with a dual coding of the surrounding around the agent. The resulting vector is given as input to the ACTOR. This coding makes it easy for the actor to generalize actions to new situations since this input contains information that lets the actor learn about the actions that are possible in each state. In addition, the ACTOR module also receives location input from the world that is used for contextual inhibition [16].

The CRITIC does not use the focal information about obstacles around the agent. Instead, it uses the location code to learn the value for each location in the environment. This is the most suitable information for learning the shortest path through an environment.

Finally, the PUNISH module uses another coding of the surrounding around the agent. The binary pattern with nine elements is 'decoded' into one of 512 distinct vectors with a single 1 at one position and 0 at the others. This decoding is used as a simplified means of getting distinct categories for environments where the agent has received punishment. In practice, all the different categories are not used, and it would be possible to dynamically create the required categories instead, but here we have opted for the simplest solution.

2. Simulations

A typical reinforcement learning problem has a multidimensional state space. This makes it difficult to visualize the problem in a way that is easy to comprehend. Therefore, a navigation task through a two-dimensional maze is often chosen since each state can be represented by a physical location. When the state space is visualized as a two dimensional surface, the solution can be described as a path from the start state to the goal state. Initially the agent has no knowledge of the state space. Therefore, the first time the agent enters the maze it has to search it through to find the goal. It is important to note that the two-dimensional layout of the state-space is not available to the agent. Our intuitions about the expected behavior can thus be misleading. Nevertheless, a maze is a useful visualization of a state-space and we have chosen a set of mazes we call 17T4U that illustrates different strengths and weaknesses of reinforcement learning algorithms (Figs. 2 and 3) [16]. The mazes superficially looks like the letter in the name of the set. We tested three algorithms in the different mazes: standard tabular Q-learning [14], the novel actor-critic architecture proposed above and the same architecture but with the punishment module disabled [7].

The Q-learning model was initiated in a way to support efficient exploration [11]. For each model and each environment, we recorded the number of steps needed to reach the goal location from the start at each trial. The number of extra steps beyond the shortest path was recorded and added for each trial to give the result graphs which show the average of 100 simulations.

3. Results

Fig. 2 shows the results for the different models on the narrow mazes. On the simple straight corridor, both the actor-critic models learn the optimal policy very quickly, while Q-learning needs about 10 trails before the optimal policy is found. The quick learning of the actor-critic variants depends on the ability to generalize the action of moving straight in a corridor to all positions in the maze.

The merit of the generalization ability is also evident in the 7-maze and the T-maze, but only when it is combined with punishment. The punishment system improves learning speed considerably by suppressing actions that lead into walls. Note that the suppression of these inappropriate actions is learned from experience.

The 4-maze was selected since it is optimally bad for the generalization abilities of the two actor-critic models. The generalized action of moving straight in a corridor will lead it to the dead end. As expected, the actor-critic model does not work well in this maze. However, the model with the punishment system is doing much better and learns faster than both the other models. In the U-maze, the results is similar and the actor-critic with punishment is again outperforming the other models.

Fig. 3 shows the results for the wide mazes. For the models tested here, the results are similar for the wide mazes as for the narrow ones. In all cases, the actor-crititc with punishment is best of the three models.

4. Discussion

The results of the simulations show that the combination of an actor-critic architecture with a punishment system results in very efficient learning, even for problems designed specifically to be as difficult as possible for this kind of architecture. The separation of the appetitive learning subsystem into an actor and a critic makes it possible to use different forms of generalization for actions and state evaluation. The addition of a punishment system dedicated to aversive learning makes the architecture even more powerful since it allows the system to learn about actions to avoid. Together, the appetitive and aversive parts of the system learns different heuristics that it can later use during exploration.

We described the novel architecture from a maze learning perspective, but the framework is much more general. The division into the three modules ACTOR, CRITIC and PUNISH can be applied also to other reinforcement learning problems. The three sys-

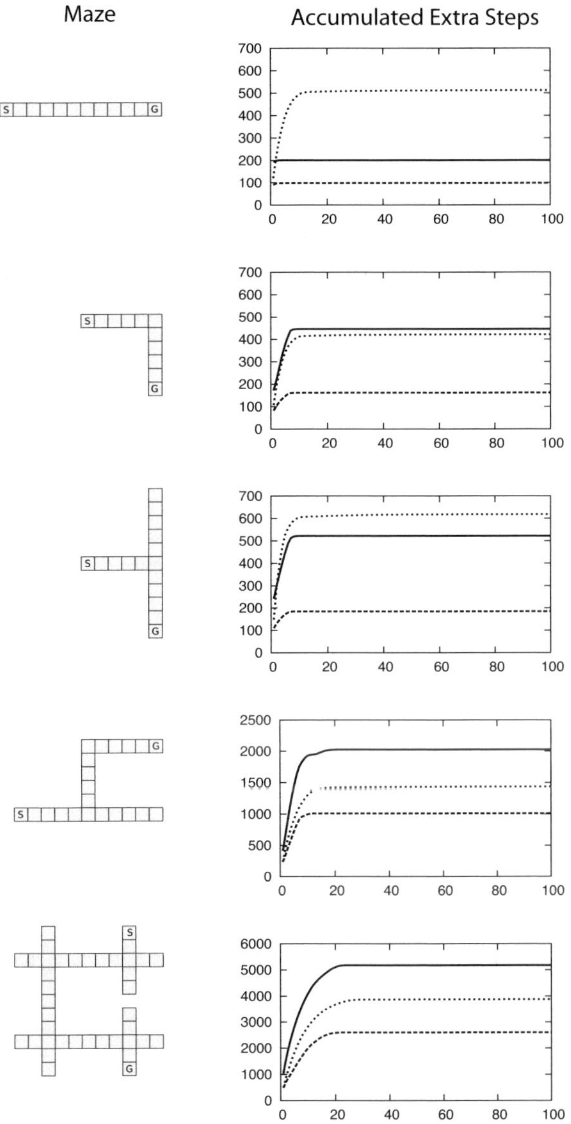

Figure 2. Results on the narrow mazes. Dotted line: Q-learning, solid line: actor-critic without punishment, striped line: actor-critic with punishment. The actor-critic architecture with punishment is best in all cases.

tems learn in three complementary ways. The ACTOR learns associations between the coding of the current state that supports generalization and potential actions in that state. This learning will generalize to other similar states which will give the agents sugegstions about what to do in new states it has never seen before based on "perceptual similarity". When the generalized actions are not successful, they will be inhibited in the current context. There is thus an interplay between generalization and specialization in the ACTOR module [16].

Unlike the ACTOR module, the CRITIC module does not generalize to similar

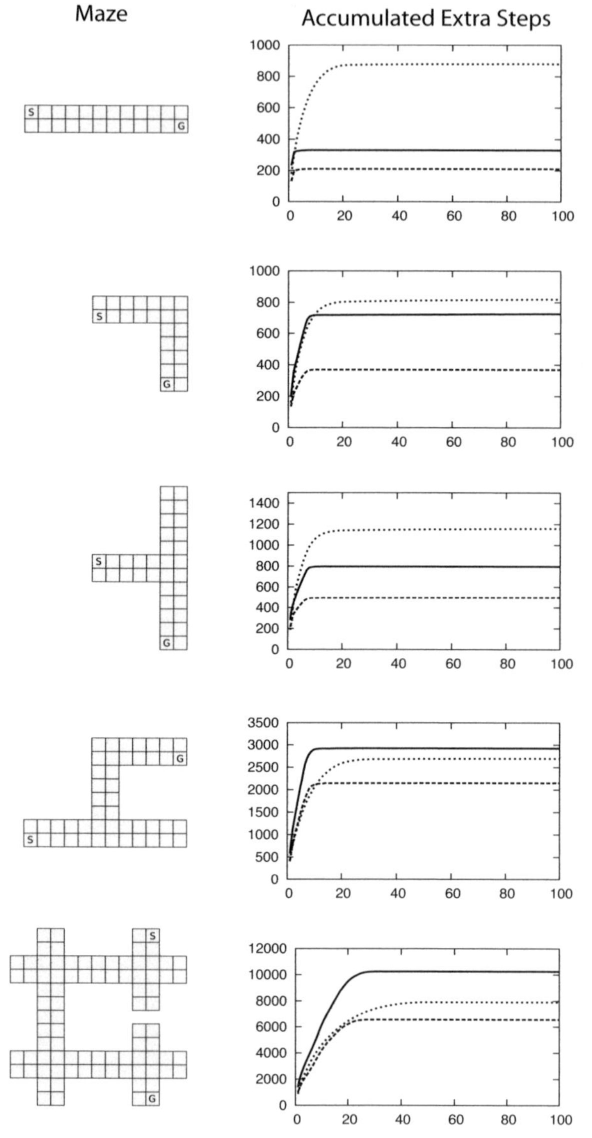

Figure 3. Results on the wide mazes. Dotted line: Q-learning, solid line: actor-critic without punishment, striped line: actor-critic with punishment. The actor-critic architecture with punishment is best in all cases.

states. The reason for this is that it attempts to learn a goal-gradient toward the goal [1]. This gradient should be based on the location with respect to the goal and not generalized based on similarity. Our earlier attempts to include contextual inhibition within a Q-learning framework did not distinguish between the role of the ACTOR and the CRITIC, and would sometimes generalize incorrectly which would slow down learning [16]. The actor-critic architecture overcomes this problem. As far as we know, this feature of the actor-critic architecture to allow more flexible generalization has not been investigated before.

The PUNISH module, finally, learns in a way that is different from both the ACTOR and the CRITIC. Like the ACTOR it uses a description of the current state rather than the location. However, unlike the ACTOR that generalizes maximally, the PUNISH module does not generalize at all. It uses different categories for each of the possible local environments around the agent. This reflects a fundamental asymmetry between reward and punishment in that rewarding situations is something that the agent will seek out again an learn more about, while punishing situation will be avoided. The agent will thus not explore potentially punishing actions again and it is important that this suppression is not extended to actions that may be advantageous in other situations.

Acknowledgements

This work was supported by the EU project MindRaces, FP6-511931.

References

[1]   Balkenius, C. (1995). *Natural intelligence in artificial creatures*. Lund University Cognitive Studies, 37.

[2]   Balkenius, C. (1996). Generalization in instrumental learning. In Maes, P., Mataric, M., Meyer, J.-A., Pollack, J., and Wilson, S. W. (Eds.), *From Animals to Animats 4: Proceedings of the Fourth International Conference on Simulation of Adaptive Behavior*. Cambridge, MA: MIT Press.

[3]   Balkenius, C., and Morén, J. (2000). A computational model of context processing. In Meyer, J-A., Berthoz, A., Floreano, D., Roitblat, H. L., Wilson, S. W. (Eds.), *From Animals to Animats 6: Proceedings of the 6th International Conference on the Simulation of Adaptive Behaviour*. Cambridge, MA: MIT Press

[4]   Balkenius, C., Morén, J. and Johansson, B. (2007). *System-level cognitive modeling with Ikaros*. Lund University Cognitive Studies, 133.

[5]   Balkenius, C. and Winberg, S. (2004). Cognitive Modeling with Context Sensitive Reinforcement Learning, *Proceedings of the AILS-04 Workshop*, 10-19.

[6]   Björne, P., and Balkenius, C. (2005). A model of attentional impairments in autism: First steps toward a computational theory. *Cognitive Systems Research, 6, 3*, 193-204.

[7]   Barto, A. G., Sutton, R. S. and Anderson, C. W. (1983) Neuronlike adaptive elements that can solve difficult learning control problems. IEEE Transactions on Systems, Man, and Cybernetics 13:835-846

[8]   Bouton, M. E. (1991). Context and retrieval in extinction and in other examples of interference in simple associative learning. In Dachowski, L. W. and Flaherty, C. F. (Eds.), Current topics in animal learning: Brain, emotion, and cognition (pp. 25Ð53). Hillsdale, NJ: Erlbaum.

[9]   French, R. M. (1999). Catastrophic Forgetting in Connectionist Networks. *Trends in Cognitive Sciences*, 3, 128-135.

[10] Hall, G. (2002) Associative Structures in Pavlovian and Instrumental Conditioning In Pashler, H. and Gallistel, R. (eds.), *StevenÕs Handbook of Experimental Psychology. Volume 3: Learning, Motivation, and Emotion*. John Wiley & Sons.

[11] Koenig, S. and Simmons, R.G. (1996).The Effect of Representation and Knowledge on Goal-Directed Exploration with Reinforcement-Learning Algorithms. *Machine Learning*, 22, (1-3), 227-250.

[12] Morén, J. (2002). *Emotion and Learning - A Computational Model of the Amygdala*, Lund University Cognitive Studies, 93.

[13] Sutton, R., and Barto, A., (1998). Reinforcement Learning: An Introduction. MIT Press, Cambridge, MA, A Bradford Book.

[14] Watkins, C. J. C. H. and Dayan, P. (1992). Q-learning. Machine Learning, Vol. 9, 279-292.

[15] Winberg, S. (2004). Contextual Inhibition in Reinforcement Learning, MSc Thesis in Cognitive Science. Lund University.

[16] Winberg, S. and Balkenius, C. (2007). Generalization and Specialization in Reinforcement Learning. In Berthouze, L. et al., *Proceedings of the seventh international conference on Epigenetic Robotics*. Lund University Cognitive Studies, 135.

Tenth Scandinavian Conference on Artificial Intelligence
A. Holst et al. (Eds.)
IOS Press, 2008

Explanatory Capabilities in the CREEK Knowledge-Intensive Case-Based Reasoner

Anders KOFOD-PETERSEN [1], Jörg CASSENS, Agnar AAMODT
Department of Computer and Information Science (IDI), Norwegian University of Science and Technology (NTNU), Trondheim, Norway

Abstract. The ability to give explanations for its reasoning and behaviour is a core capability of an intelligent system. There are a number of different goals a user can have towards such explanations. This paper presents how the knowledge intensive case-based reasoning framework CREEK can support some of these different goals in an ambient intelligence setting.

Keywords. Case-based reasoning, ambient intelligence, explanation

Introduction

Explanations have been identified as one of the most important aspects of intelligent systems in general [1,2,3], and for ambient intelligent systems in particular [4]. When systems are assigned a kind of responsibility from their users, and exhibit pro-active behaviour, explanations are often the most important way to instil trust. This is especial true in ambient intelligent systems where the main interface often is behavioural.

Recent developments in ubiquitous and pervasive computing have shown that to achieve the visions proposed, systems must have far more complicated capabilities than initially identified by Weiser [5]. This has lead to the developments jointly labelled as *ambient intelligence* [6]. Ambient intelligence is defined as a system's ability to appreciate its environment, be aware of persons present, and respond to these persons needs in an intelligent manner.

We have earlier demonstrated how *case-based reasoning*, combined with a socio-technical analysis of the domain, can be utilised as a means of achieving ambient intelligence [7,8]. The use of case-based reasoning [9] is partly motivated by understanding reasoning as an explanation process [10]. Our understanding of similar occurrences of a situation assist us in comprehending stories, in such a way that details omitted or implicitly assumed do not make a story incomprehensible.

We have previously presented a framework for explanations in intelligent systems with a special focus on case-based reasoning [2]. Specifically, we identified five goals that explanations can satisfy.

---

[1]Corresponding Author: Department of Computer and Information Science, Norwegian University of Science and Technology, 7048 Trondheim, Norway; E-mail: anderpe@idi.ntnu.no

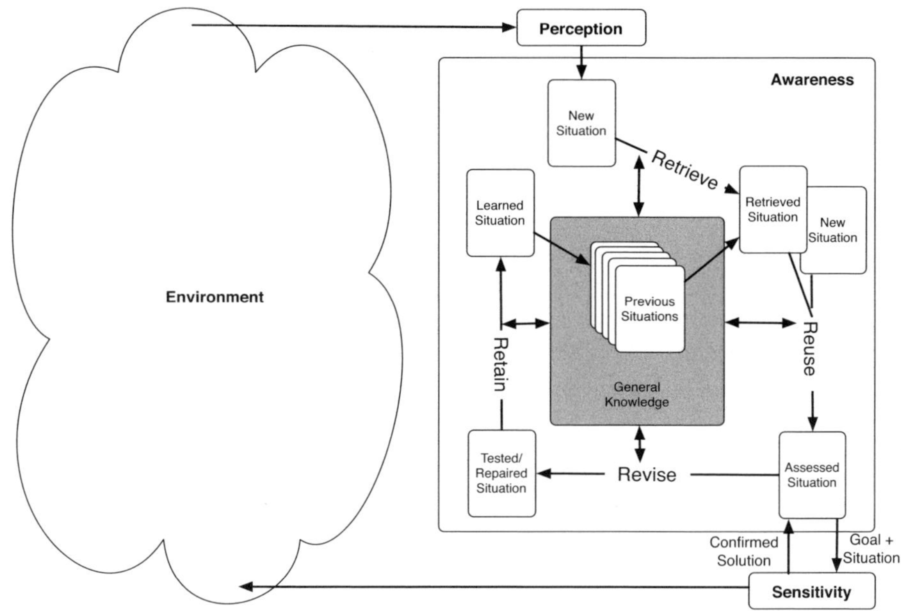

Figure 1. The Case-based Reasoning Cycle in Ambient Intelligence

The work presented here demonstrates the current state of the explanatory capabilities of the knowledge-intensive case based reasoning system CREEK [11]. In particular viewed in the light of the five explanation goals identified in [2].

The rest of the paper is organised as follows: Firstly, a short introduction to the CREEK system, and how it is used in an ambient intelligent setting, is given. Secondly, an overview of the five explanation goals and how they fit into the ambient intelligence paradigm is given. This is followed by a description of how CREEK achieves the three goals which it is capable of supporting. Finally, a short summary and an outlook on future work is presented.

CREEK and Ambient Intelligence

Case-based reasoning approaches the reasoning process, not by the classic approach of rules or general knowledge, but by using episodic memory. The knowledge base consists of situations experienced by the system and the solution to the problem in these situations (cases).

A case-based reasoning system can, to some degree, be perceived as a rule-based system with very long rules. A case's findings can be viewed as a problem's antecedent and its solution as the consequence. However, they differ in several important ways: *i)* rules are patterns, whereas cases are constants; *ii)* rules are retrieved based on exact matching, where cases only require partial matching; *iii)* rules are small, independent, and consistent pieces of domain knowledge, cases can be large chunks of, potentially redundant, domain knowledge.

Table 1. Context and Explanations

	Context Awareness	**Context Sensitivity**
System Centric	Generate an explanation to **recognise** the situation	**Identify** the behaviour the system should expose
User Centric	**Elucidate** why the system identifies a particular situation	**Explicate** why a certain behaviour was chosen

Case-based reasoning has commonly approached the matching of a newly encountered situation to the existing case base by comparing *surface* features. The features are the findings, or description of a case, and are often represented as attribute-value pairs. Other approaches include comparison of *structural* properties. Structural features may contain explicit structural information, i.e. internal dependencies among features within the case itself, or implicitly through an additional model of general domain relationships that contains concepts referred to in the case. Such an approach tends to be more computational expensive than purely syntactical comparison, yet it often produces more relevant cases [12].

The CREEK method [11,13], which is used in the work presented here, is a *knowledge-intensive* case-based reasoning architecture especially developed to approach problem-solving and learning in open and weak-theory domains. CREEK contains structural features by linking flat case structure to a multi-relational network of concepts in the case. The main asset of CREEK is the fact that the cases are submerged into the general domain knowledge. This model is realised through a multi-relational semantic network, where object-oriented, frame-based representation is used to capture both cases and domain knowledge.

Modelling of knowledge in CREEK is a combination of a top-down process for the initial knowledge acquisition, and a bottom-up process of continuous learning by retaining cases. The top-down process is to acquire and develop the conceptual model required to define the domain model, to define the case contents and structure, and to manually described an initial set of case. To facilitate this knowledge acquisition, and the reasoning process, CREEK is equipped with a top-level ontology, which encompasses the high-level concepts and relations required.

CREEK has been experimentally used within an ambient intelligent environment for hospital wards [8]. Figure 1 depicts how the case-based reasoning cycle [9] has been adapted to an ambient intelligent environment. The knowledge model was developed by executing an ethnographical study at the local university hospital [7,14].

The Five Explanation Goals

Sørmo et al. [2] describe five different explanation goals that an intelligent system should be able to satisfy.

The goal of *transparency* is concerned with the system's ability to explain how an answer was reached. *Justification* deals with the ability to explain why the answer is good. When dealing with the importance of a question asked, *relevance* is the goal that must be satisfied. *Conceptualisation* is the goal that handles the meaning of concepts. Finally, *learning* is in itself a goal, as it teaches us about the domain in question. These goals are defined from the perspective of a human user. His expectations on what constitutes a good explanation is situation dependent and has a historic dimension [15].

We have previously described how context awareness and sensitivity are related to explanations seen from either a user-centric or system-centric perspective [8]. Table 1 describes these relationships. In previous work we have described how all five goals are related to an ambient intelligent system. In the work presented here, we will only investigate the three goals that CREEK currently supports.

Explanation Goals in CREEK

Transparency Goal

The transparency goal is concerned with a system's ability to explain how an answer was reached. In the case of the user centric perspective, a system can elucidate (see Table 1) why it assumes that a particular situation has been identified correctly.

CREEK approaches this by visualising why a known situation (case) matches the ongoing situation. Figure 2 depicts the matching of two cases: `US_V_OL9_1302_Car` being the unsolved new case and `V_OL9_1305_Car_S` being the known case. CREEK displays the way the two cases are related, thus achieving the transparency goal.

If we look at the new case, we can see that by following the relations through to the know case we are aware of the match. `US_V_OL9_1302_Car` is connected to `US_UC_V_OL9_1302_Car` through the `has context` relation. The `has context` relation points to a context that encapsulates all findings of a case. This context has several parts, all connected through the `has part` relation. If we look at the `has part` relation that connects to `EC_V_OL9_1302_Car` (the environmental context), is again connected to the person `SPL8`, who is a nurse[2]. `SPL8` is again connected to the unsolved case through `EC_V_OL9_1305_Car_S` (environmental context) and `UC_V_OL9_1305_Car_S`.

By looking at Figure 2 we can also observe that both cases are connected through other findings. We can observe that both cases share the `GroupLeaderRole` and `ExaminationResponsibleRole`. Finally, both cases have a `Time` that is very close to the other: `1040` versus `1002`. We will examine the closeness of these times in the justification goal.

Justification Goal

The justification goal is closely related to the transparency goal. Where transparency is concerned with presenting the reasoning trace, justification deals with the ability to explain why an answer is good. Justification is often preferable over transparency, as simply displaying the reasoning trace is not always sufficient, it can even be counter productive [16,17]. In the case of the user-centric perspective, a system can elucidate (see Table 1), by justification, why it has classified a situation correctly.

CREEK allows the user to investigate why two concepts are matched, in particular when they do not match syntactically. When using the CREEK interface it is possible to investigate all the findings used when matching two cases. This is of particular interest when matches occur that are not based on surface features, or syntactical match, but rather on semantic similarity.

---

[2]The fact that SPL8 is a nurse can be observed by exploring the knowledge base.

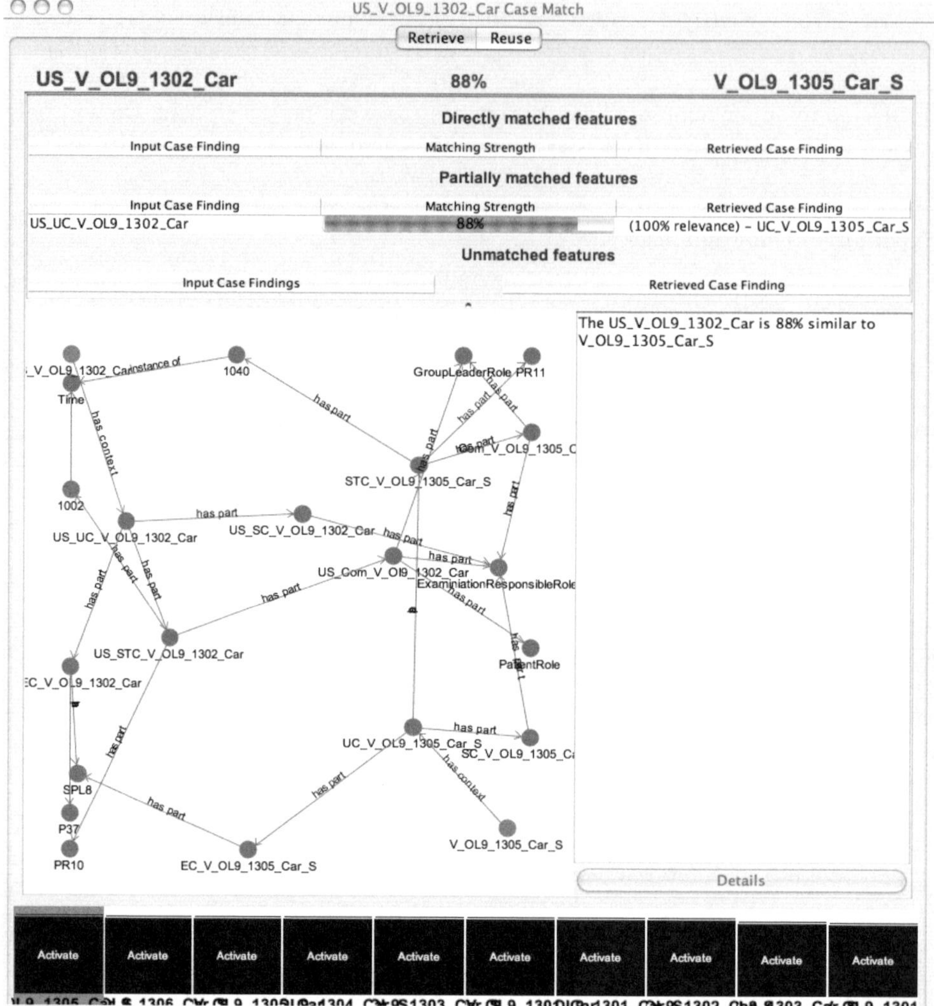

Figure 2. Transparency goal in CREEK

For example, if we look at the time in the two example cases, we can see that one of the situations is occurring at 1002 and one at 1040. Looking at Figure 3 we can see that CREEK calculates that the two values are 95% similar, as times varies from 09:50 to 16:10[3]. In this case, CREEK has justified its assumption that the two points in time are close.

Conceptualisation Goal

The conceptualisation goal deals with the meaning of concepts. When we examined Figure 2 we found that both situations (cases) contained SPL8, and we noted that it was

---

[3]Please note that due to internal representational issues time is represented as integers. Thus, time is not correctly represented. However, for matching purposes these values are sufficient.

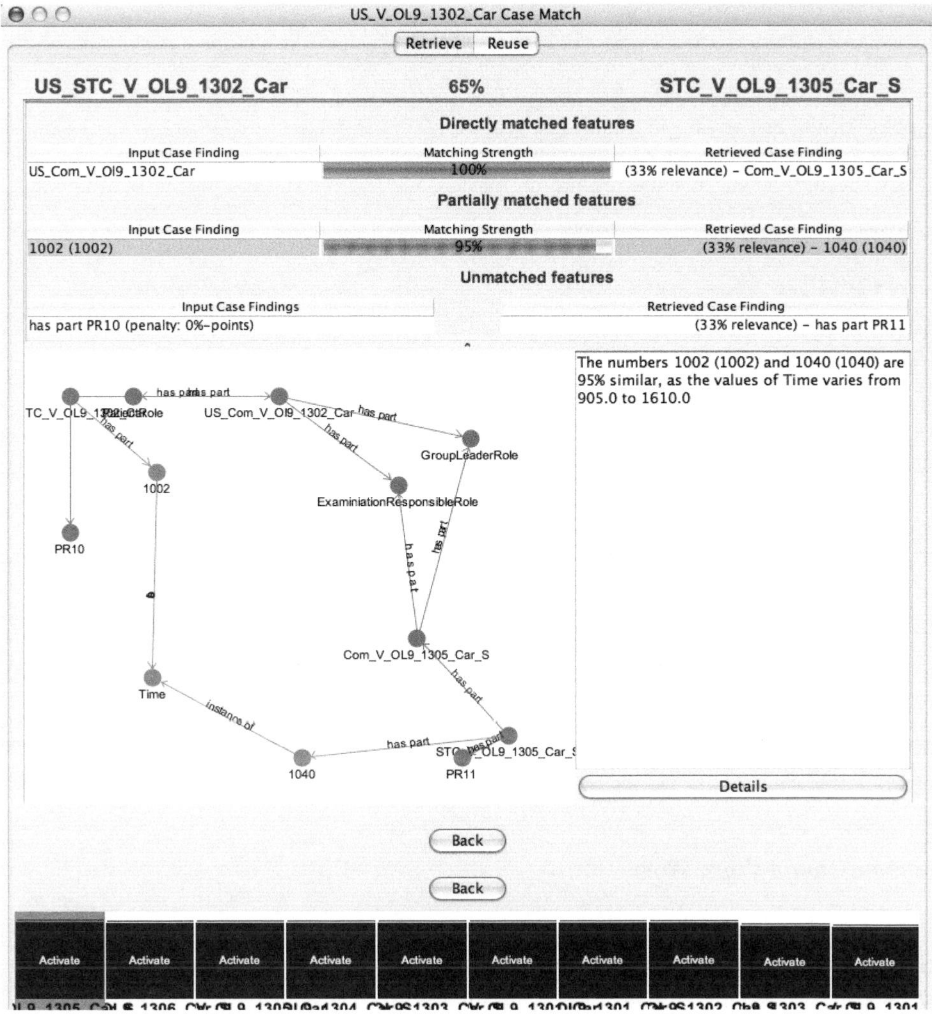

Figure 3. Justification goal in CREEK

a nurse. However, to explain the concept `SPL8` we can examine the knowledge base contained in CREEK. Figure 4 shows a small subset of the knowledge base used.

When we examine the knowledge base, we can start with the concept `Thing`. According to the top-ontology in CREEK all concepts are at some point, through potential many levels of the multi-relational semantic network, either a subclass or an instance of `Thing`.

If we look closer at `Nurse` we can see that it `Consumes` an information source name `FAMSOS`, which is short for family and social issues. This information is offered by (among others) `Patients`. We can further examine the specific `Nurse` instance `SPL8`, and we can see that it is `cast in` the `Role` of `GroupLeaderRole`. Going back to Figure 2, this role was present in both cases. Finally, the location of `SPL8` is `LK4`, which is an instance of a `DoctorOffice`, which again is a subclass of a `Location`.

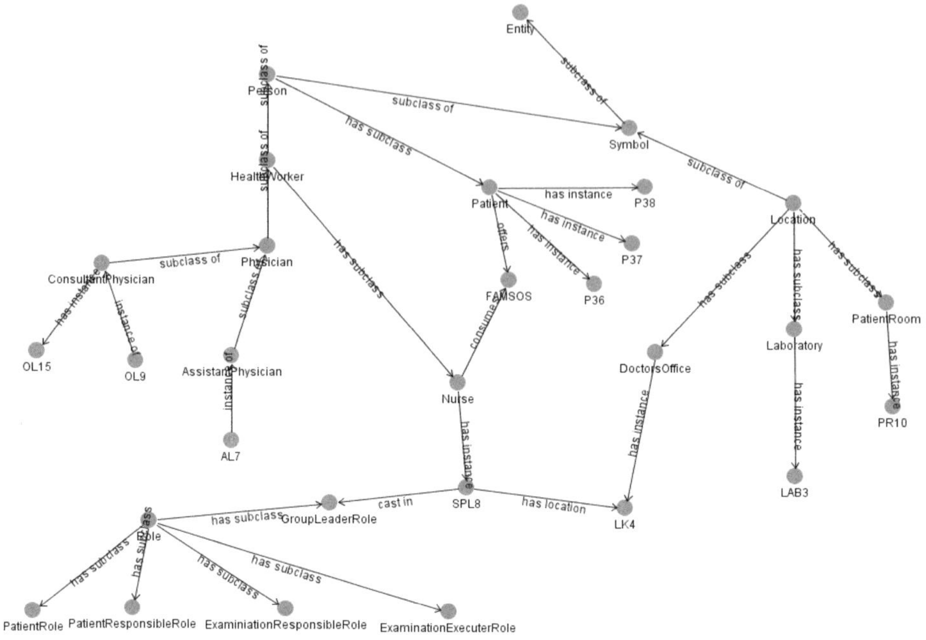

Figure 4. Conceptualisation goal in CREEK

Inspecting the knowledge model is the means of achieving the conceptualisation goal in CREEK.

Summary and Future Work

In this paper, we have described how the knowledge intensive case-based reasoner CREEK can support different user goals. We have taken a user-centric perspective, enhancing the system's communication with the user. In particular, we have shown examples for how we support the *transparency*, the *justification*, and the *conceptualisation* goals. For *transparency* and *justification*, we have focused on elucidating the system's reasoning, that means we have described how the system delivers an explanation to the user which explains why a particular situation was identified. Support of the *conceptualisation* goal in the way we have outlined can be useful both for elucidation and explication, which is an explanation targeting the behaviour of the system.

One of the future research areas we are currently exploring is the support of the *relevance* and the *learning* goal. The learning goal is special in the sense that it focuses on the user's interest in the application domain (hence the real world), and not on some particular behaviour of the system. It is mainly important to be supported in intelligent tutoring applications. Therefore, we concentrate on the *relevance* goal.

Another area of future work deals with the question of how to support the different user goals with the means of behavioural interfaces. The main form of interaction engaged in by the user of an ambient intelligent system is determined by the behaviour of that system. This implies that we have to focus on means to transport explanations on different channels than traditional computer displays.

Acknowledgements

Part of this work has been supported by Accenture Innovation Lab Norway.

References

[1] Leake, D.B.: Evaluating Explanations: A Content Theory. Lawrence Erlbaum Associates (1992)

[2] Sørmo, F., Cassens, J., Aamodt, A.: Explanation in case-based reasoning – perspectives and goals. Artificial Intelligence Review **24** (2005) 109–143

[3] Roth-Berghofer, T.R., Cassens, J.: Mapping goals and kinds of explanations to the knowledge containers of case-based reasoning systems. In Muñoz-Avila, H., Ricci, F., eds.: Case Based Reasoning Research and Development – ICCBR 2005. Volume 3630 of LNAI., Chicago, Springer (2005) 451–464

[4] Kofod-Petersen, A., Cassens, J.: Explanations and context in ambient intelligent systems. In kokinov, B., Richardson, D.C., Roth-Berhofer, T.R., Vieu, L., eds.: Modeling and Using Context, proceedings of the 6th International and Interdisciplinary Conference (CONTEXT 2007). Volume 4635 of Lecture Notes in Artificial Intelligence., Roskilde, Denmark, Springer Verlag (2007) 303–316

[5] Weiser, M.: The computer for the 21st century. Scientific American (1991) 94–104

[6] Ducatel, K., Bogdanowicz, M., Scapolo, F., Leijten, J., Burgelman, J.C.: ISTAG scenarios for ambient intelligence in 2010. Technical report, IST Advisory Group (2001)

[7] Kofod-Petersen, A., Cassens, J.: Using activity theory to model context awareness. In Roth-Berghofer, T.R., Schulz, S., Leake, D.B., eds.: Modeling and Retrieval of Context: Second International Workshop, MRC 2005, Revised Selected Papers. Volume 3946 of Lecture Notes in Computer Science., Edinburgh, UK, Springer Verlag (2006) 1–17

[8] Kofod-Petersen, A., Aamodt, A.: Contextualised ambient intelligence through case-based reasoning. In Roth-Berghofer, T.R., Göker, M.H., Güvenir, H.A., eds.: Proceedings of the Eighth European Conference on Case-Based Reasoning (ECCBR 2006). Volume 4106 of Lecture Notes in Computer Science., Ölüdeniz, Turkey, Springer Verlag (2006) 211–225

[9] Aamodt, A., Plaza, E.: Case-based reasoning: Foundational issues, methodological variations, and system approaches. AI Communications **7** (1994) 39–59

[10] Schank, R.C.: Explanation Patterens – Understanding Mechanically and Creatively. Lawrence Erlbaum, New York (1986)

[11] Aamodt, A.: Knowledge-intensive case-based reasoning in Creek. In Funk, P., Calero, P.A.G., eds.: Advances in case-based reasoning, 7th European Conference, ECCBR 2004, Proceedings. (2004) 1–15

[12] López de Mántaras, R., McSherry, D., Bridge, D., Leake, D., Smyth, B., Craw, S., Faltings, B., Maher, M.L., Cox, M., Forbus, K., Keane, M., Aamodt, A., Watson, I.: Retrieval, reuse, revision, and retention in case-based reasoning. Knowledge Engineering Review **20** (2005) 215–240

[13] Aamodt, A.: A knowledge-intensive, integrated approach to problem solving and sustained learning. PhD thesis, University of Trondheim, Norwegian Institute of Technology, Department of Computer Science (1991) University Microfilms PUB 92-08460.

[14] Cassens, J., Kofod-Petersen, A.: Using activity theory to model context awareness: a qualitative case study. In: Proceedings of the 19th International Florida Artificial Intelligence Research Society Conference, Florida, USA, AAAI Press (2006) 619–624

[15] Leake, D.B.: Goal-based explanation evaluation. In: Goal-Driven Learning. MIT Press, Cambridge (1995) 251–285

[16] Majchrzak, A., Gasser, L.: On using artificial intelligence to integrate the design of organizational and process change in US manufacturing. AI and Society **5** (1991) 321–338

[17] Gregor, S., Benbasat, I.: Explanations from intelligent systems: Theoretical foundations and implications for practice. MIS Quarterly **23** (1999) 497–530

Tenth Scandinavian Conference on Artificial Intelligence
A. Holst et al. (Eds.)
IOS Press, 2008

Case-based Reasoning for Ontology Engineering

Eva BLOMQVIST

Jönköping University, Sweden. eva.blomqvist@jth.hj.se

Abstract. When developing semantic applications, constructing the underlying ontologies is a crucial part. Construction of both Semantic Web and enterprise ontologies need to be semi-automatic in order to reduce the effort required and the
need for expert ontology engineers. Another important issue is to introduce knowledge reuse in the ontology construction process. By basing our semi-automatic
method on the principles of case-based reasoning (CBR) we envision a novel semi-
automatic ontology construction approach and also a novel application of case-
based reasoning. The development of OntoCase is still ongoing work, in this paper
we report mainly on the motivation for using CBR and the possible benefits of this.

Keywords. Ontology Engineering, Ontology Learning, Case-based Reasoning

Introduction

Ontology engineering has for a long time been considered a manual process, but it is very
resource demanding. Especially in fields like the Semantic Web, where many ontologies
needed are more light-weight and reliability requirements are less strict, semi-automatic
approaches are emerging. Semi-automatic tools reduce both the total construction effort
and the need for specific ontology engineering expertise. An important issue is also to introduce knowledge reuse in the ontology construction process. Common practises of the
domain should be exploited, as well as drawing on best practises in ontology engineering. One way of doing this is through ontology patterns. Case-based reasoning (CBR)
is a methodology also focussing on the notion of reuse. By combining the CBR viewpoint with the use of patterns the OntoCase approach intends to apply a novel view of
semi-automatic ontology construction.

The following section briefly introduces some background together with related
work. In section 2 we analyse the suitability of CBR to ontology engineering and subsequently in section 3 the proposed phases of the OntoCase approach are described. Finally,
the paper is concluded with a summary and outlook in section 4.

1. Background and Related Work

In our research we adopt the commonly used ontology definition from Gruber [13], stat-
ing that an ontology is a formal explicit specification of a shared conceptualisation. We
do not restrict our research to one specific ontology representation formalism, but the ap-

proach assumes the possibility to reduce the ontology to a semantic network-like graph, although this might also mean a loss of information. An enterprise ontology is an ontology with a specific enterprise as domain, intended for some enterprise application.

1.1. Ontology Patterns

We generally define the notion of ontology engineering pattern as *a set of ontological entities, structures or construction principles that recur, either exactly replicated or in an adapted form, within some set of ontologies or is envisioned to recur within some future set of ontologies.* This notion of pattern includes the general pattern mining view, where the aim is to find regularities in some set of objects. We restrict this view slightly to only consider any connected set (with connected referring to the ontology as a graph). Finding such patterns is quite close to the CBR idea of retaining solutions. Additionally the definition includes the view of patterns as predefined templates for constructing solutions. In our research we aim to exploit a combination of both views.

For specific ontology languages, template-like patterns to help engineers construct well-structured ontologies exist (proposed for example by W3C [20]). Another example is the notion of "semantic patterns" for describing implementation independent logical constructs [18]. Similar to software design patterns are the conceptual ontology design patterns [12]. We are in the OntoCase approach mainly interested in patterns on the design and architecture level (see previous classification by Blomqvist [6]). We describe the notion of ontology design patterns generally as self-contained ontology templates for solving a restricted modelling problem. An ontology architecture pattern is a pattern describing the overall structure of an ontology.

1.2. Semi-automatic Ontology Engineering

Semi-automatic ontology construction is often denoted ontology learning (OL). Most of the semi-automatic approaches focus on techniques for text analysis in order to extract mainly suggestions for concepts and relations from a text corpus input. None of the existing semi-automatic approaches exploit ontology patterns. Most recent systems use a variety of text analysis techniques (see [9], [11], [19] and [14]). A problem with the use of a text corpus as input is that not all information is explicitly stated. Some approaches use additional knowledge sources for enhancing the ontology construction, one way to reduce the impact of this problem is also to use ontology patterns.

Ontology matching is a field that aims to assist ontology reuse in ontology engineering [17] [10], both syntactic and semantic techniques are generally combined. The OntoCase approach is not an ontology matching approach as such, still we use many of the same techniques for our pattern matching, like string matching and dictionary look-up of terms. Our approach is also related to search and ranking of ontologies, like described by Alani et al. [2]. Most ontology search engines expect a very simple query (keywords) that is evaluated against the available set of ontologies, while in our case the query will be an ontology (similarly to Anutaraiya et al. [3]).

1.3. Case-based Reasoning

Case-based reasoning (CBR) is, according to for example Aamodt and Plaza [1], aiming to use previous experiences to solve new problems. It is worth noting that this is an idea similar to patterns. CBR is generally depicted as a cycle of four phases (retrieve, reuse, revise and retain), all using the stored knowledge in the central case base. In addition to the stored cases, the case base might also contain general domain knowledge. A specific branch of CBR is textual CBR (TCBR) that focuses on approaches using natural language texts. Weber et al. [21] describe four open research questions of this area, containing how to get from a textual representation of a case to a structured representation and how to automate approaches. Our approach addresses these research questions in the setting of semi-automatic enterprise ontology construction. Recent developments of CBR also use "soft" computing (as noted by Pal and Shiu [16]).

A number of variations of case-based reasoning can be listed [1]. A "true" case-based reasoning method is distinguished by the complexity of the case structure and stored information, and also by the ability to modify the retrieved solutions to a new situation. Although an extensive literature search has been conducted, no approach using CBR for ontology engineering has been found. Some related approaches can be noted though, most similar seems to be the concept map extension and knowledge acquisition techniques applied by Leake et al. [15] when using previously created concepts maps as past cases when constructing and extending new ones. That approach store complete concept maps as cases, while our approach is focused on storing patterns instead of complete previous cases.

1.3.1. Benefits of CBR and When to Use it?

A summary concerning some of the benefits and drawbacks of using case-based reasoning is presented by Pal and Shiu [16]. Some of the benefits listed are to reduced the load on knowledge acquisition tasks, learning from the past, reasoning with incomplete, imprecise or insufficient information, and reflecting human reasoning and means of explanation. Based on these benefits the authors suggest some guidelines as to help determining when CBR is the right method to choose [16]. The guidelines are expressed as 5 questions to ask when considering to use, or construct, a CBR system:

1. Does the domain have an underlying model?
2. Are there exceptions and novel cases?
3. Do cases recur?
4. Is there significant benefit in adapting past solutions?
5. Are relevant previous cases obtainable?

If there is no clear underlying model that can be completely understood, there are many exceptions to the rules that govern the world, but similar cases still reoccur, then the problem might be suitable for a CBR solution. Additionally there must be past solutions available and it must be clear that it is more beneficial to reuse these than to start over.

2. Is CBR Suitable for Ontology Engineering?

First we refer to the questions presented in the last section in order to motivate the suitability of CBR. The first question concerns the domain, and ontology construction is certainly a very tough problem to model completely, not all underlying mechanisms are fully understood. Additionally there are exceptions and novel cases, depending on the problem at hand. Still, some general principles do apply for different kinds of ontologies.

For example when discussing enterprise ontologies, including the organisation structure in the ontology will probably be very common.

The fourth question is harder to answer, is there really any benefit in adapting an old solution rather than constructing a new one? There are two main benefits with knowledge reuse, to avoid common mistakes in modelling and to make the modelling easier and faster, but this has not been shown to hold empirically. Finally, answering the fifth question is also not straight forward. If complete ontologies are considered this probably does not hold, but if instead smaller parts, like the ontology patterns already mentioned, are envisioned this is most likely a reasonable assumption.

When comparing our initial ideas for OntoCase (as described in previous publications [5] [7]) with the general idea of CBR the methodologies are quite similar. The arrival of a new case would in terms of OntoCase mean the arrival of a new text corpus with the intention of constructing an ontology. The problem can be expressed as finding the ontology that best represents the domain of the input text corpus, and in addition the problem could be further described by a set of optional competency questions. The retrieval step would then correspond to extracting ontological evidence from the text, then retrieving a set of possibly relevant patterns (partial past cases) and evaluating that set for relevance. The final task in the retrieval step is to choose what patterns to reuse.

The following phase of CBR is reuse, in OntoCase reuse of the patterns to propose an ontology for the current input. This phase contains the specialisation and adaptation of the patterns and the composition of the adapted patterns into an ontology. The revise step of CBR corresponds to evaluation and revision of the ontology. The retain step is connected to the construction and refinement of the patterns, pattern extraction from solutions is still future work but is planned as a part of OntoCase.

3. OntoCase

The following sections describe the general outline of the OntoCase approach (illustrated in Figure 1), and details on the retrieval and reuse phases that are currently being implemented as a prototype system.

3.1. Initial Experiment

As an initial experiment a partial version of the OntoCase approach was tested and evaluated, for a description of this see previous publications by Blomqvist et al. [5]. In this experiment only the first two phases of the cycle were implemented, mainly restricting the method to a pattern selection and combination approach (in CBR terms very simple retrieval and reuse). The process steps included were focused on extraction of terms and relations from the input text corpus, comparing this to the concepts and relations of the patterns, and computing a similarity score for each pattern. Patterns above a user-defined threshold were selected and combined through a naive approach, discarding parts that did not have appropriate support.

When compared to the analysed input (details on the evaluation can also be found in previous publications [5]), the automatically constructed ontology covered only about a third of the ontological primitives extracted from text after pattern specialisation. The reason is partly a small pattern catalogue, but when compared to the manually con-

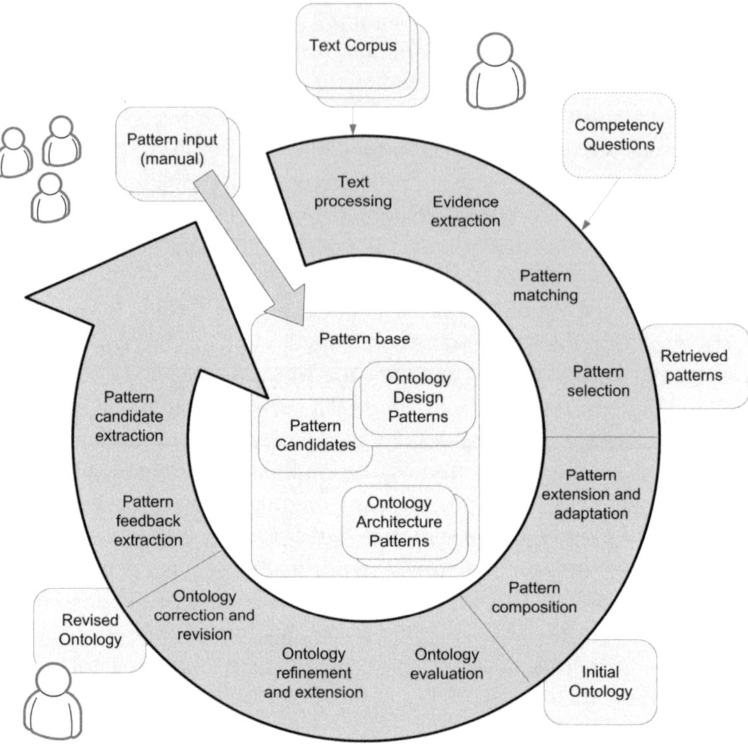

Figure 1. The OntoCase Approach.

structed ontology it was mainly quite specific terms that were missing. A selection process is not enough to cover the scope, since patterns are too abstract compared to a text corpus. Additionally, some abstract information was missing since this is not explicit in the texts. This experiment led us to believe that further refinement of the pattern selection, further adaptation of the patterns when specialised and further revision steps were needed, and this is the basis for our adoption of a CBR viewpoint.

3.2. OntoCase Overview

One of the main elements of a CBR approach is the case base and its content. In the OntoCase approach (illustrated in Figure 1), the case base corresponds to a pattern catalogue, containing both ontology design and architecture patterns and pattern candidates (which are retained partial solutions that have not been generalised and validated as actual patterns). The design patterns are constructed for automatic use and are therefore small self-contained ontologies described in some ontology representation language (examples by the author [4] and others [12] can be found in additional publications). In the future we intend to also add competency questions to the patterns in the pattern base and match those competency questions to requirements from the user, but this is still future work.

The pattern base is currently realised in the form of a database, containing metadata of each pattern, pointers to the actual pattern file, and connections between patterns. The metadata constitute the pattern base index and is currently based on the labels of the core concepts of each pattern and additional optional information about the pattern. Connections to other patterns can be of two kinds, either the pattern is a variant of another pattern or it is just related to another pattern. Additionally we would like to include provenance information and the origin of the pattern, e.g. if the pattern was originally part of a top-level ontology this could be used later when composing patterns.

In the OntoCase approach there is an uncertainty inherent in all the described steps. Each primitive found in the analysis of the input has a certain degree of confidence associated with it. The pattern primitives match input primitives only to a certain extent, and the levels of confidence are transferred onto the constructed ontology.

3.2.1. Retrieval

The retrieval phase consists of four distinct steps; input pre-processing, ontology extraction, pattern matching and pattern selection. The first two steps of the retrieval phase concerns how to extract a representation of the input text corpus. This text processing and analysis is the main focus of many of the existing OL approaches, as stated in section 1.2, therefore developing new solutions for this is not the main focus of our research. Instead we are assuming that an existing OL approach is used, which will at a minimum provide a set of extracted terms and relations between those terms.

The third step of the retrieval phase concerns how to compare the input representation to the pattern base and fourth step includes how to select appropriate patterns. When viewing the matching on an abstract level it is similar to ontology matching. The matching method developed is additionally inspired by ontology ranking schemes, although our approach draws heavily on the richer structure of the input. We have proposed a ranking scheme based on four different factors (as recently presented by Blomqvist [8]); concept and relation coverage, density of relations and semantic proximity. The pattern selection in the fourth step is made based on choosing patterns in the ranking order and computing the resulting total coverage over the input representation. Selection should continue until a sufficient coverage is reached or no more patterns can be selected.

3.2.2. Reuse

The reuse phase is concerned with specialising and composing the patterns into an initial solution ontology and contains two steps that are iteratively applied until all selected patterns have been used. The combination process uses the architecture pattern chosen by the user (if present) to guide the composition, while iterating over all selected patterns. The basic rule is to only include those parts of a pattern that had some match in the input representation. With this as background the first step involves pattern specialisation and adaptation, i.e. selecting only matched concepts, synonyms, as well as relations and extending these pattern parts with additional information from the extracted input representation. The process is enhanced by a set of heuristics, intended to create a more well-structured ontology. Such a heuristic is for example to use the transitive property of taxonomic relations, including more taxonomic relations to keep the ontology connected.

The second step of this phase is pattern composition, which is done based on both the information contained in the pattern base and on the matching information produced in the retrieval phase. Overlaps needs to be resolved and the patterns composed into an initial ontology. Pattern composition can be aided by the origins of the patterns (like patterns extracted from top-level ontologies), the matching results from the retrieval step, or by additional ontology matching methods.

3.2.3. Revise and Retain - Future Work

The revision phase will contain three main steps; first evaluating the constructed ontology, next refining and extending it with missing information, and finally correcting and revising it to improve coherence and correctness as well as the fit to the specific case at hand. For this phase, one main objective is to compensate the missing background information of input texts. Some missing parts have already been added with the help of patterns, but still we can see from the initial experiment mentioned previously that this can probably be improved even further. In this case we have to use external sources of information to try and attach primitives to the ontology in a structured way. In addition another step of the revision phase will focus on reduction of redundancy and resolving inconsistencies in the ontology.

The final phase contains two main steps, the task of generating pattern changes and feedback and the task of extracting new pattern candidates for storage in the pattern base (and for future study by human experts and possible promotion to a pattern status). When retaining solutions we have mainly been inspired by approaches to ontology modularisation, to find coherent parts of the ontology that might constitute suggestions for new patterns is similar to module discovery. This can be done by traversing the taxonomy and finding pattern candidates, and through heuristics these candidates can be restricted in their size and structure. We envision some user involvement in this step, validating and possibly generalising the candidates before inclusion in the pattern base. The feedback process for existing patterns involves the recalculation of confidence values and applying changes in patterns.

4. Summary and Outlook

To conclude the comparison between CBR and OL (specifically the OntoCase approach), we can note that our semi-automatic approach for constructing ontologies using patterns actually do have a lot in common with CBR and that the CBR methodology fits well to such a problem. This paper has been kept on a very general level when it comes to CBR methods though, not going into detail in representation and realisation issues, but adding the matching of competency questions to OntoCase would take a further step into the direction of pure CBR.

We have presented our CBR-inspired approach for pattern-based ontology construction in brief, but initial experiments (see referred papers) have already indicated the usefulness of ontology patterns for supporting semi-automatic enterprise ontology construction. This research provides a balanced hybrid approach somewhere between manual ontology engineering using patterns and a completely case-based system. Patterns could be constructed both manually and discovered automatically. We believe that this is a novel application area of CBR (and TCBR) that has a promising future.

The paper describes ongoing research but the first two phases of the approach are already realised, and initial experiments have provided promising indications. Although no experiment results can yet be presented for the latest improvements of OntoCase, it adds several steps to improve the output compared to existing OL approaches. It remains to implement the complete OntoCase cycle and conduct thorough evaluations. We envision that iterative approaches exploiting knowledge reuse and uncertainty, are really the future of semi-automatic ontology construction.

Acknowledgements

We would like to thank the anonymous reviewers for their comments which helped improve this paper. Parts of the work was conducted within the Media Information Logistics project, funded by the foundation *Carl-Olof och Jenz Hamrins Stiftelse*.

References

[1]　A. Aamodt and E. Plaza, 'Case-based reasoning: Foundational issues , methodological variations, and system approaches', *AICom*, **7**, 39–59, (1994). IOS Press.

[2]　Harith Alani and Christopher Brewster, 'Ontology Ranking based on the Analysis of Concept Structures', in *Proceedings of K-CAP'05*, Banff, Alberta, Canada, (October 2005).

[3]　Chutiporn Anutariya, Rachanee Ungrangsi, and Vilas Wuwongse, 'Sqore: A framework for semantic query based ontology retrieval', *Advances in Databases: Concepts, Systems and Applications*, (2007).

[4]　E. Blomqvist, 'Fully automatic construction of enterprise ontologies using design patterns: Initial method and first experiences', in *Proc. of OTM'05 (ODBASE)*, Agia Napa, Cyprus, (2005).

[5]　E. Blomqvist, A. Öhgren, and K. Sandkuhl, 'Ontology Construction in an Enterprise Context: Comparing and Evaluating two Approaches', in *Proc. of ICEIS'06*, Paphos, Cyprus, (May 2006).

[6]　E. Blomqvist and K. Sandkuhl, 'Patterns in Ontology Engineering: Classification of Ontology Patterns', in *Proc. of ICEIS2005*, Miami Beach, Florida, (May 24-28 2005).

[7]　Eva Blomqvist, 'Ontocase - a pattern-based ontology construction approach', in *Proccedings of OTM 2007: ODBASE - The 6th International Conference on Ontologies, DataBases, and Applications of Semantics*, Vilamoura, Algarve, Portugal, (November 25-30 2007).

[8]　Eva Blomqvist, 'Pattern ranking for semi-automatic ontology construction', in *Proceedings of SAC2008*, Fortaleza, Brazil, (March 2008).

[9]　Philipp Cimiano, *Ontology Learning and Population from Text: Algorithms, Evaluation and Applications*, Springer Science, 2006.

[10]　Jerome Euzenat and Pavel Shvaiko, *Ontology Matching*, Springer Berlin Heidelberg, 2007.

[11]　Blaz Fortuna, Marko Grobelnik, and Dunja Mladenic, 'Semi-automatic Data-driven Ontology Construction System', in *Proc. of IS-2006*, Ljubljana, Slovenia, (2006).

[12]　A. Gangemi, 'Ontology Design Patterns for Semantic Web Content', in *Proceedings of ISWC 2005*, volume 3729 of *LNCS*, pp. 262–276. Springer, (2005).

[13]　T. Gruber, 'A translation approach to portable ontology specifications', in *Knowledge Acquisition*, volume 5, pp. 199–220, (1993).

[14]　Jose Iria, Christopher Brewster, Fabio Ciravegna, and Yorick Wilks, 'An Incremental Tri-partite Approach to Ontology Learning', in *Proc. of LREC2006*, Genoa, (May 2006).

[15]　David B. Leake, Ana Maguitman, Thomas Reichherzer, Alberto Cañas, Marco Carvalho, Marco Arguedas, Sofia Brenes, and Tom Eskridge, 'Aiding knowledge capture by searching for extensions of knowledge models', in *Proceedings of the Second International Conference on Knowledge Capture (K-Cap 2003)*, (2003).

[16]　S. K. Pal and S. Shiu, *Foundations of Soft Case-based Reasoning*, John Wiley & Sons Inc, 2004.

[17]　Pavel Shvaiko and Jerome Euzenat, 'A Survey of Schema-based Matching Approaches', *Journal on Data Semantics*, **IV**, 146–171, (2005). LNCS Springer-verlag.

[18]　S. Staab, M. Erdmann, and A. Maedche, 'Engineering Ontologies using Semantic Patterns', in *Proceedings of the IJCAI-01 Workshop on E-business & The Intelligent Web*, Seattle, (2001).

[19]　Paola Velardi, Roberto Navigli, Allessandro Cucchiarelli, and Francesca Neri, 'Evaluation of OntoLearn, a methodology for automatic learning of domain ontologies', in *Ontology Learning from Text: Methods, Evaluation and Applications*, IOS Press, (2005).

[20]　W3C-SWBPD, 'Semantic Web Best Practices and Deployment Working Group'. Available at: http://www.w3.org/2001/sw/BestPractices/, 2004.

[21]　Rosina O. Weber, Kevin D. Ashley, and Stefanie Brüninghaus, 'Textual case-based reasoning', *The Knowledge Engineering Review*, **20**(3), 255–260, (2006).

Tenth Scandinavian Conference on Artificial Intelligence
A. Holst et al. (Eds.)
IOS Press, 2008

DEFECT PREDICTION IN HOT STRIP ROLLING USING ANN AND SVM

Manu HIETANIEMI [a], Ulla ELSILÄ [b], Perttu LAURINEN [b] and Juha RÖNING [b]

[a] *manu@ee.oulu.fi*
[b] *University of Oulu, Department of Electrical Engineering*
Computer Engineering Laboratory, Intelligent Systems Group
PO BOX 4500, FIN-90401 Oulu, Finland

Abstract.

One of the largest factors affecting the loss for steel manufacturing are defects in the steel strips produced. Therefore the prediction of these defects forehand would be very important. In this study we used classifiers - feedforward neural networks and a support vector machine - to solve this problem. We also used different kinds of feature selection methods such as a preprocessing step for the classifiers. As a result, these two classifiers confirmed the same grade of classification error in this study.

Keywords. Hot steel rolling, feature selection, classification, neural networks, support vector machine

Introduction

Due to the complexity and the deficiencies in existing physical models of the hot strip rolling process, defects are quite common when steel strips are produced. The defects are typically a result of improper temperatures or dimension measures. The thickest strips that are produced in the hot strip mill of this study (height from 6.50 mm to 20 mm) were chosen in the classification, because the defects are most common in these. Defects occur in approximately one out of four steel strips and this leads to further inspection by an inspector and additional operations, leading to a considerable financial loss for the production. Thus, there is a need for finding these failures beforehand.

The amount of data and measurements is huge; the relation can potentially be non-linear and also involves a lot of uncertainty, whereupon the traditional physical estimators are almost useless. Therefore the prediction of these failures by a proper classifier, e.g. artificial neural network (ANN) or support vector machine (SVM) methods, was the main goal of this study. There are a lot of existing studies on hot strip rolling using classifiers, but they are concentrated on modelling optimized rolling process control parameters *i.e.* temperatures [1], rolling force [2]. However, we had the opposite approach in the sense that the parameters of the rolling process were predetermined and the defect prediction had to be made on these parameters.

ANNs and SVMs are useful tools for comparison because they have a lot of different characteristics. While ANNs can suffer from multiple local extrema, the solution of a SVM is global and unique. The model selecting for ANN, *i.e.* hidden layers, the number of neurons and the functions that are utilized, are predetermined, whereas the supervised SVM training determines its parameters based on the available data, although you need to adjust the hyperparameters properly. Also, the ANN uses only empirical risk minimization whereas the SVM uses structural risk minimization [3]. The structural risk minimization principle finds the best solution in terms of empirical risk but also the simplest in terms of the model complexity. The large number of features on the dataset and their significance for the classification was also an important issue in the study. Thus the complexity of the dataset led to different kinds of approaches in the preprocessing stage.

1. Hot Strip Rolling Process

The data used was gathered from the hot strip mill of Ruukki in Raahe, Finland. The mill with its pyrometers is illustrated in Figure 1. Slab dimensions, the chemical composition of the slabs as well as target values of the rolling process are collected from the production planning computer of the process control system. Before rolling, the slabs are heated in reheating furnaces. At the time of the collection of the used datasets, there was one walking beam furnace and three pusher type furnaces. After discharging, the slab is rolled at the reversing roughing mill, typically in seven passes from the thickness of some 210 millimeters to a target thickness of *e.g.* 30 millimeters. After roughing, the rolling stock is called a transfer bar. Next, the transfer bar goes through the finishing mill. In the case of the most recent datasets, a coil box had been added on the line immediately before the finishing mill. The coil box makes rolling of bigger coils possible and facilitates more uniform temperature control of the transfer bar. After finishing, the rolling stock, which is now called the hot strip, enters the cooling area where the targeted temperature profile of the strip is achieved. Finally, the strip is coiled at the down-coiler.

During the rolling process, many measurements are made and some of the meter positions are shown in Figure 1. Temperatures are measured at several places from the furnace up to the coiler; the width at the rougher and after finishing; and the thickness, profile, flatness, and speed of the strip are measured after the finishing line. Also, time stamps and durations of the various process stages are recorded. From these measurements, the process control system calculates properties of the rolling stock: mean values, variations, segmented values, deviations from the targets, classification, which are subsequently stored in the database.

Since the actual rolling process after the heating is fast, with a duration of a mere few minutes, the process is very sensitive to various errors. The maintenance of the right and uniform temperature during the process is a particularly challenging task. At any moment during the rolling, the automation system or the rolling mill operator may store a strip-specific retention code in the database. Each product with this type of code has to be checked manually and sometimes reshaped before it can be approved for selling. In this study, these products are collectively termed retained samples.

2. Dataset

On the basis of a previous study "Defect prediction in hot strip rolling" [4], the original dataset was reduced by 83% from over 200 to 37 features with basic statistical analysis

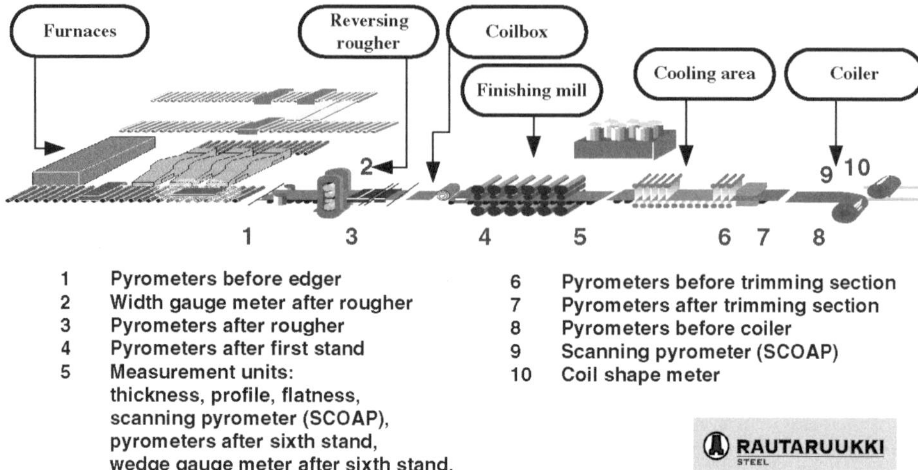

Figure 1. Illustrated hot strip rolling mill in Rautaruukki, Raahe, Finland

and linear correlation, and according to advice received from the rolling experts. These remaining 37 features included different kinds of material properties, temperature measurements, dimensional measurements and rolling properties of the steel slab. The continuous features were scaled from 0 to 1. The class features, which had discrete values, were also separated into components, *e.g.* if a feature had four possible values, it was separated into four different binary features with a value of 0 or 1. The dataset eventually consisted of 77 features and 6004 measurements. 25.5 % of these examples included the retention code.

3. Classification Methods

3.1. Artificial Neural Network

A feedforward multilayer perceptron (MLP) neural network model was used with a back-propagation algorithm to minimize the errors at the output [5]. The dataset (with 6004 samples) was divided as follows: half for training, one quarter for testing and the last quarter for validation.

Training was executed with (i) the Levenberg-Marquardt algorithm, which appears to be the fastest method for training moderate-sized feedforward neural networks [6,7], and (ii) the Scale conjugate gradient algorithm [5]. The selected transfer function was a log-sigmoid function, which is commonly used in back propagation networks partly because it is differentiable. It takes the input, which can have any value between plus and minus infinity, and compresses the output into the range of 0 to 1.

The decision regarding how many hidden layers should be used was limited to one or two. It has been proven that a three-layer feedforward network (*i.e.* input layer, one hidden layer and output layer) with (N - 1) hidden neurons can give any N input-target relations precisely [6]. The same size input in a four-layer-network *i.e.* two hidden layers, can give the target relations with a negligibly small error using only (N / 2) + 3 hidden neurons. So using only one or two hidden layers was the obvious choice. The number of

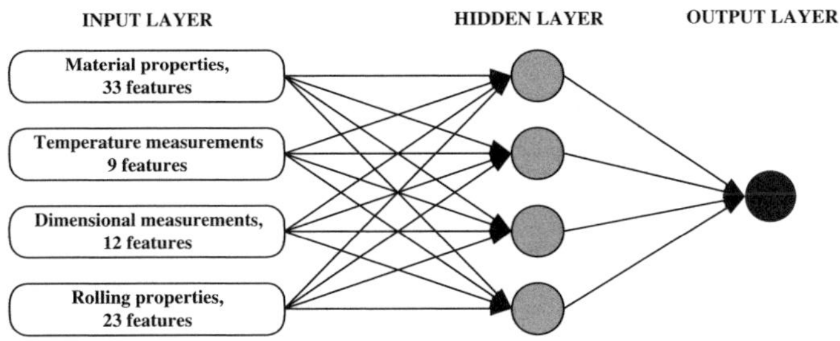

Figure 2. Illustration of the feedforward neural network with the available features in input, a single hidden layer and an output layer.

neurons was optimized case-specificly depending on the number of features, which was verified by the validation dataset.

3.2. *Support Vector Machine*

A support vector machine with a Gaussian Radial Basis Function (RBF) kernel was used. The most important part of a SVM is the selection of the hyperparameters. But the optimal spread of the RBF and the corresponding penalty parameter were attained by pinpointing a large interval of possibilities and verifying the results with cross-validation. In optimization a "LibSVM" tool was used [8]. However, some manual adjustment on the bias and the threshold of the predictions were done to get more accurate results for the test set.

With the use of a non-linear RFB kernel in an SVM, we can map any non-linear input function into high dimensional feature spaces that are illustrated in Figure 3. This leads to a convex linear optimization problem, which is relatively easy to calculate. This way we can obtain a global optimum and overfitting is not problem in the sense that it is in an ANN.

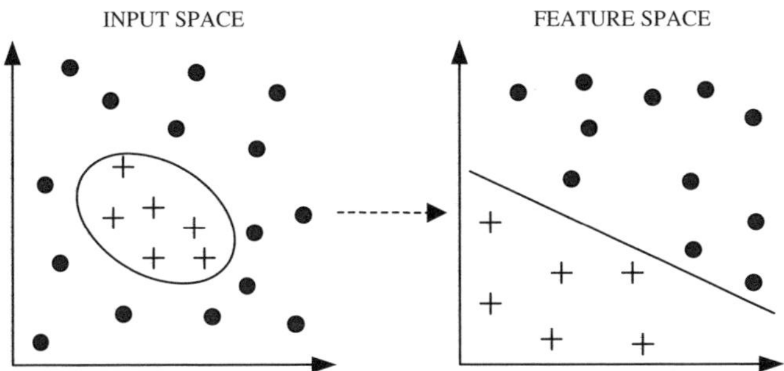

Figure 3. Illustrates the two-class classification problem, where the input is mapped on a higher dimensional feature space, which leads to a linear classification problem.

4. Feature Selection

4.1. Forward/Backward Feature Selection Algorithm

The main method for pre-processing was the so-called "Forward Backward Feature Se-lecting" algorithm (FBFS) which has also been used in *e.g.* adaptive context selection [9]. The purpose of this technique was to select only the most suitable features for the dataset. The features were selected one by one into the dataset as long as the result got better, and along the way it was possible to drop one out if it became worth it. But this technique was only necessary for the ANN because the large number of features in the dataset creates huge computational demands. However, the computational complexity of SVM does not depend on the dimensionality of the input space.

4.2. Self-organizing Maps and K-Means Clustering

On the basis of a previous study "Defect prediction in hot strip rolling" [4], which was done for the same dataset, there was a lot of useful information on the features and their segmentation in proportion to the retentions. The study was utilized using the self-organizing maps, originally developed by Kohonen [10], which are an unsupervised learning method that organizes n-dimensional input space into a two dimensional line of knots, where each knot includes similar samples of each other measured by Euclidian distance. By the help of SOMs we can analyse the significance of the input features in relation to the other features. The SOMs were done in many stages where unsignificant features were excluded from the dataset. After the final stage 16 most meaningful fea-tures were left in the dataset. These were clustered by using k-means clustering algo-rithm. This 16 feature dataset was also used in the results in comparison to other feature selection methods.

4.3. Grouping Features

With the information obtained by the aforementioned clustering and analytic evaluation of the most significant and advantageous features gave us three features that we used in grouping the dataset. From the boundaries of these features we attained 9 different more homogenous groups.

Classification within these groups did not improve the results, however, but we found an interesting group that had a significantly low retention percentage, which we isolated from the classification input. This group had only 2.1% of retentions, and it contained 145 examples, 2.4% of all the examples. Hence, it could be left out of classification due to the small percentage of retentions, which could not be achieved by prediction.

5. Results

In the classification problem of two classes, *i.e.* 0 and 1, the confidence value for the predictions given by the classifier on each sample are given from 0 to 1. In this case we used a boundary point of 0.5 *i.e.* the samples predicted below 0.5 are rounded downwards to 0 and samples with a prediction of 0.5 or greater are rounded up to 1. Results obtained

CLASSIFIER	FEATURES	TOTAL ERROR
ANN(LM)	FBFS (12-feat.)	17.5%
ANN(LM)	Clustering (16-feat.)	17.6%
ANN(LM)	All features	17.7%
ANN(SCG)	FBFS (12-feat.)	17.8%
ANN(SCG)	Clustering (16-feat.)	18.1%
ANN(SCG)	All features	17.6%
SVM	FBFS(12-feat.)	19.8%
SVM	Clustering (16-feat.)	18.7%
SVM	All features	18.1%

Table 1. Comparison of results obtained by all classifiers

using this binary type of classification are shown in Table 1. As we can see, the ANN works most effectively with the FBFS algorithm and the SVM is most effective when all the features are included in the dataset. Although these results in Table 1 are comparable, they are useless in the sense that the prediction error for retained samples are on average 45% and 5% for the successful samples.

This led to an approach that gave a stronger weight to the retained samples that were predicted correctly. It was obtained with using supervised training and then manually adjusting the threshold and bias in terms of the training data and verifying these results with a test set. Due to this adjusting the total loss of classification increased while the prediction error for retained samples decreased, which is illustrated in Table 2 for the ANN and in Table 3 for the SVM, where the predictions are in the columns and the true values in the rows.

Due to these unsatisfactory results obtained by only using this classical binary -type of classification there was a need to examine where the errors were located. This procedure would enable us to find intervals on the distribution of the classification, where the predictions would be comparatively reliable. In Figures 4 and 5 we have examined the distribution of the classification errors on the confidence values with respect to one decimal. On the x-axis we have the confidence value given by the classifier *e.g.* if all samples would be classified correctly then the figures would contain only gray colored successful samples on the left from 0.0 to 0.5 and the black colored samples would lie on the right from 0.5 to 1.0. With this technique we obtain reliability levels for the classifications given by the classifier *i.e.* if the NN gives a confidence value from 0.9 to 1.0, we can tell that it is a sample with a retention code of 96% certainty. The largest percentage of the incorrectly predicted samples lies close to probability 0.5 on both classifiers, which is the most problematic area. This problem area is slightly wider for the ANN (from 0.4 to 0.7) than it is for the SVM (from 0.4 to 0.6), where the prediction error is greater than 25%. If these problem areas would be removed from the classification set, we could predict more than three quarters of the samples with about 90% accuracy.

6. Discussion and Conclusions

The study was made at the steel plant of Ruukki due its high financial significance. This kind of approach could work, but in our point of view the dataset is missing some valuable information. This information could be attained by adding some pyrometer in the

ANN	Successful	Retention	True codes
Successful	1556	610	2166
Retention	206	557	763
Predicted codes	1762	1167	2929

Table 2. Error percentage of samples with retention code 27.0% and 28.0% respectively for the successful samples. 27.7% in total. The rows indicate the true codes and the columns the predicted codes for the samples.

SVM	Successful	Retention	True codes
Successful	1620	546	2166
Retention	222	541	763
Predicted codes	1842	1087	2929

Table 3. Error percentage of samples with retention code 29.1% and 25.2% respectively for the successful samples. 26.2% in total. The rows indicate the true codes and the columns the predicted codes for the samples.

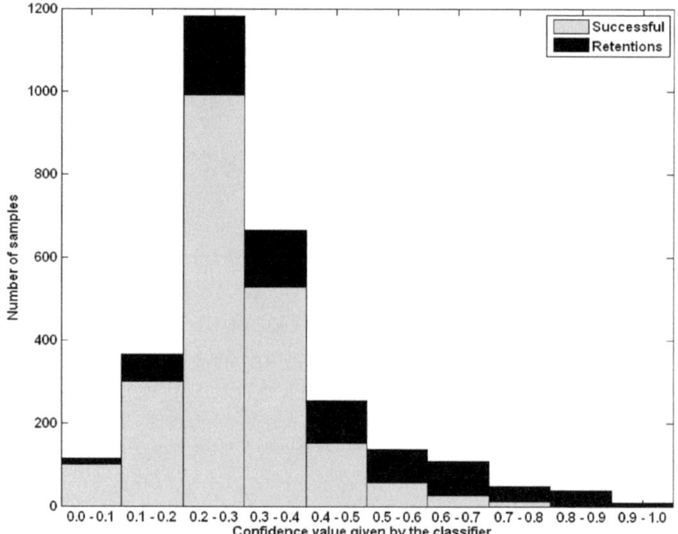

Figure 4. Predictions made by SVM

production line or improving the existing physical models. Also these physical models are related in large part to the parameters that are estimated beforehand and used in classification. Because of this, many parameters may have more or less random error, which makes the classification more unreliable. We have nevertheless shown that the classifiers performs quite similarly in this subject with regard to the classification error, although the distributions are segmented quite differently.

With respect to the distribution of the confidence values and the reliability levels given by the classifiers there could be some closer inspection, *i.e.* clustering, on the boundaries of confidence values. This would make it possible to find homogenous groups in the predictions, which could be classified correctly to a large degree.

A different kind of approach could be the combination of the online rolling process parameter optimization and the defect classifier. In this case the rolling parameters could be optimized for instance by a genetic algorithm and the defect classifier would verify

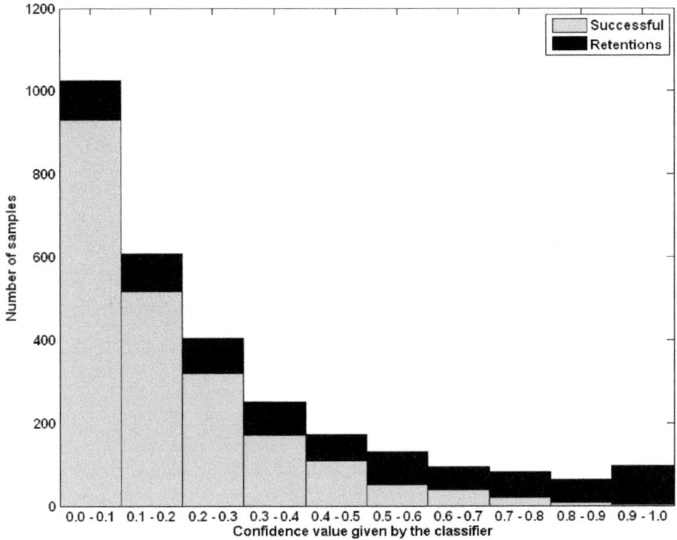

Figure 5. Predictions made by NN(SCG)

that no defects occur, and if some defects would appear, then the genetic algorithm could find the second best solution, in terms of the optimal, that does not cause any defects.

References

[1]　P. Laurinen and J. Roning, An adaptive neural network model for predicting the post roughing mill temperature of steel slabs in the reheating furnace, *Journal of Materials Processing Technology* **168** (2005), 423–430.

[2]　T. Fechner, D. Neumerkel and I. Keller, Adaptive neural network filter for steel rolling, *IEEE International Conference on Neural Networks* **6** (1994), 3915–3920.

[3]　V. N. Vapnik, *The Nature of Statistical Learning Theory,* , New York: Springer-Verlag, (1995).

[4]　U. Elsila and J. Roning, Defect prediction in hot strip rolling, *Ironmaking & Steelmaking* **3** (1993), 241–248.

[5]　C. M. Bishop, *Neural Networks for Pattern Recognition*, Oxford University Press, (1995).

[6]　M. T. Hagan and H. B. Demuth, *Neural Network Design*, MA: PWS Publishing, (1996).

[7]　W. H. Chen and J. Y. Shih, Comparison of support vector machines and back propagation neural networks in forecasting the six major stock markets, *Int. J. Electronic Finance* **1**, (2006), 49–67.

[8]　C. C. Chang and C. J. Lin, LIBSVM: a library for support vector machines, (2001), Software available at http://www.csie.ntu.edu.tw/cjlin/libsvm.

[9]　W. Jiang and A. Ortega, Forward/backward adaptive context selection with applications to motion vector field encoding,*International Conference on Image Processing*, **2**, (1997), 168–171.

[10]　T. Kohonen, *Self-Organizing Maps*, Springer-Verlag, (1995)

Tenth Scandinavian Conference on Artificial Intelligence
A. Holst et al. (Eds.)
IOS Press, 2008

A Framework For Human-Aware Robot Planning

Marcello CIRILLO, Lars KARLSSON and Alessandro SAFFIOTTI
AASS Mobile Robotics Lab, Örebro University, Sweden

Abstract. Robots that share their workspace with humans, like household or service robots, need to take into account the presence of humans when planning their actions. In this paper, we present a framework for human-aware planning in which we consider three kinds of human-robot interaction. We focus in particular on the core module of the framework, a human-aware planner that generates a sequence of actions for a robot, taking into account the status of the environment, the goals of the robot and the forecasted plan of the human. We present a first realization of this planner, together with two simple experiments that demonstrate the feasibility of our approach.

Keywords. Robot task planning, Human-aware planning, Human-robot interaction, Intelligent environments

1. Introduction

Until now, robots have been confined into special working cells under controlled conditions, and have been applied mostly to industrial automation. Now, the interest of the public for home robots is increasing, and people are looking at robots as a new mean to improve the quality of their everyday life. The aging of the population, for instance, could open a wide space for new robotic applications [10]. The robots could then become silent workers, precious butlers and, eventually, friendly helpers in our houses.

The presence of humans introduces other challenges besides how the robots should interact with them. It also has a profound influence on how the robots perform high level reasoning and especially plan their actions. Most AI planning systems use a model in which the world is in a particular state, the robot executes a specific action, and the world changes to another state, and so on. This state may be to some extent unpredictable, but it is the robot's choice of actions that determines what the next states can be. In other words, the robot is in control. However, humans are agents that act independently of the robot, and they are only partially observable. Thus, when planning, the robot needs to consider two different processes affecting the state, both its own actions and the actions of the human.

There has been a number of approaches to planning in partially observable and non-deterministic/stochastic environments for mobile robots, and as mentioned, the presence of human actors introduces partial observability. POMDPs [7], which can deal with sensing and uncertainty, have featured prominently among these, such as the robot Xavier [9]. However, these works tend to be focused on navigation tasks. Considering humans as a

Figure 1. An example of human-aware robot planning.

source of uncertainty, one can point to some work on planning with external/exogenous events, which in principle can be caused by humans. An early example is the work of Blythe [4], which used Bayesian nets to compute the probability of success in the presence of external events. In the robotic field, some works have considered human-robot co-habitation. Often these works take a viewpoint which is different from the one adopted here, by focusing on aspects such as security (e.g., within MORPHA [6]) or acceptable motion (e.g., within COGNIRON [1]). The problem of task planning in the presence of humans is currently completely open, although some researchers have started exploring the issue [2,3].

In this paper, we present a framework for human-aware robot task planning in which the human(s) and the robot(s) both have their own goals, but the robots should prepare their own plan taking into account the presence of the humans. We classify the types of human robot interaction that we consider into three categories:

1. Both human and robot have goals, that are different. The robot should try to avoid interference with the human (implicit cooperation)
2. The human has a goal (or a set of goals) and the robot should help to accomplish it. The robot becomes a butler for the human
3. The robot has a goal to accomplish and needs some extra help. In this case, it is the robot that asks for help from the human

Figure 1 shows an example of the intended interaction in case 1.

The three kinds of interaction are ordered by increasing complexity and highlight the steps that are needed in order to bring the two worlds, of the humans and of the intelligent systems, to a closer cooperation. In this paper, we propose a general framework to address the problem of robot task planning and execution within the above categories. The full study and realization of this framework is an ambitious goal, and in this paper we offer a small but concrete first step by proposing a human-aware planner that deals with the first category under restrictive assumptions.

In the next section we present our framework, including an hypothetical example of its intended working. Section 3 presents the first version of our human-aware plan-

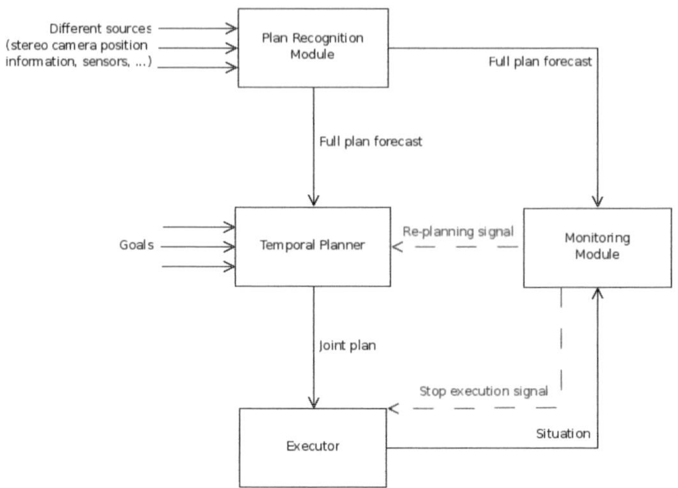

Figure 2. The proposed framework for human-aware robot planning.

ner, while in Section 4 we report two simple experiments that show the validity of this planner. Section 5 concludes.

2. The Overall Framework

To plan safely and effectively in the presence of human, the robot should be aware of the actions performed by the human and should be able to produce a forecast of the human's next actions. Taking into account the forecast, the robot can then make a plan of its own, avoiding any unwanted interference, assisting the human when needed, and, in the most complex case previously described, requesting assistance from the part of the human when this request does not cause discomfort to the inhabitant of the environment.

2.1. Architecture

This idea above is embodied in the architecture sketched in Figure 2. This schema does not describe an implemented system, but rather the proposed organization of functionalities needed to realize human-aware planning. The intent of this schema is to clarify the place and role, in the overall human-aware planning problem, of the planner described in the next section.

Plan Recognition Module   The task of this module is to provide the robot with the needed awareness of the actions and intentions of the human(s), by recognizing their actions and forecasting their plans. This module receives as input information from different sources, and it produces, at each time t, a forecast of the possible plans of the human(s) in the environment. Every forecasted plan may be associated with its likelihood. As time passes, the set of plans and their likelihoods are updated as new actions are detected. Human plan recognition is a very active area of research (see, e.g., [5]). In our work, we plan to use existing state of the art systems for this module.

Temporal Planner   The temporal planner is the main focus of the research presented in this work. It receives as inputs goals and the human's plan forecast. The output of this module is a temporal, probabilistic joint plan of both robot(s) and human(s). Since it is not certain which plan each human is performing, then the robot plans must be branched to take into account different possibilities. The plan is both temporal (absolute time and time dependencies between actions are taken into account) and probabilistic (actions may fail or lead to different outcomes). The full joint plan of both human(s) and robot(s) is then passed to the executor.

Executor   The executor puts the robot plan into action. Information about the current situation is then sent to the monitoring module.

Monitoring Module   The monitoring module provides a continuous control over the robot plan execution, ensuring that time constraints are respected and implementing some strong safety policies to protect the human inhabitants. In case inconsistencies are found, the monitor can stop the plan execution and request a new plan generation.

The importance of the monitoring capability lays in the fact that our main objective is to allow the cooperation between two worlds that are, for their nature, strongly different. The goal of synchronizing and keeping them consistent raises a number of open research issues. In every moment the robot should be aware of the overall situation, understanding what is the plan of the human and verifying that the actions of the robot do not interfere with the people present in the environment. The robot should verify as well that its plan is still consistent both with the human's needs and with the overall situation, that is, the robot's plan may have to be changed not only because of possible external events, but also because of the unpredicted actions of humans.

2.2. Example

We illustrate the intended working of the above framework by way of a hypothetical example. We assume a household pervaded by sensors and intelligent devices, which provide input to the plan recognition module. For instance, the information that the user is watching TV could be acquired by a stereocamera on the ceiling and then validated by a pressure sensor on the couch and by the fact that the TV is on.

Figure 3 graphically illustrates the example. The four lines at the bottom represent the predicted plans of the inhabitant generated by the plan recognition module. In the example, at time *t0* the user is observed sitting on the couch and the system identifies three possible patterns of actions: the human may want to read a book (**b**), watch television (**c**) or make a phone call (**d**). As time passes and new data are available, some plans that seemed possible are discarded and new possibilities are identified. In the example, at time *t1* the human is observed taking off his glasses, and the system identifies the new possible plan to take a rest (**a**). Then, at time *t2*, the user is observed turning off the phone, and the corresponding plan (**d**) is discarded as not consistent.

At time *t2* the temporal planner receives a goal, and it generates the probabilistic temporal robot plan represented by the upper part of Figure 3. This plan contains conditional branches: actions that are applicable if the human real plan is (**a**) may be not an adequate choice in case the plan is in fact (**b**) or (**c**). Each action of the robot plan (represented in the figure by the capital letter **A**) is applicable to a subset of the possible human plans. The robot will then start to execute the actions that correspond to the

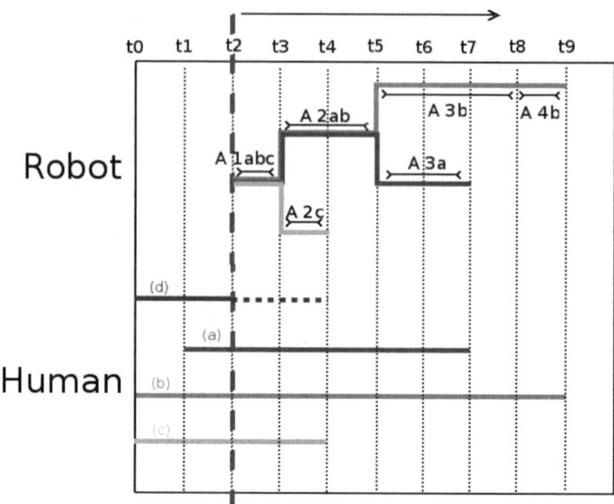

Figure 3. Graphical representation of the output of human-aware planning. The *x* axis represents time, quantized in slots. The lower part of the picture represents the possible human plans generated by the plan recognition module. The upper part represents a conditional robot plan generated by the human-aware planner. Branches in the robot plan specify courses of robot's actions corresponding to different human plans.

human's predicted plan with the highest likelihood. The monitoring module will ensure both the safety of the human and the soundness of the execution.

3. A Human-Aware Planner

In this paper, we focus on the human-aware planning module (that is, the "temporal planner" box in Figure 2), its design and implementation. As we said, human-aware planning involves a number of totally open research issues. Therefore, we adopt an incremental approach to the problem, starting our work with a very simplified scenario and, with each step of our research, relaxing some constraints to tackle more general cases. The complexity of the research problem requires simple, even unrealistic assumptions as starting point. For instance, in the first step we present in this paper, we assume the presence of a single human and of a single robot in the environment. Moreover, we assume that every action of the human ends in a deterministic way and we exclude the possibility for the human to change his intentions in the middle of an action: every activity that is started must be concluded without any interruption.

The input for the planner is a single plan for the human, that is, a linear sequence of actions split in discrete time slots (the expansion of the planner to handle multiple human plan with different levels of confidence is part of our future work). The planner produces a plan according to the goals of the robot, the state of the environment, the constraints imposed by the sequence of actions of the human and the cost of the actions that the robot can perform. From a more technical prospective, we use as a starting point PTLPlan [8], a probabilistic conditional planner that we extend to perform our first experiments on human-aware planning.

The extended planner works as follows. It takes as input:

1. A planning domain description specifying both the actions the robot can perform, and those of the human. Action are specified in terms of preconditions and

effects; the latter may be context dependent and/or stochastic, and may involve sensing (for the robot). In other words, the actions are of the type commonly found in POMDPs.

2. The robot's current belief state, including the topology of the environment and the estimated positions of the robot and the human.
3. A hypothesis about the plan of the human, as a sequence of actions.
4. A goal

In this first step, we make the following assumptions on the forecasted plan for the human:

- The forecast received by the planner is limited to one single plan.
- In the human plan there are no conditional branches.
- The forecast does not contain parallel actions.
- The duration of the actions is fixed.

Notice, however, that the actions of the human can have non-deterministic effects with associated probabilities.

In the original planning algorithm, the planner starts from the current belief state and then tries different actions, resulting in new belief states from which the algorithm can continue its search. If an action involves sensing and can result in different observations, then that action will result in several different belief states (one for each potential observation) and the planner will consider them all. The algorithm takes advantage of user-specified control rules (specified in temporal logic) to prune certain sequences of belief states. The algorithm continues until a plan (or policy) is found for which a goal state is reached with sufficient probability. That plan is conditional on the observations that the robot may do. For instance, it may contain branches like "if the door is observed to be open, then move to the bedroom".

The extended, human-aware, version of the algorithm simply applies the next action in the human's plan after the robot tries to apply its own action. Hence, each application of a robot action yields one or more new belief states which include the effects of both the robot's and the human's action, and a new human plan where the last applied action has been removed. Non-determinism of the human's actions is handled thanks to the ability of PTLPlan to consider actions with non-deterministic effects. The output of the planner is a joint plan, a list of human actions coupled with the ones that the robot performs at the same time.

4. An Illustrative Experiment

We have performed some simple experiments with the human-aware planner, in which we simulate the input from the plan recognition module using synthetic data and we analyze the output without actually executing it. The goal is to test the behaviour of the planner when human constraints are provided. The human plan is composed by a sequence of linear actions, quantized in time slots of 5 minutes each. Therefore, an action may take several time steps to complete (e.g., if the human cooks for 18 minutes, the system will split his action in 4 basic units). In this experiments, all actions are deterministic. The human's actions are passed to the planner as a list and then a joint plan is generated, as we will see in the following.

Time	Human action	Robot action		Time	Human action	Robot action
0	(MOVE KITCHEN)	(MOVE LIVINGROOM)		0	(MOVE KITCHEN)	(MOVE LIVINGROOM)
1	(COOK)	(STAY LIVINGROOM)		1	(COOK)	(STAY LIVINGROOM)
4	(EAT)	(STAY LIVINGROOM)		3	(EAT)	(STAY LIVINGROOM)
7	(WASHDISHES)	(STAY LIVINGROOM)		5	(WASHDISHES)	(STAY LIVINGROOM)
9	(MOVE LIVINGROOM)	(CLEAN LIVINGROOM)		6	(OUTSIDE)	(STAY LIVINGROOM)
10	(READ LIVINGROOM)	(MOVE BEDROOM)		10	(OUTSIDE)	(STAY LIVINGROOM)
11	(READ LIVINGROOM)	(STAY BEDROOM)		24	(MOVE KITCHEN)	(STAY LIVINGROOM)
24	(WATCHTV)	(STAY BEDROOM)		25	(COOK)	(STAY LIVINGROOM)
42	(MOVE KITCHEN)	(STAY BEDROOM)		34	(EAT)	(STAY LIVINGROOM)
43	(COOK)	(STAY BEDROOM)		38	(EAT)	(CLEAN LIVINGROOM)
48	(EAT)	(STAY BEDROOM)		40	(EAT)	(MOVE BEDROOM)
53	(WASHDISHES)	(CLEAN BEDROOM)		41	(EAT)	(CLEAN BEDROOM)
54	(MOVE BEDROOM)	(MOVE KITCHEN)		42	(MOVE LIVINGROOM)	(MOVE KITCHEN)
55	(REST)	(CLEAN KITCHEN)		43	(WATCHTV)	(CLEAN KITCHEN)
65	(REST)	(CLEAN KITCHEN)		53	(WATCHTV)	(CLEAN KITCHEN)

Table 1. Left: full joint plan of Johanna and the cleaning robot, during a typical week day. Right: full joint plan of Johanna and the cleaning robot, during a Sunday. Since actions take usually more than a single time step, only time steps when the human or the robot start a new action are displayed.

The scenario we consider involves one human, an elderly person that lives alone, and one robot, a floor cleaner that can perform three basic actions: stay idle in a room, move to another room, and clean. The apartment is composed by three rooms: the bedroom, the livingroom and the kitchen. The human, Johanna, can perform different actions that we assume can be recognized by the system: she can cook, eat, wash the dishes, watch TV, read (both in the bedroom and in the livingroom) or she can go out for a walk. Some of her actions affect the cleanliness of the apartment (e.g., cooking produces more dirt on the kitchen floor) and this information is known to the planner. To further simplify the scenario, we assume that the days of Johanna are driven by a quite strict routine, which means that the plan recognition module can safely guess the activities of Johanna by observing a few cues, e.g., the day of the week, the wake-up time, the clothes she wears, and so on.

The cleaner is not allowed to start its activity until Johanna is awake and she leaves her bedroom. After that time, it can start performing its job with some strict limitations: the robot can never clean a room where Johanna is present in order to avoid any disturbances, and it must wait in rooms where no human is present to avoid her to stumble into it by accident. Every action of the robot has a cost in terms of battery consumption. The most expensive action is cleaning. Moving from one room to the other is less expensive, while the cheapest action is to wait still in a room.

We consider here two sample runs corresponding to two typical days in Johanna's life. In the first one, a normal week day, she wakes up early in the morning, she cooks her breakfast and eat it. She washes the dishes and then move to the living room, to read and to watch TV. Then, at lunch time, she moves back to the kitchen, prepares and consumes her lunch, washes again the dishes and then goes to the bedroom to have a one-hour rest. The second run considers a typical Sunday. Johanna wakes up later than usual, she has a quick breakfast (cooking, eating and washing the dishes) and then she goes out for a walk. At about half past eleven, she comes back home, she spends more time than usual to prepare a Sunday meal and to consume it. Finally, she moves into the living room to watch TV.

For each run, the input to the planner is the guessed plan of Johanna, and the goal is to have the apartment clean at the end of the day. The corresponding outputs from the planner are shown in Tables 1. Each row in the tables lists the time step and the actions of both the human and the robot that start at that time. Time 0 is the time when Johanna first leaves her bedroom in the morning. As it can be seen, the robot adapts its plan to the behaviour of the human, performing its tasks without disturbing the inhabitant or threatening her safety, according to the above constraints. It remains inactive as much as possible, in order to avoid useless power consumption and then performing the necessary actions to leave the apartment clean at the end of the day.

5. Conclusions

In this paper we have presented a framework to cope with the issues that arise in human-aware planning. Considering the complexity of the problem, we focused our research on the core module of the framework, a planner that takes into account the actions of the human(s) in the environment. Although we made strong simplifying assumptions regarding the plan of the human in our first step, our experiments confirm the feasibility of our approach. The simulated robot performs its tasks without interfering with the human, considering her actions and plans.

We explored so far only the first kind of human-robot interaction defined in the introduction. Our future work will focus first on relaxing the above assumptions and then on increasing the complexity of the interaction level between human and robot. We also intend to introduce into the environment more agents, both robotic and human.

6. Acknowledgments

This work has been supported by CUGS (Swedish national computer science graduate school) and by the Swedish KK foundation.

References

[1]   E. Akin Sisbot, A. Clodic, L.F. Marin, M. Fontmarty, L. Brèthes, and R. Alami. Implementing a human-aware robot system. In *Proc. of the ROMAN Symposium*, pages 727–732, 2006.

[2]   R. Alami, A. Clodic, V. Montreuil, E.A. Sisbot, and R. Chatila. Task planning for human-robot interaction. In *sOc-EUSAI '05: Proc. of the 2005 joint conference on Smart objects and ambient intelligence*, pages 81–85, New York, NY, USA, 2005.

[3]   R. Alami, A. Clodic, V. Montreuil, E.A. Sisbot, and R. Chatila. Toward human-aware robot task planning. In *AAAI Spring Symp 'To boldly go where no human-robot team has gone before'*, pages 39–46, 2006.

[4]   J. Blythe. Planning with external events. In *UAI '94: Proc. of the Tenth Annual Conference on Uncertainty in Artificial Intelligence*, pages 94–101, Seattle, Washington,USA, 1994.

[5]   B. Bouchard, S. Giroux, and A. Bouzouane. A smart home agent for plan recognition of cognitively-impaired patients. *Journal of Computers*, 1(5):53–62, 2006.

[6]   B. Graf, M. Hans, and R.D. Schraft. Mobile robot assistants: issues for dependable operation in direct cooperation with humans. IEEE *Robotics and Automation Magazine*, 11(2):67–77, 2004.

[7]   L.P. Kaebling, M.L. Littman, and A.R. Cassandra. Planning and acting in partially observable stochastic domains. *Artificial Intelligence*, 101(1–2):99–134, 1998.

[8]   L. Karlsson. Conditional progressive planning under uncertainty. In *Proc. of the 17th Int. Joint Conference on Artificial Intelligence (IJCAI)*, pages 431–438, 2001.

[9]   S. Koenig and R. Simmons. Xavier: A robot navigation system based on partially observable markov decision process models. In Kortenkamp, Bonasso, and Murphy, editors, *Artificial intelligence based mobile robotics: case studies of successful robot systems*, pages 91–122. MIT Press, 1998.

[10] A. Tapus, M.J. Mataric, and B. Scassellati. The grand challenges in socially assistive robotics. IEEE *Robotics & Automation Magazine*, 14(1):35–42, Mar 2007.

Tenth Scandinavian Conference on Artificial Intelligence
A. Holst et al. (Eds.)
IOS Press, 2008

The Problem of Object Recognition in the Presence of Noise in Original Data

V. N. VAGIN[1], M. V. FOMINA, and A. V. KULIKOV
Moscow Power Engineering Institute (Technical University),
Krasnokazarmennaya 14, 111250 Moscow, Russia

Abstract. The problem of object generalization with account for the necessity of processing the incomplete and inconsistent information stored in real databases is considered. It is suggested to use means of rough sets theory and decision trees to generalize the information stored in real databases. Noise models are presented, and a noise effect on the operation of generalization algorithms using the methods of building decision trees is developed. The algorithm for unknown values reconstruction in learning samples subjected to the noise effect based on the nearest neighbour method is proposed. The results of program modeling are brought out.

Keywords: knowledge acquisition and discovery, data mining, rough sets, decision tree, noise model, learning sample.

Introduction

Knowledge discovery in databases (DB) is important for many technical, social, and economic problems. Up-to-date DBs contain such a huge quantity of information that it is practically impossible to analyze this information manually to acquire valuable knowledge for decisions making. The systems for automatic knowledge discovery in DB are capable of analyzing "raw" data and presenting the extracted information faster and with more success than an analyst could find it himself. At first we consider setting up the generalization problem and the methods of its decision. Then the noise models and prediction of unknown values in accordance with the nearest neighbour method in learning samples are viewed. And finally modeling of the algorithm of decision tree building in the presence of noise and classification results both in the absence of noise and in its presence are given.

1. Setting up the generalization problem

Knowledge discovery in DB is closely connected with the solution of the inductive concept formation problem or the generalization problem.

Let us give the formulation of feature-based concept generalization [1].

Let $O = \{o_1, o_2, ..., o_n\}$ be a set of objects that can be represented in an *intelligent decision support system* (IDSS). Each object is characterized by r attributes: A_1, A_2, ... , A_r. Denote by $Dom(A_1), Dom(A_2), ... , Dom(A_r)$ the sets of admissible values of

---

[1] vagin@appmat.ru, m_fomina2000@mail.ru, av_kulikov@mail.ru

features where $Dom(A_k)=\{x_1, x_2, \ldots x_{q_k}\}$, $1 \le k \le r$, q_k is the number of different values of the feature A_k. Thus, each object $o_i \in O$, $1 \le i \le n$ is represented as a set of feature values, i.e., $o_i = \{x_{i1}, x_{i2}, \ldots, x_{ir}\}$, where $x_{ik} \in Dom(A_k)$, $1 \le k \le q_k$. Such a description of an object is called *a feature description*. Quantitative, qualitative, or scaled features can be used as object features [1].

Let O be the set of all objects represented in a certain IDSS; let V be the set of *positive objects* related to some concept and let W be the set of *negative objects*. We will consider the case where $O = V \cup W$, $V \cap W = \varnothing$, $W = \bigcup_i W_i$, and $W_i \cap W_j = \varnothing \; (i \ne j)$. Let K be a non-empty set of objects such that $K = K^+ \cup K^-$, where $K^+ \subset V$ and $K^- \subset W$. We call K a *learning sample*. Based on the learning sample, it is necessary to build a rule separating positive and negative objects of a learning sample.

Thus, the concept is formed if one manages to build a decision rule which, for any example from a learning sample, indicates whether this example belongs to the concept or not. The algorithms that we study form a decision in the form of rules of the type "IF condition, THEN the desired concept." The condition is represented in the form of a logical function in which the boolean variables reflecting the feature values are connected by logical connectives. The decision rule is correct if, in further operation, it successfully recognizes the objects which originally did not belong to the learning sample.

The presence of noise in data changes the above setting up of the generalization problem both at the stage of building decision rules and at the stage of the object classification. First of all, the original learning sample K is replaced by the sample K' in which distorted values or missing values of features occur with a certain probability. We consider the solution of the concept generalization problem using the method of decision trees [2, 3] with the combination of the rough set approach [4, 5].

2. The generalization algorithm in the absence of noise

A rough set is defined by the assignment of upper and lower boundaries of a certain set called the approximations of this set. Each element of the lower approximation is certainly an element of the set. Each element that does not belong to the upper approximation is certainly not an element of the set. The difference in the upper and lower approximations of a rough set forms the so-called boundary region. The element of the boundary region is probably (but not certainly) an element of the set. Similarly to fuzzy sets, rough sets are mathematical conception for the work with fuzziness in data.

The **G**eneralized **I**terative algorithm based on the **R**ough **S**et approach (GIRS) has been developed by authors [6] and consists of the following stages: search of equivalence classes of the indiscernibility relation, search of upper and lower approximations, search of a reduct of the decision system and construction of decision rules. Moreover there is a discretization stage that is applied to process attributes (further, instead of the notion "feature" we will use the notion "attribute") with a continuous domain. In the given algorithm we combined the discretization of quantitative attributes with the search of significant attributes. A certain set of significant attributes is called a *reduct*. Therefore the process of searching a reduct is viewed as a search of attributes belonging to approximate reducts. An approximate reduct is a generalization of a reduct where generalization is understood as the result of forming significant attributes on the basis of the rough set approach [4, 5]. The application of approximate reducts is very useful in processing incomplete and "noisy" data.

The implemented experiments show that the developed algorithm allows to reduce time for searching the significant attributes essentially due to combination with a discretization process. For all data sets taken into the comparison, this algorithm has shown classification accuracy as good as other generalization algorithms, and in some cases surpasses it. The average accuracy of classification is approximately 89.26% (see Table 1). It is necessary to note that the classification accuracy received by our algorithm for most learning samples is higher than classification accuracy achieved by the methods of decision tree induction (ID3, ID4, ID5R, C4.5).

3. Noise models

Assume that examples in a learning sample contain noise, i.e., attribute values may be missing or be distorted. The noise arises due to following causes: incorrect measurement of the input parameters; wrong description of parameter values by an expert; the use of damaged measurement devices; and data lost in transmitting and storing the information [7].

We study two noise models:

1. The noise connected with the absence of attribute values (an attribute value did not manage to measure). For each attribute A, a domain of admissible values includes the value "not known." Such a value corresponding to the situation, when the true value of an attribute has been lost, is denoted by N (Not known). Thus, individual examples of a learning sample K' contain a certain quantity of attributes with the values "not known" [7].

2. The noise connected with the distortion of certain attribute values in a learning sample. Moreover, the true value is replaced by one admissible, but wrong, value (the values are mixed).

Further, we consider the work of the generalization algorithm in the presence of noise in original data. Our purpose is to assess the classification accuracy of examples in a control sample by increasing a noise level in this sample.

4. Prediction of unknown values by the nearest neighbour method

Let a sample with a noise, K', be given; moreover, let the attributes taking both discrete and continuous values be subjected to distortions. Consider the problem of using the objects of a learning sample K' in building a decision tree T and in conducting the examination using this tree.

Let $o_i \in K'$ be an object of the sample; $o_i = <x_{i1}, \ldots , x_{ir}>$. Among all the values of its attributes, there are attributes with the value N (Not known). These attributes may be both discrete and continuous.

The decision tree is a tree in which each nonfinite node accomplishes checking of some condition, and in case a node is finite, it gives out a decision for the element being considered. In order to perform the classification of the given example, it is necessary to start with the root node. Then, we go along the decision tree from the root to the leaves until the finite node (or a leaf) is reached. In each nonfinite node one of the conditions is verified. Depending on the result of verification, the corresponding branch is chosen for further movement along the tree.

Building a decision tree while having examples with unknown values leads to multivariant decisions. Therefore, we try to find the possibility for recovering these unknown values. One of the simplest approaches can be the nearest neighbour method which was proposed for the classification of the unknown object X on the basis of consideration of several objects with the known classification nearest to it. The decision on the assignment of the object X to one or another class is made by information analysis on whether these nearest neighbours belong to one or another class. We can use even a simple count of votes to do this. The parameter defining a number of nearest objects, on basis of which a possible value of an unknown attribute is found, is called "the nearest neighbour number". The given method is implemented in the RECOVERY algorithm that was considered in detail in [8].

5. The RECOVERY algorithm of building a decision tree

Let us consider the possibility of using this algorithm for solving the problems of inductive concept generation. We propose the algorithm "Induction of **Decision Tree** with restoring **Unknown Values**" (IDTUV) that includes the procedure of recovery of unknown values when there is noise in learning sample examples. When unknown values of attributes are recovered, one of algorithms of building decision trees is used. Examples for which we could not restore the unknown values are removed from a learning sample.

Below, we present the pseudocode of the IDTUV algorithm.

    Algorithm IDUTV
     Given: $K = K^+ \cup K^-$
      Obtain: the decision tree T.
      Beginning
         Obtaining $K = K^+ \cup K^-$
       For all informative attributes of objects of K
       repeat
        beginning of the loop
         If there is an unknown value of the attribute
         then apply the **RECOVERY** algorithm.
        end of the loop
       If informative attributes have continuous values
       then apply algorithm **C4.5**.
       else apply the algorithm **ID3**
       End if
       Output T, the decision tree.
      End of IDTUV.

6. Modeling the algorithm of building the decision tree in the presence of noise

The program IDTUV is implemented in the Delphi 7.0 programming system with the use of Borland Database Engine (BDE) for the access to databases. It performs the following main functions:
- builds the classification model (a decision tree) on the basis of the learning sample;
- forms production rules corresponding to the constructed tree;
- recognizes (classifies) objects using a decision tree.

We present experiment results carried out on the following four data groups from the known collection of the test data sets of California University of Informatics and Computer Engineering "UCI Machine Learning Repository" [9]:
1. Data of Monk's problems;
2. Medical data: diagnostics of heart diseases (Heart);
3. Repository of data of the StatLog project:
    - diagnostics of diabetes diseases (Diabetes);
    - australian credit (Australian);
4. Other data sets (from the field of biology and judicial-investigation practice).

6.1. Classification results under the absence of noise

The results obtained on the basis of comparison of classification results on presented methods are given in Table 1. The classification is performed by algorithms ID3, C4.5, CN2, CART5, GIRS, IDTUV under the absence of noise. Classification results have shown that, in the absence of noise, the algorithm IDTUV operates not worse than other algorithms but the best result has shown by the algorithm GIRS.

Table 1. Experimental results on research of classification accuracy without noise

Data set	Classification accuracy in a sample, %					
	ID3	C4.5	CN2	CART5	IDTUV	GIRS
Glass	62.79	65.89	66.01	44.86	67.62	70.10
Heart	77.78	77.04	77.95	80.00	84.37	86.37
Diabetes	66.23	70.84	71.10	74.09	76.38	81.00
Monks-2	65.00	69.91	69.00	63.20	78.94	83.10
Australian	78.26	85.36	79.60	85.51	80.59	88.30
Monks-1	81.25	75.70	100.00	83.34	79.65	100
Adult	83.53	84.46	84.00	81.59	85.69	-
Monks-3	90.28	97.20	89.00	97.22	95.29	94.44
Mushroom	100.00	100.00	100.00	100.00	100	100
Soybean	100.00	95.56	91.43	98.00	100	100
Average	80.51	82.20	82.81	80.78	84.81	89.26

Since the algorithms ID3, C4.5, CN2, CART5 do not treat examples with unknown values, the introduction of noise was not performed at this stage.

6.2. Classification results of examples with noise

Since the main task of experiments is to estimate the noise effect on results of building classification rules and recognition of test examples, we decided not to include chaotic noise in fields of any attributes in test tables. To introduce distortions, we used the most informative attribute of a table, that is located at the root of a decision tree. Obviously, changes in values of such informative attribute can affect most essentially the results of the generalization algorithm operation. Assume that an attribute that is not a root one is subjected to distortions. Then, its effect on the results of classification is either extremely weak or may not manifest itself at all (for example, in case this attribute does not belong to the path to the leaf of a decision tree).

6.3. Research of the effect of the nearest neighbour number on the classification accuracy in examples with unknown values

The purpose of the experiment is to check up the influence of the parameter "the nearest neighbour number" used in the IDTUV algorithm in the process of building a decision tree for a noisy learning sample on the classification accuracy of test examples (see Table 2). The analogous results are presented in Table 3 for the GIRS algorithm.

Table 2. Experimental results on research of the influence of the nearest neighbour number on the classification accuracy in the IDTUV algorithm

Data sets	The nearest neighbour number	Classification accuracy in a sample, %					
		No noise	Noise 5%	Noise 10%	Noise 20%	Noise 30%	Noise 40%	Average
Heart	1	84.37	83.57	83.37	**83.28**	82.45	**82.16**	82.97
	5		**84.53**	83.68	82.37	82.18	81.11	82.77
	9		84.43	**83.75**	82.84	**82.59**	81.90	83.10
	33		84.42	**83.75**	82.88	82.36	82.14	**83.11**
	89		84.42	**83.75**	82.88	82.36	82.14	**83.11**
Australian	1	80.59	80.72	80.92	81.06	82.22	82.35	81.45
	5		81.44	81.40	82.46	82.18	81.64	81.82
	9		81.72	81.21	82.36	82.76	**83.28**	82.26
	33		**82.15**	**82.62**	**82.83**	83.10	83.25	**82.79**
	299		**82.15**	**82.62**	**82.83**	83.10	83.25	**82.79**
Monks-1	1	79.65	82.37	**89.49**	86.69	86.29	85.07	85.98
	5		**84.42**	85.25	89.87	89.57	82.37	86.30
	9		83.44	87.78	**91.70**	**90.71**	87.97	**88.32**
	33		81.23	82.13	91.06	90.05	**88.96**	86.69
Monks-3	1	95.29	93.95	93.09	94.75	92.04	93.67	93.50
	5		94.44	93.02	94.18	92.80	94.44	93.78
	9		94.83	**94.80**	95.24	94.15	94.71	94.75
	33		**95.14**	94.79	**95.37**	**94.67**	**94.77**	**94.95**
Tic-Tac-Toe	1	90.50	90.55	89.07	87.99	86.88	86.19	88.14
	5		90.63	90.19	89.47	88.63	87.37	89.26
	9		90.90	90.40	89.79	**89.39**	88.56	89.81
	33		90.83	**90.59**	90.46	88.68	88.84	89.88
	77		**91.18**	90.55	**90.52**	89.02	**88.88**	**90.03**

The noise model "the absence of an attribute value" has been used. For bringing in distortions, the most informative attribute located in the root of a decision tree has been chosen. The situations of noise presence in 5%, 10%, 20%, 30% and 40% on a chosen attribute were considered and the effect "the nearest neighbour number" on the classification accuracy for each of the given noise level was analyzed. To reduce a chance of introducing noise in a sample, there were produced three experiment series for each noise level. In each series, noise was brought in an original learning sample anew. Then we use each of chosen parameter values for "the nearest neighbour number" to recover the unknown values in accordance with "the nearest neighbour" method and build a decision tree on the basis of which the classification of test examples has been made. Each series of experiments have been produced in accordance with 10-fold cross-validation or bootstrap methods. For each noise level and the nearest neighbour number as an assessment of classification accuracy, the average value of three experiments series is taken.

As it is shown in Table 2, for different data collections, distinct dependencies of the classification accuracy from the nearest neighbour number are obtained. So, for the data collection "Australian credit", "the third Monk's task" and "The game in Tic-Tac-Toe", it is preferably to have the large value of this parameter; for the data set "Diagnostics of heart diseases" and "The first Monk's task", there was brought out no dependency of the classification accuracy from a researched parameter.

In table cells where the classification accuracy is represented, maximal values of the classification accuracy are marked by the bold type.

Table 3. Experimental results on research of the influence of the nearest neighbour number on the classification accuracy in the GIRS algorithm

Data sets	The nearest neighbour number	Classification accuracy in a sample, %						
		No noise	Noise 5%	Noise 10%	Noise 20%	Noise 30%	Noise 40%	Average
Heart	1	86.37	**86.28**	86.16	**86.26**	84.39	83.72	**85.36**
	5		85.58	85.40	85.74	84.39	**84.79**	85.18
	9		85.75	86.15	85.93	83.78	84.16	85.15
	33		**86.28**	**86.36**	86.23	**84.51**	83.15	85.31
	89		86.06	**86.36**	85.60	83.84	83.43	85.06
Australian	1	88.30	**88.64**	**88.12**	88.18	88.09	**87.69**	**88.14**
	5		88.53	87.67	**88.44**	**88.31**	87.42	88.07
	9		88.20	87.66	88.33	87.88	87.29	87.87
	33		88.40	87.62	88.29	87.89	87.11	87.86
	299		88.40	87.62	88.29	87.89	87.11	87.86
Monks-1	1	100.0	**100.0**	98.15	95.75	96.3	95.76	97.19
	5		**100.0**	99.54	96.83	94.52	92.82	96.74
	9		**100.0**	99.23	98.3	96.18	97.53	98.25
	33		**100.0**	**100.0**	**99.07**	**98.61**	**97.99**	**99.13**
Monks-3	1	94.44	94.44	93.90	94.48	94.48	88.27	93.11
	5		**95.06**	**95.14**	94.60	**94.83**	89.58	93.84
	9		**95.06**	94.06	**94.71**	93.90	90.58	93.66
	33		**95.06**	94.29	94.60	94.29	**93.05**	**94.26**
Tic-Tac-Toe	1	85.07	83.87	83.40	82.00	80.84	80.42	82.11
	5		84.17	84.80	83.29	**84.25**	**83.35**	83.97
	9		84.74	84.15	**84.33**	83.92	82.85	**84.00**
	33		**85.03**	84.56	83.42	82.76	82.99	83.75
	77		84.14	**84.86**	82.55	83.36	82.93	83.57

The results of influence of the effect "the nearest neighbour number" on the classification accuracy for each of the given noise level for the GIRS algorithm are analyzed. As it is shown in Table 3, for distinct data sets, the different dependencies of the classification accuracy from the nearest neighbour number are displayed. So, for the data set "Tic-Tac-Toe", the most effective is use of the average nearest neighbour number (i.e. 5 – 9); for the first and third "Monk's task", great values of this parameter are preferable; for "Diagnostics of heart diseases" and "Australian credit", such dependency is absent at all.

Conclusions

We considered the problem of information generalization and examined the ways of its solution under the presence of noise in original data.

The noise models in DB tables, consequences of which are the absence of attribute values or the distortion of attribute values in a learning sample, have been considered. The algorithms GIRS, IDTUV allowing to process learning samples, containing examples with unknown or distorted values, have been suggested. The system of building generalized concepts using the obtained theoretical results has been developed and programmly implemented.

The obtained results have shown that the algorithms GIRS and IDTUV in combination with the recovery algorithm essentially enhance the classification accuracy of examples in the presence of noise in data.

References

[1]   V. N. Vagin, E.Ju. Golovina, A.A. Zagoryanskaya, M.V. Fomina. Exact and Plausible Inference in Intelligent Systems. /Ed. by V.N. Vagin, D.A. Pospelov.-M.: FizMatLit, , 2004, 704p. (in Russian).

[2] Quinlan J.R. Induction of Decision Trees// Machine Learning, Vol.1, 1986, 81-106

[3] Quinlan J.R. Improved Use of Continuous Attributes in C 4.5//Journal of Artifical Intelligence Reseach, Vol. 4, 1996, 77-90

[4]   J. Bazan, A Comparison of Dynamic and Non-dynamic Rough Set Methods for Extracting Laws from Decision Tables//Rough Sets in Knowledge Discovery 1.: Methodology and Application/ Ed. by L.Polkowski, A.Skowron. Heidelberg: Phisica-Verlag, 1998, 321-365.

[5]   H. S. Nguyen, S. H. Nguyen. Discretization Methodsin Data Mining// Rough Sets in Knowledge Discovery 1: Methodology and Application/ Ed. by L.Polkowski, A.Skowron. Heidelberg: Phisica-Verlag, 1998, 451-482.

[6]   V.N. Vagin, A.V. Kulikov , M.V. Fomina. The Development of the Generalization Algorithm Based on the Rough Set Theory./ Intern. Journal "Information Theories&Applications", Vol.13, Nu. 3, 2006, 255-262.

[7]   V. Mookerjee, M. Mannino, R. Gilson, Improving the Performance Stability of Inductive Expert Systems under Input Noise.// Information Systems Research. 1995, Vol.6, Nu.4, 328-356 .

[8]   A. M. Berisha , V. N. Vagin, A.V.Kulikov, M.V.Fomina. Methods of Knowledge Discovery in "Noisy" Databases./ Journal of Computer and Systems Sciences International. Vol. 44, Nu. 6, 2005, 973-987.

[9] C.J.Merz, P.M.Murphy. UCI Repository of Machine Learning Datasets, 1998, Information and Computer Science University of California, Irvine, CA 92697-3425 http://www.ics.uci.edu/mlearn/ MLRepository.html.

Tenth Scandinavian Conference on Artificial Intelligence
A. Holst et al. (Eds.)
IOS Press, 2008

Troubleshooting when Action Costs are Dependent with Application to a Truck Engine

Håkan WARNQUIST [a], Mattias NYBERG [b] and Petter SÄBY [a]

[a] *Service Methods Framework Development, Scania, SE-151 87 Södertälje, Sweden*
[b] *Department of Electrical Engineering, Linköping University, SE-581 83 Linköping, Sweden*

Abstract. We propose a troubleshooting algorithm that can troubleshoot systems with dependent action costs. When actions are performed they may change the way the system is decomposed and affect the cost of future actions. We present a way to model this by extending the traditional troubleshooting model with an additional state that describes which parts of the system that are decomposed. The proposed troubleshooting algorithm searches an AND/OR graph with the aim of finding the repair plan that minimizes the expected cost of repair. We present the heuristics needed to speed up the search and make it competitive with other troubleshooting algorithms. Finally, the performance of the algorithm is evaluated on a probabilistic model of a fuel injection system of a truck. We show that the expected cost of repair can be reduced when compared with an algorithm from previous literature.

Keywords. Fault Diagnosis, Decision Theoretic Troubleshooting

Introduction

In many troubleshooting algorithms, where the aim is to minimize the expected cost of repair, action costs are assumed to be independent [1][2]. For complex systems such as modern trucks it can be unrealistic to make this assumption. When troubleshooting a truck, the mechanic sometimes must decompose large parts of the truck to find the faulty component in need for repair, i.e. the cab needs to be tilted and components need to be decomposed. This can be very time consuming. Depending on which actions that have previously been performed, the cost of performing other actions may vary. For trucks it is often the case that the vehicle has to be fully reassembled to test if everything is functioning properly. If the wrong repair is made the vehicle has to be decomposed again. Therefore, when mechanics repair trucks they sometimes repair more components than necessary to avoid spending too much time decomposing and assembling the vehicle.

The problem of troubleshooting with dependent action costs is addressed in [3]. There, actions are grouped in clusters such that when an action is performed within a cluster the other actions in the same cluster become cheaper. One limitation of this method is that the clusters are not allowed to be nested. Instead, in this paper we propose to model the action costs to be dependent on which parts of the system that are decomposed. This allows a more flexible description of the action costs. We propose a troubleshooting algorithm that can troubleshoot systems with this type of dependent action costs. In contrast to some other troubleshooting algorithms [1][2][4] it may choose to repair more components than necessary before reassembling, if this can reduce the total expected cost of repair. The algorithm is evaluated on a probabilistic model of the fuel injection system of a truck. On this same model the performance of the algorithm is compared with an implementation of the decision theoretic troubleshooting algorithm proposed by Breese and Heckerman [1]. The result of the comparison shows that the here proposed algorithm can reduce the expected cost of repair significantly. The algorithm is based on an AND/OR search [5] which easily becomes computationally intractable, but with the right heuristics the search can be made in reasonable time.

The outline of the paper is as follows. In Section 1 we describe the troubleshooting model and how the dependent action costs are modeled. Section 2 describes the search algorithm and the heuristics that are used. In Section 3 the performance of the algorithm is evaluated on a model of the fuel injection system of a truck. Also, the performance of the algorithm is compared with the algorithm proposed in [6]. Finally, we conclude in Section 4.

1. The Troubleshooting Model

The troubleshooting model consists of two separated states, the *decomposition state*, describing which parts of the system that are accessible, and the *fault state*, describing which component that is faulty. The decomposition state is completely observable while the fault state is not directly observable. In this section we describe the different states of the model and the actions that can be performed.

1.1. Fault State and Belief State

The state describing which component of the modeled system that is faulty, is called the *fault state*. This state is not directly observable, otherwise there would be no need for troubleshooting. Instead, the probability of being in a certain fault state is estimated from a probabilistic model of the system using the current information at hand, such as observations and earlier performed actions, as done in [6] and [2]. The probability distribution of the fault states represents our belief in which components are faulty. Such a distribution is commonly called a *belief state* [5].

1.2. Actions

The fault state is changed by performing actions on the system. When an action is performed a new belief state can be inferred from the previous belief state and from the new information that may have been gained from the action. This type of inference is also made in [6] and [2]. We distinguish between actions that gain information, *testing actions*, and actions that revokes faults, *fault revoking actions*. The testing actions and the fault revoking actions correspond to the *questions* and the *repair actions* in [2] respectively. When a testing action is performed we retrieve a new belief state for every possible outcome of the test. When a fault revoking action is performed a single new belief state can be calculated simply by moving probability mass from fault states where the revoked fault is faulty onto fault states where it is not.

For a given belief state not all actions are relevant. For example, if we are sure that the batteries are working properly we do not need to consider fault revoking actions such as "replace batteries" or testing actions such as "measure fluid level in batteries." Relevant actions that we allow to be considered, are called *applicable actions*.

Definition 1 (Applicable Action). An action a is an *applicable action* if after it is performed, the resulting belief state, b_{after}, is different from the prior belief state, b_{before}, i.e. $b_{after} \neq b_{before}$.

1.3. Modeling the Decomposition State

Consider a bicycle. Before the inner tube on the wheel of a bicycle can be changed, the wheel has to be dismounted and the tire has to be taken off. The time required for dismounting the wheel and removing the tire can be considered affecting the cost of the action *change inner tube*. A dismounted wheel is not considered to be a fault, just a normal step of the repair process, and the mechanic will always know if it is mounted or not, so there is no need to represent this fact in the belief state.

To represent parts of the system that can be taken apart during a normal repair process we introduce the *decomposition state*. This state is fully observable. The parts of the system that can be taken apart are called *decomposable units*. The notion of a decomposition state was introduced in a series of master theses [7][8][9] with the aim of troubleshooting trucks using theory from [1][6][2].

Definition 2 (Decomposition State). The *decomposition state* $\delta = [d_1, d_1, \ldots]$ is a vector, where each element d_i represents a *decomposable unit* of the system. Each element is in one of the modes *decomposed* or *assembled*.

Each action may require one or more of the decomposable units to be in a certain mode. Further, decomposing a decomposable unit may require other decomposable units to be in the mode *decomposed*. This relation between the elements of a decomposition state can be described by a directed acyclic graph, see Figure 1. Each node represents a decomposable unit and requires its parents to be in the mode *decomposed*, before itself can be decomposed. Before a node can be assembled, all its children have to be in the mode *assembled*.

Changing the mode of a decomposable unit is associated with a certain cost. When actions are performed, the cost of making the transition necessary to meet the requirements of the action is added to the cost of performing the action. Note that the transitions in the decomposition state are not treated as actions themselves. A transition in the decomposition state occur only when it is required by an action that is performed. This makes the cost of performing an action dependent of previously performed actions.

Example. Consider a decomposition state where all decomposable units in Figure 1 are assembled. The cost of an action that requires d_7 to be decomposed is increased with the cost of decomposing d_1, d_2, d_4, d_5, and d_7. Afterward we wish to perform an action that requires d_1 to be assembled. The cost of this transition in the decomposition state is the cost of assembling d_1, d_4, and d_7.

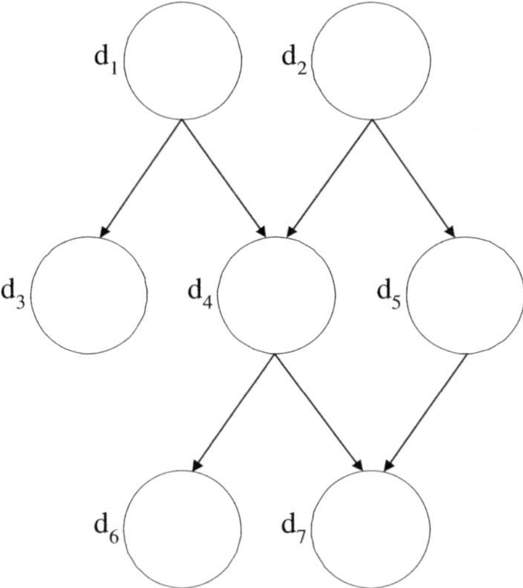

Figure 1. The relation between elements in the decomposition state. Each node, d_i, represents an individual decomposable unit. The top layer represents the outer, easily reachable parts of the system and the lower levels represent parts deeper down in the system.

2. The Search Algorithm

As in [1] the troubleshooting is incremental. At every step of the troubleshooting process, based on the current information and on the system model, the best action is calculated with the aim of minimizing the expected cost of repair. The system is considered to be repaired when the probability in the belief state for the fault free state is approximately one.

In our algorithm the choice of action is calculated by searching through alternative action plans as done in [10] and [11]. This is in contrast to [6] where the idea of deciding which action to take by searching is abandoned in favor of directly choosing the action that has the best relation between the probability of having a certain fault, given the information at hand, and the cost of performing the action. In this paper, as in [2], we will call this relation the *efficiency* of an action. When choosing actions based on efficiencies the computational complexity is significantly lower compared to complete searching. Even though, a complete AND/OR search is exponential in time, with heuristics that limit the branching factor and search depth, the search can be performed in reasonable time and still provide satisfactory results. With a precise heuristic value, forward pruning can be made with only a small loss in optimality.

2.1. The AND/OR Tree Representation

For each fault revoking action it is possible to calculate a single new belief state and for each testing action it is possible to calculate the resulting belief state for each possible outcome of the test. The relation between belief states, actions, and observations can be described as an AND/OR tree [12]. It is a directed tree with nodes of two types: OR nodes representing alternative ways of solving the problem, and AND nodes representing problem decomposition into subproblems, all of which need to be solved [13].

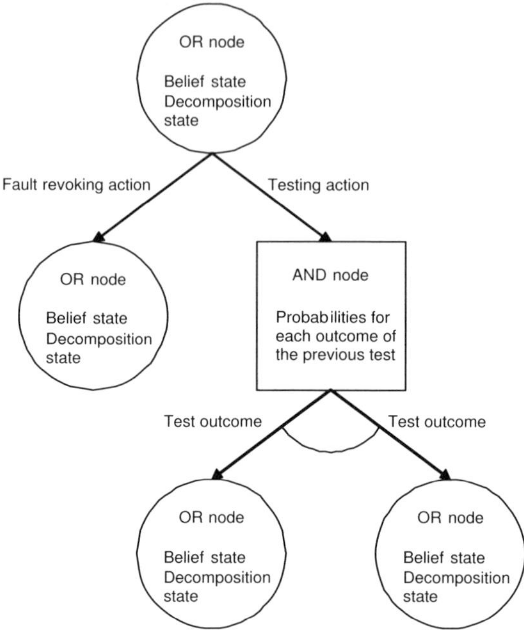

Figure 2. OR nodes have one child for each *applicable action* given the belief state of the node. AND nodes have one child for every possible outcome of the corresponding testing action. The children of an AND node are always OR nodes.

A fault revoking action defines the edge between two OR nodes and a testing action defines the edge from an OR node to an AND node. The test outcomes define the edges from an AND node to its children. Every OR node is labeled with a belief state and a decomposition state and every AND node is labeled with the probabilities for each outcome of the previous testing action. The root node of the AND/OR tree is always an OR node containing the initial belief state and initial decomposition state. Figure 2 illustrates the structure of the AND/OR tree.

2.2. Minimal Expected Cost of Repair

The search algorithm finds the choice of actions that minimizes the expected cost of repair. Let $c(n, m)$ be the cost of performing the action on the edge between the OR node n and its child m. Included in this cost are the costs of making the necessary transitions in the decomposition state. Let $p(n, m)$ be the probability of the test outcome associated with the child m of the AND node n. A goal node is an OR node where the system is in a fault free state. When a goal node is reached all that needs to be done is to restore the system to a fully assembled state. Let $r(n)$ be the cost of restoring the decomposition state of the goal node n to the fully assembled state. The minimal expected cost of repair for a node n is calculated as

$$C_{min}(n) = \begin{cases} r(n) & \text{if } n \text{ is an goal node} \\ \min_{m \in ch(n)} \big(c(n,m) + C_{min}(m)\big) & \text{if } n \text{ is an OR node} \\ \sum_{m \in ch(n)} p(n,m)C_{min}(m) & \text{if } n \text{ is an AND node} \end{cases} \tag{1}$$

Where $ch(n)$ is the set of all children of n. Further details on how (1) is derived can be found in [14].

The minimal expected cost of the entire tree is C_{min} of the root node. The goal for the search algorithm is to find the choice of actions that satisfies (1).

2.3. Searching the Tree

The algorithm searches the AND/OR tree using a recursive depth first search strategy. For every expanded node it maintains values for lower bound $lb(n)$, upper bound $ub(n)$, as well as a heuristic value $h(n)$.

The lower bound is calculated as the cost of repairing the system if one could make a "perfect test" that gains full information of the underlying fault state. Since there are no negative costs and since all faults must be repaired, $lb(n) \leq C_{min}(n)$. This method is calculating the lower bound is also used in [15].

The upper bound is the best solution found so far. The upper bound of a node is inherited from its parent and is updated as the algorithm backtracks. For children of AND nodes, the inherited upper bound corresponds to their share of the parent's upper bound,

$$ub(m) = \frac{ub(n) - \sum_{\substack{m' \in ch(n) \\ m' \neq m}} p(n,m')lb(m')}{p(n,m)} \tag{2}$$

where n is the parent node of m [14]. Nodes where the lower bound is greater than the upper bound can be pruned.

When choosing which node to expand next, the children of an AND node are sorted in a descending order according to the value of the probability $p(n,m)$. The children of an OR node are sorted in an ascending order according to their heuristic value $h(n)$. If the child is an OR node, this value is calculated as

$$h(n) = lb(n) + c_{entropy}H(n) \tag{3}$$

where $H(n)$ is the *entropy* [16] of the belief state in node n and $c_{entropy}$ is a parameter which can be thought of as the mean cost of reducing entropy. AND nodes do not contain belief states so the heuristic value cannot be calculated in the same way. Instead, the heuristic value of an AND node is calculated by weighting the heuristic values of its children, which are OR nodes, with their probability:

$$h(n) = \sum_{m \in ch(n)} p(n,m)h(m) \tag{4}$$

We wish that the heuristic value is an estimate of the minimal expected cost of repair, i.e. $h(n) \approx C_{min}(n)$. Given a set of training data where the true minimal expected cost of repair C_{min} is known for every node, the parameter $c_{entropy}$ is estimated using the least square method in (3) where $C_{min}(n)$ is substituted for $h(n)$.

So far the algorithm is guaranteed to find the optimal solution that satisfies (1), but for complex problems finding this can be computationally intractable. If the heuristic is accurate enough, the branching factor can be limited to allow forward pruning with little loss in optimality. With an additional limit to the search depth, the algorithm can be guaranteed to finish within reasonable time.

3. Performance of the Algorithm on the Fuel Injection System Model

A precondition for solving troubleshooting problems by searching is that the search algorithm finds its solution adequately fast. In [8] an existing fuel injection system of a truck is modeled as a Bayesian network [17]. The actions that can be performed on the fuel injection system are strongly dependent on its decomposition state. We let the algorithm find the optimal solution for troubleshooting the fuel injection system starting from randomly generated inputs. When using the heuristic based on entropy (3), the optimal solution was found in average among the first two branches searched [14]. This allows us to put a tight limit on the branching factor to make a deeper search.

In [9], Breese and Heckerman's decision theoretic troubleshooting algorithm [6] is evaluated in a series of experiments on the fuel injection system model. In these experiments, a Monte Carlo simulation of the complete repair process is made. The set up consists of a simulated fuel injection system that has a predefined fault. When a testing action is performed the resulting observation is generated randomly according to probabilities from the probability model. The total cost of repair is the cost of all actions performed until the system is verified to be free of faults. In each experiment a different fault is predefined and the average of the total cost of repair is measured.

We repeated the same series of experiments under the same conditions using the here proposed search algorithm. In average over all experiments, the cost of repair was 32% less. The greatest differences in costs are in cases where the faulty component is hard to isolate and the risk of making the wrong repair is high. In these cases, when a repair is made, several expensive transitions in the decomposition state have to be made to verify if the repair is correct. Our algorithm avoids this by repairing several faults before returning to a fully assembled decomposition state whenever this is beneficial. A more detailed analysis of these experiments can be found in [14].

4. Conclusions

When troubleshooting large mechanical systems such as trucks it is not always realistic to assume that the cost of performing actions are independent of previously performed actions. Therefore the troubleshooting model in [6] has been extended with the decomposition state that describes which parts of the system that are assembled or decomposed. We proposed a new troubleshooting algorithm that finds the best action to perform by searching an AND/OR tree using a heuristic based on entropy. In the experiments on the fuel injection system, we showed that the expected cost of repair can be reduced significantly when using the here proposed search algorithm compared to when using the method proposed in [6].

Acknowledgments

We would like to thank Anders Florén, Hans Ivendal, Göran Johansson, Mats Karlsson, Per Nyblom, Anna Pernestål, and Jan Sterner for many fruitful and interesting discussions. We would also like to thank Katja Lotz, Jonatan Mossberg, and Helena Sundberg for supplying us with data and algorithms needed for the experiments.

References

[1] J.S. Breese and D. Heckerman. Decision-theoretic troubleshooting: A framework for repair and experiment. In *Proceedings of the Twelfth Conference on Uncertainty in Artificial Intelligence*, pages 124–132, San Fransisco, 1996. Morgan Kaufmann.

[2] H. Langseth and F.V. Jensen. Decision theoretic troubleshooting of coherent systems. *Reliability Engineering and Systems Safety*, 80(1):49–62, april 2002.

[3] Helge Langseth and Finn V. Jensen. Heuristics for two extensions of basic troubleshooting. In *Proceedings of the 7th Scandinavian Conference on Artificial Intelligence, SCAI'01, Frontiers in Artificial Intelligence and Applciations*, pages 80–89, 2001.

[4] D. Gillblad, A. Holst, and R. Steinert. Fault-tolerant incremental diagnosis with limited historical data. Technical report, Swedish Institute of Computer Science, Kista, 2006.

[5] S. Russell and P. Norvig. *Artificial Intelligence: A Modern Approach*. Prentice Hall, Englewood Cliffs, 2003.

[6] D. Heckerman, J. Breese, and K. Rommelse. Decision-theoretic troubleshooting. In *Communications of the ACM 38*, pages 49–57, 1995.

[7] K. Lotz. Optimizing guided troubleshooting using interactive tests and bayesian networks with an application to diesel engine diagnosis. Master's thesis, Department of Mathematics, Royal Institute of Technology, 2007.

[8] J. Mossberg. Bayesian modeling of a diesel injection system for optimal troubleshooting. Master's thesis, Department of Mathematics, Royal Institute of Technology, 2007.

[9] H. Sundberg. Decision-theoretic troubleshooting using bayesian networks - guided troubleshooting of a diesel injection system. Master's thesis, School of Computer Science and Communication, Royal Institute of Technology, 2007.

[10] P. P. Faure, X. Olive, L. Travé-Massuyès, and H. Poulard. AGENDA: Automatic GENeration of DiAgnosis trees. In *Journées Doctorales d'Automatique JDA'01*, pages 203–214, 2001.

[11] Xavier Olive, Louise Trave Massuyes, and Hervé Poulard. AO* variant methods for automatic generation of near-optimal diagnosis trees. In *14th International Workshop on Principles of Diagnosis (DX'03)*, pages 169–174, 2003.

[12] M. Ghalab, D. Nau, and P. Traverso. *Automated Planning*. Morgan Kaufmann, San Francisco, 2004.

[13] R. Dechter and R. Marinescu. And/or search spaces for graphical models. *Artificial Intelligence 171*, pages 73–106, 2007.

[14] H. Warnquist and P. Säby. Conditional planning for troubleshooting and repair in a partially observable environment. Master's thesis, Department of Computer and Information Science, Linköping University, 2008. Not yet published as of submission date.

[15] Marta Vomlelová and Jiří Vomlel. Troubleshooting: Np-hardness and solution mehtods. In *Proceedings of the Fifth Workshop on Uncertainty Processing, WUPES'2000*, 2000.

[16] R.M. Gray. *Entropy and Information Theory*. Springer, New York, 1990.

[17] Finn V. Jensen. *An Introduction to Bayesian Networks*. Springer, 1996.

Tenth Scandinavian Conference on Artificial Intelligence
A. Holst et al. (Eds.)
IOS Press, 2008

A Sparse Regularized Least-Squares Preference Learning Algorithm

Evgeni TSIVTSIVADZE, Tapio PAHIKKALA, Antti AIROLA, Jorma BOBERG, and
Tapio SALAKOSKI

Turku Centre for Computer Science (TUCS)
Department of Information Technology
University of Turku, Joukahaisenkatu 3-5 B
20520 Turku, Finland
email: firstname.lastname@utu.fi

Abstract. Learning preferences between objects constitutes a challenging task that
notably differs from standard classification or regression problems. The objective
involves prediction of ordering of the data points. Furthermore, methods for learning preference relations usually are computationally more demanding than standard
classification or regression methods. Recently, we have proposed a kernel based
preference learning algorithm, called RankRLS, whose computational complexity
is cubic with respect to the number of training examples. The algorithm is based
on minimizing a regularized least-squares approximation of a ranking error function that counts the number of incorrectly ranked pairs of data points. When non-
linear kernel functions are used, the training of the algorithm might be infeasible if
the amount of examples is large. In this paper, we propose a sparse approximation
of RankRLS whose training complexity is considerably lower than that of basic
RankRLS. In our experiments, we consider parse ranking, a common problem in
natural language processing. We show that sparse RankRLS significantly outperforms basic RankRLS in this task. To conclude, the advantage of sparse RankRLS
is the computational efficiency when dealing with large amounts of training data
together with high dimensional feature representations.

1. Introduction

Recently, learning preference relations has received a lot of attention in machine learning
research. Generally, the task can be cast as learning a function that is capable of ranking data points according to some given preference relation. The ranking algorithms are
widely used in many areas such as information retrieval [6], natural language processing
[2], et cetera.

In many cases the preference learning problem is reduced to classification of data
point pairs, where one pair is preferred to the other one [5]. A major drawback associated with this approach is that the number of data point pairs grows quadratically with
respect to the size of the dataset, making the training of a preference learner too expensive for large datasets. In [7], we proposed RankRLS whose computational complexity
is the same as that of the standard RLS regression [12], even though RankRLS takes
account of the data point pairs instead of the individual data points. A similar algorithm

was proposed independently by [3]. The computational complexity of the kernel version of RankRLS is $O(m^3)$, where m is the size of the training set. In practise, also this may be infeasible for very large training sets. In this paper, we propose sparse RankRLS, a sparse regularized least-squares algorithm for learning preference relations. The computational complexity of sparse RankRLS is $O(mr^2)$. In fact, r can be selected to be much smaller than m and in some cases it can be considered as a constant. Thus, our algorithm can efficiently perform ranking using a large amount of training data together with high dimensional feature representations.

Sparse RankRLS can be used to learn pairwise preferences from scored data. In our setting, every data point provided to the algorithm consists of an input and its real valued score. The algorithm can be used for both object ranking and label ranking tasks (see e.g. [4] for in depth discussion about these types of tasks). However, in this paper we consider only label ranking. Therefore, we define every input to consist of an object and its label.

As an example, we consider the task of parse ranking, a common problem in natural language processing. In this case, each input consists of a sentence and its parse. That is, the sentence and the parse are considered as an object and a label, respectively. We are given a set of sentences and each sentence is associated with a set of parses. The task is to find the correct ordering of the parses of a sentence. We are not interested in preferences between parses associated with different sentences. Thus, the only relevant input pairs are the ones that are associated with the same sentence. As another example one can consider information retrieval task where we are given a set of web-search results obtained with a set of queries. The aim is to rank them according to the user preference. In this case, we are not interested in the order of the web documents obtained from different queries.

Training of the existing kernel based ranking algorithms, such as RankSVM [5], may be infeasible when the size of the training set is large. This is especially the case when nonlinear kernel functions are used. In this study, we suggest that sparse RankRLS makes it possible to take advantage of much more data in the training process than the non-sparse kernel methods do.

2. Ranking Task

We construct a training set from a given set of m data points. A data point $z = (x, y)$ consist of an input $x \in \mathcal{X}$ and its score $y \in \mathbb{R}$, where $\mathcal{X}$, called the input space, can be any set. We say that a data point $z = (x, y)$ is preferred to $z' = (x', y')$ if $y > y'$ and vice versa. We call data points tied if $y = y'$. In this paper, we consider label ranking (see e.g. [4]), where every input consists of an object and its label. An input pair is considered relevant if both inputs are associated with the same object. In parse ranking tasks, for example, each object is a sentence and the labels associated with it are parses generated for the sentence. The score of an input indicates how well the parse included in the input matches the correct parse of the sentence.

Following [7], we define an undirected graph whose vertices correspond to the training inputs. Two vertices in the graph are connected with an edge if the corresponding pair of inputs is relevant to the task. Let $W \in \mathbb{R}^{m \times m}$ denote the adjacency matrix of the graph. That is, $W_{i,j} = 1$ when the vertices indexed by i and j are connected, and $W_{i,j} = 0$ otherwise. Further, let $X = (x_1, \ldots, x_m) \in (\mathcal{X}^m)^T$ be a sequence of inputs, where $(\mathcal{X}^m)^T$ denotes the set of row vectors whose elements belong to $\mathcal{X}$. We also define $Y = (y_1, \ldots, y_m)^T \in \mathbb{R}^m$ to be a sequence of the corresponding scores. Finally, we consider a training set to be the triple $S = (X, Y, W)$.

Let us denote $\mathbb{R}^{\mathcal{X}} = \{f : \mathcal{X} \to \mathbb{R}\}$, and let $\mathcal{H} \subseteq \mathbb{R}^{\mathcal{X}}$ be the hypothesis space. Further, let $f(X) = (f(x_1), \ldots, f(x_m))^T$. We measure how well a hypothesis $f \in \mathcal{H}$ is able to predict the direction of preference for the input pairs that are relevant to the task with the following function known as the disagreement or ranking error:

$$d(f(X), Y, W) = \frac{1}{N} \sum_{i,j=1}^{m} W_{i,j} \frac{1}{2} \left| \text{sign}(y_i - y_j) - \text{sign}(f(x_i) - f(x_j)) \right|, \quad (1)$$

where $N = \sum_{i,j=1}^{m} W_{i,j}$ and $\text{sign}(\cdot)$ is the signum function.

3. Regularization

In order to construct an algorithm that selects a hypothesis f from $\mathcal{H}$, we have to define an appropriate cost function that measures how well the hypotheses fit the training data. We would also like to avoid too complex hypotheses that overfit at the training phase and are not able to generalize to unseen data. To give a formal representation of these aims, we follow [13] and consider the framework of regularized kernel methods in which $\mathcal{H}$ is so-called reproducing kernel Hilbert space (RKHS) defined by a positive definite kernel function k. The kernel functions (see e.g. [14]) are defined as follows. Let $\mathcal{F}$ denote the feature vector space. For any mapping $\Phi : \mathcal{X} \to \mathcal{F}$, the inner product $k(x, x') = \langle \Phi(x), \Phi(x') \rangle$ of the mapped data points is called a kernel function. Using RKHS as our hypothesis space, we define the learning algorithm as

$$\mathcal{A}(S) = \underset{f \in \mathcal{H}}{\text{argmin}} \, J(f),$$

where

$$J(f) = c(f(X), Y, W) + \lambda \| f \|_k^2, \quad (2)$$

$f(X) = (f(x_1), \ldots, f(x_m))^T$, c is a real valued cost function, and $\lambda \in \mathbb{R}_+$ is a regularization parameter controlling the tradeoff between the cost on the training set and the complexity of the hypothesis. By the generalized representer theorem ([13]), the minimizer of (2) has the following form:

$$f(x) = \sum_{i=1}^{m} a_i k(x, x_i), \quad (3)$$

where $a_i \in \mathbb{R}$. Using this notation, we rewrite $f(X) = KA$ and $\| f \|_k^2 = A^T K A$, where $A = (a_1, \ldots, a_m)^T$.

It would be natural to use the disagreement error (1) as a cost function, however, it is well known that this leads to intractable optimization problem. Thus, following [7], we use a least-squares approximation of (1), that is, regressing the differences $y_i - y_j$ with $f(x_i) - f(x_j)$:

$$c(f(X), Y, W) = \frac{1}{2} \sum_{i,j=1}^{m} W_{i,j}((y_i - y_j) - (f(x_i) - f(x_j)))^2. \tag{4}$$

Note also that when using (4), not only the sign of $y_i - y_j$ but also its magnitude is included in the objective function (2).

Let $L = D - W$ be the Laplacian matrix [1] of the graph W, where D is the degree matrix of W. That is, D is a diagonal matrix whose entries are defined as

$$D_{i,i} = \sum_{j=1}^{m} W_{i,j}. \tag{5}$$

We observe that for any vector $p \in \mathbb{R}^m$ and an undirected weighted graph W with m vertices, we can write

$$\frac{1}{2} \sum_{i,j-1}^{m} W_{i,j}(p_i - p_j)^2 = p^T D p - p^T W p = p^T L p.$$

Therefore, by selecting $p = Y - KA$, we rewrite the cost function (4) in a matrix form as

$$c(f(X), Y, W) = (Y - KA)^T L (Y - KA).$$

The RankRLS algorithm can be presented in matrix form as

$$A(S) = \underset{A}{\operatorname{argmin}}\, J(A),$$

where

$$J(A) = (Y - KA)^T L (Y - KA) + \lambda A^T K A. \tag{6}$$

As shown in [7], the minimizer of (6) is

$$A = (KLK + \lambda K)^{-1} KLY. \tag{7}$$

The computational complexity of the matrix inversion operation involved in (7) is $O(m^3)$. In practice, this makes the RLS training procedure infeasible when the amount of data available is large. Next, we propose a solution for this problem.

4. Sparse RankRLS

In this section, we propose an algorithm that is based on a similar kind of idea as the subset of regressors method [9,15] for the standard regularized least-squares regression. For in depth discussion of this type of techniques, we refer to [11].

Let $M = \{1, \ldots, m\}$ be the index set in which the indices refer to the examples in the training set and let $R \subseteq M, |R| = r$. By Z_{RM} we denote the submatrix of $Z \in \mathbb{R}^{m \times m}$ that contains only the rows indexed by R. Further, Z_{RR} denotes a submatrix of Z having only rows and columns indexed by R.

Now we consider instead of (3) a solution that allows only the training instances indexed by R to have nonzero coefficient, that is,

$$f(x) = \sum_{i \in R} a_i k(x, x_i).$$

We call the training examples indexed by R basis vectors. The problem of finding this type of hypothesis can be solved by finding the coefficients a_i, where $i \in R$. We observe that $f(X) = K_{MR}A$ and $\|f\|_k^2 = A^T K_{RR} A$, where a coefficient vector $A \in \mathbb{R}^r$, determines the sparse approximation of the minimizer of (2). Using these definitions, we present a method we call sparse RankRLS:

$$\mathcal{A}(S) = \underset{A \in \mathbb{R}^r}{\operatorname{argmin}} J(A)$$

and

$$J(A) = (Y - K_{MR}A)^T L(Y - K_{MR}A) + \lambda A^T K_{RR} A.$$

We take the derivative of $J(A)$ with respect to A:

$$\frac{d}{dA} J(A) = -2K_{RM} L(Y - K_{MR}A) + 2\lambda K_{RR} A$$

$$= -2K_{RM} LY + (2K_{RM} L K_{MR} + 2\lambda K_{RR})A$$

We set the derivative to zero and solve with respect to A:

$$A = (K_{RM} L K_{MR} + \lambda K_{RR})^{-1} K_{RM} LY. \tag{8}$$

The calculation of the solution (8) requires multiplications with a $m \times m$ matrix L which might be infeasible in practise. However, it can be performed efficiently using the following method.

Let $B \in \mathbb{R}^{m \times q}$, where q is number of objects in the training set. The value of $B_{i,j}$ is 1 when the ith input is associated with the jth object and 0 otherwise. Then matrix W can be written as $W = BB^T$. Now, the multiplication $K_{RM} L K_{MR}$ can be written as

$$K_{RM} L K_{MR} = K_{RM}(DK_{MR} - B(B^T K_{MR})),$$

where D is the diagonal degree matrix whose entries are defined in (5). The multiplication $K_{RM} LY$ can be done analogously. The computational complexity of the inversion operation used on $r \times r$ matrices is $O(r^3)$. The complexity of the matrix multiplications is $O(mr^2)$, because B contains only m nonzero elements. Selecting r to be much smaller than m, the overall training complexity of the sparse RankRLS algorithm is $O(mr^2)$.

Clearly, the selection of the index set R may have an influence on results obtained by our method. Different approaches for selecting R are discussed, for example, in [12]. There, it was found that simply selecting the elements of R randomly performs no worse than more sophisticated methods.

4.1. Efficient Training via Decompositions

One advantage of using sparse RankRLS instead of other ranking methods is efficient selection of regularization parameter. Using Cholesky decompositions for K_{RR}, we can rewrite the solution (8) as follows:

$$A = (K_{RM}LK_{MR} + \lambda CC^T)^{-1}K_{RM}LY,$$

where $K_{RR} = CC^T$. Now,

$$\begin{aligned}
(K_{RM}LK_{MR} + \lambda CC^T)^{-1} &= (CC^{-1}K_{RM}LK_{MR}(C^T)^{-1}C^T + \lambda CC^T)^{-1} \\
&= (C^T)^{-1}(C^{-1}K_{RM}LK_{MR}(C^T)^{-1} + \lambda I)^{-1}C^{-1} \\
&= (C^T)^{-1}(V\Lambda V^T + \lambda I)^{-1}C^{-1} \\
&= (C^T)^{-1}V\hat{\Lambda}_\lambda V^T C^{-1},
\end{aligned}$$

where $V\Lambda V^T$ is the eigen decomposition of $C^{-1}K_{RM}LK_{MR}(C^T)^{-1}$ with V, Λ being the eigenvector matrix and diagonal matrix containing the corresponding eigenvalues, respectively, and $\hat{\Lambda}_\lambda = (\Lambda + \lambda I)^{-1}$. Therefore, we rewrite the solution (8) as follows:

$$A = (C^T)^{-1}V\hat{\Lambda}_\lambda V^T C^{-1}K_{RM}LY.$$

The decompositions and the inversion of C can be calculated in $O(r^3)$ time, and hence the overall training complexity is not increased. The computational cost of calculating $\hat{\Lambda}_\lambda$ is $O(r)$, since $(\Lambda + \lambda I)$ is a diagonal matrix. When the matrices $V^T C^{-1}K_{RM}LY \in \mathbb{R}^{r \times 1}$ and $(C^T)^{-1}V \in \mathbb{R}^{r \times r}$ are stored in memory, the subsequent training with different values of regularization parameters can be performed in $O(r^2)$ time.

5. Experiments

We evaluate the performance of sparse RankRLS on the task of ranking of the parses of an unseen sentence. We use the BioInfer corpus [10] which consists of 1100 manually annotated sentences. A detailed description of the parse ranking problem and the data used in the experiments is given in [16]. Each sentence is associated with a set of candidate parses. The manual annotation of the sentence, present in the corpus, provides the correct parse. Further, each candidate parse is associated with a goodness score that indicates how close to the correct parse it is. The correct ranking of the parses associated with the same sentence is determined by this score. While the scoring induces a total or-

Basic RLS Regressor	Sparse RLS Regressor	Basic RankRLS	Sparse RankRLS
0.27	0.24	0.23	0.21

Table 1. Comparison of the parse ranking performances of RLS regressor, sparse RLS regressor, basic RankRLS, and sparse RankRLS using the disagreement error (1) as the performance evaluation measure.

der over the whole set of parses, the preferences between parses associated with different sentences are not considered in the parse ranking task.

As a similarity measure for parses, we use the best performing graph kernel considered in [8]. The disagreement error (1) is used to measure the performance of the ranking algorithms. The error is calculated for each sentence separately and the performance is averaged over all sentences. We have previously shown that basic RankRLS significantly outperforms the basic RLS regressor in the parse ranking task [7]. As shown in Section 4, with sparse RankRLS it is possible to take advantage of much more training data than with basic RankRLS only with a small increase in computational complexity. In our experiments, we test how beneficial this is by comparing sparse RankRLS with basic RankRLS. Furthermore, we make a comparison with basic and sparse RLS regressors. As the basis vectors of the sparse algorithms, we use the training examples of the non-sparse ones, while adding more examples as non-basis vectors. We select 500 sentences for the training of rankers. For basic RankRLS we randomly select 5 parses per sentence, and for sparse RankRLS we use additional 15 randomly selected parses per sentence as non-basis vectors. Thus, $m = 10000$ and $r = 2500$ for the sparse methods.

The algorithms have the regularization parameter λ that controls the trade-off between the minimization of the training error and the complexity of the learned function. Further, kernel function has parameters too. We evaluate the performance of sparse RankRLS as well as other baseline methods by performing a 10-fold cross-validation on the sentence level so that all parses generated from the same sentence would always be in the same fold. We use 500 sentences for the parameter estimation and the rest are reserved for the final evaluation. The appropriate values of the regularization and the kernel parameters are determined by grid search with 10-fold cross-validation on the parameter estimation data. The parameter selection is performed separately for each experiment.

Finally, the algorithms are trained on the whole parameter estimation data set with the best found parameter values and tested with the sentences reserved for the final validation. The results of the validation are presented in Table 1. The results show that the sparse RankRLS algorithm notably outperforms RLS regressor, sparse RLS regressor, and basic RankRLS. Furthermore, to test the statistical significance of the performance differences between the sparse RankRLS algorithm and the other methods, we conducted Wilcoxon signed-ranks tests. The sentences reserved for the final validation are considered as independent trials. We observed that the performance differences are statistically significant ($p < 0.05$).

6. Conclusion

We propose sparse RankRLS, a sparse regularized least-squares algorithm, for learning preference relations. The computational complexity of the algorithm is $O(mr^2)$, where m is the number of training examples, and r is much smaller than m. We formulate the algorithm within the kernel framework. The key feature of the algorithm is the ability to efficiently train the ranker with large amounts of data in high dimensional feature spaces, thus improving the ranking performance. This is achieved by finding a sparse solution to the regularized least-squares problem. In our experiments, we consider parse ranking task. It is shown that sparse RankRLS significantly outperforms basic RLS regressor, sparse RLS regressor, and basic RankRLS.

Acknowledgments

This work has been supported by Tekes, the Finnish Funding Agency for Technology and Innovation. We would like to thank CSC, the Finnish IT center for science, for providing us extensive computing resources.

References

[1]   R. A. Brualdi and H. J. Ryser. *Combinatorial Matrix Theory*. Cambridge University Press, 1991.

[2]   M. Collins. Discriminative reranking for natural language parsing. In *Proceedings of the 17th International Conference on Machine Learning*, pages 175–182, San Francisco, CA, USA, 2000. Morgan Kaufmann Publishers Inc.

[3]   C. Cortes, M. Mohri, and A. Rastogi. Magnitude-preserving ranking algorithms. In Z. Ghahramani, editor, *Proceedings of the 24th Annual International Conference on Machine Learning*, pages 169–176. Omnipress, 2007.

[4]   J. Fürnkranz and E. Hüllermeier. Preference learning. *Künstliche Intelligenz*, 19(1):60–61, 2005.

[5]   R. Herbrich, T. Graepel, and K. Obermayer. Support vector learning for ordinal regression. In *Proceedings of the Ninth International Conference on Articial Neural Networks*, pages 97–102, London, 1999. Institute of Electrical Engineers.

[6]   T. Joachims. Optimizing search engines using clickthrough data. In *Proceedings of the ACM Conference on Knowledge Discovery and Data Mining*, pages 133–142, New York, NY, USA, 2002. ACM Press.

[7]   T. Pahikkala, E. Tsivtsivadze, A. Airola, J. Boberg, and T. Salakoski. Learning to rank with pairwise regularized least-squares. In T. Joachims, H. Li, T.-Y. Liu, and C. Zhai, editors, *SIGIR 2007 Workshop on Learning to Rank for Information Retrieval*, pages 27–33, 2007.

[8]   T. Pahikkala, E. Tsivtsivadze, J. Boberg, and T. Salakoski. Graph kernels versus graph representations: a case study in parse ranking. In T. Gärtner, G. C. Garriga, and T. Meinl, editors, *Proceedings of the ECML/PKDD'06 workshop on Mining and Learning with Graphs (MLG'06)*, Berlin, Germany, 2006.

[9]   T. Poggio and F. Girosi. Networks for approximation and learning. *Proceedings of the IEEE*, 78(9), 1990.

[10]   S. Pyysalo, F. Ginter, J. Heimonen, J. Björne, J. Boberg, J. Järvinen, and T. Salakoski. BioInfer: A corpus for information extraction in the biomedical domain. *BMC Bioinformatics*, 8:50, 2007.

[11]   J. Quinonero-Candela, C. E. Rasmussen, and C. K. I. Williams. Approximation methods for gaussian process regression. In L. Bottou, O. Chapelle, D. DeCoste, and J. Weston, editors, *Large-Scale Kernel Machines*, pages 203–224. MIT Press, Cambridge, Ma, USA, 09 2007.

[12]   R. Rifkin, G. Yeo, and T. Poggio. Regularized least-squares classification. In J. Suykens, G. Horvath, S. Basu, C. Micchelli, and J. Vandewalle, editors, *Advances in Learning Theory: Methods, Model and Applications*, volume 190 of *NATO Science Series III: Computer and System Sciences*, pages 131–154, Amsterdam, 2003. IOS Press.

[13]   B. Schölkopf, R. Herbrich, and A. J. Smola. A generalized representer theorem. In D. Helmbold and R. Williamson, editors, *Proceedings of the 14th Annual Conference on Computational Learning Theory*, pages 416–426, Berlin, Germany, 2001. Springer.

[14]   B. Schölkopf and A. J. Smola. *Learning with kernels*. MIT Press, Cambridge, Massachusetts, 2002.

[15]   A. J. Smola and B. Schölkopf. Sparse greedy matrix approximation for machine learning. In P. Langley, editor, *Proceedings of the Seventeenth International Conference on Machine Learning*, pages 911–918, San Francisco, Ca, 2000. Morgan Kaufmann Publishers Inc.

[16]   E. Tsivtsivadze, T. Pahikkala, S. Pyysalo, J. Boberg, A. Mylläri, and T. Salakoski. Regularized least-squares for parse ranking. In A. F. Famili, J. N. Kok, J. M. Peña, A. Siebes, and A. J. Feelders, editors, *Advances in Intelligent Data Analysis VI*, pages 464–474. Springer, 2005.

Tenth Scandinavian Conference on Artificial Intelligence
A. Holst et al. (Eds.)
IOS Press, 2008

Supporting Maritime Situation Awareness Using Self Organizing Maps and Gaussian Mixture Models

Maria RIVEIRO, Fredrik JOHANSSON, Göran FALKMAN and Tom ZIEMKE

School of Humanities and Informatics, University of Skövde,
Box 408, SE-541 28 Skövde, Sweden
{maria.riveiro, fredrik.johansson, goran.falkman, tom.ziemke}@his.se

Abstract. Maritime situation awareness is of importance in a lot of areas – e.g. detection of weapon smuggling in military peacekeeping operations, and harbor traffic control missions for the coast guard. In this paper, we have combined the use of Self Organizing Maps with Gaussian Mixture Models, in order to enable situation awareness by detecting deviations from normal behavior in an unsupervised way. Initial results show that simple anomalies can be detected using this approach.

Keywords. anomaly detection, situation awareness, data mining, surveillance

Introduction

Detection of unusual vessel activities has been identified as an important objective for enabling maritime situation awareness in the homeland security domain [1]. Human operators trying to establish maritime situation awareness are often overloaded by information from many different sources, such as different surveillance radars and automatic identification systems. In order to help them cope with this information overload we have aimed at developing a methodology that makes it possible to filter out vessels automatically, by building a model over normal behavior which we can detect deviations from.

As mentioned in [2], many approaches for improved maritime situation awareness require human users to specify prior knowledge of what constitutes normal behavior. Since surveillance operations of today and tomorrow often are and will be conducted against unconventional adversaries with unknown or rapidly varying doctrines, there is a need for unsupervised learning techniques. Examples of such techniques are the automated anomaly detection processor described in [2], the trajectory clusterer reported in [3], and the neural network approach described in [1]. An unsupervised Bayesian network approach where expert knowledge can be exploited if available has been suggested in [4]. We have here taken an unsupervised approach similar to the one outlined in [2], i.e. a combination of a Self Organizing Map (SOM) and a Gaussian Mixture Model (GMM).

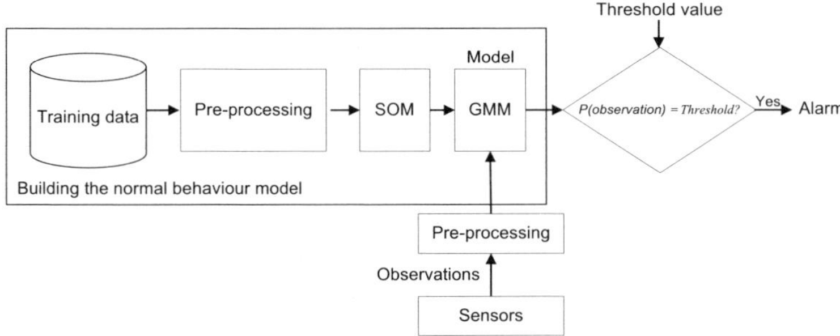

Figure 1. Schema of the anomaly detector.

1. Methodology

Anomalies can be defined as deviations from normalcy. By building models of normal data and using these models to detect deviations from the normal model in observed data, it may become possible to detect anomalous behavior. Events that are classified as anomalies can be flagged as alerts and trigger an alarm to a human operator. The method for anomaly detection presented in this paper is based on two assumptions. Firstly, anomalous events have to be sufficiently different from normal events in order to be detectable. Secondly, the training set should be free from anomalous events, otherwise it is possible that the normal model is influenced by anomalies.

A schematic diagram of the anomaly detector is shown in figure 1. The detector (based on the work presented in [2]) builds a normal behavioral model using a neural network clustering algorithm, the SOM (see section 1.1), over the training data set. Prior knowledge is not required, since the SOM learns what is normal via iteration over the training data. In order to quantify probabilities of normal and anomalous behaviors, the detector uses a GMM (see section 1.2) coupled with the use of Bayes' theorem (see section 1.3). Once the model of the normal behavior is established, the detector can be used on the test data (that represent real world observations, e.g. from sensor readings). For each new observation, $P(observation_{vesselID})$ is calculated. A sliding window over the m most recent observations is used to calculate an average probability value. If the probability value is lower than a given threshold, the detector will flag the vessel as anomalous.

We will here focus on single object anomalies (e.g. speeding), i.e. relationships between objects (e.g. two vessels about to collide) are not considered.

1.1. Clustering using a Self Organizing Map

A SOM can be seen as a clustering algorithm based on a neural network. It takes a set of n-dimensional training data as input and clusters it into a smaller set of n-dimensional nodes, also known as model vectors. These model vectors tend to move toward regions with a high training data density, and the final nodes are found by minimizing the distance of the training data from the model vectors [2]. The n-dimensional training data can for example consist of attributes such as object type, heading, and speed.

The output from the SOM is useful for classification, and can be used for representing a compressed representation of a "normal picture", however, it does not provide a complete solution to the anomaly detection problem since there are many events that do not clearly fall into these well-defined clusters. Therefore, a GMM has been used on top of the SOM.

1.2. Statistical characterization of clusters using a Gaussian Mixture Model

A GMM is a statistical model in which the overall probability distribution is synthesized from a weighted sum of individual Gaussian distributions (where the sum always is vaguer than the individual distributions themselves).

$$P(x_1, ..., x_n) = \sum_m \pi_m P_m(x_1, ..., x_n).$$ (1)

The individual distributions, P_m, in this case correspond to the model vectors that were the output from the SOM. Each model vector is characterized by a n-dimensional Gaussian probability density function. The mean of each individual probability density function is given by the final weights for the model vector, while the variance is given by the dispersion of training data around the model vector. Since the probability density function is a multivariate Gaussian distribution, it can be calculated by

$$P_m(x_1, ..., x_n) = \frac{1}{\sqrt{(2\pi)^n |\Sigma|^{(1/2)}}} \exp\left(-\frac{1}{2}(x - \mu)^T \Sigma^{-1}(x - \mu)\right),$$ (2)

where μ is the mean vector, Σ is the covariance matrix, and $|\Sigma|$ is the determinant of Σ.

The mixing proportions π_m in equation 1 are measures on the weights of each individual model vector. The mixing proportions correspond to the probability of each map unit to be selected as the best matching unit in the SOM (see figures 4(a) and 4(b)).

1.3. Calculation of probabilities using Bayes' theorem

The clustering and the creation of the GMM is done once. When new observations arrive, the GMM can be used to quantify the likelihood $P(d|H = normal)$ for obtaining the observation d given the learned model of what is to be considered as a normal event. However, the quantity we want to calculate is the probability of a normal event, given the observed data, i.e. $P(H = normal|d)$ (in order to calculate the probability of an anomalous event given the observed data, we just take the complement $1 - P(H = normal|d)$). To calculate these probabilities from the likelihood we have to use Bayes' theorem:

$$P(H = normal|d) = \frac{P(d|H = normal)P(H = normal)}{\sum_{h \in H} P(d|h)P(h)}.$$ (3)

The prior probability $P(H = normal)$ adjusts the detection threshold and can be fine-tuned by the human operator in order to get an acceptable ratio between the detection rate and the false positive rate. Otherwise it reflects the expected relative frequency between the number of normal observations and the total number of observations. The denominator in equation 3 can be seen as a normalization constant. In order to calculate this normalization constant we need to know the quantity $P(d|H = anomaly)$, which not is known since we have not built such a model. Hence, we conclude that

$$P(H = normal|d) \propto P(d|H = normal)P(H = normal).$$ (4)

2. Detection of vessel anomalies

This section describes the characteristics of the data used in the learning process and the evaluation and preliminary results obtained.

2.1. Data set description

The training and test data has been provided by Saab Microwave Systems. It has been generated using the ground target simulator GTSIM, described in [5]. Since the training data is synthetic, it does not include any anomalies. Thereby the assumption that the training set should be free from anomalous events is valid.

The original data consists of a large set of observations with a number of attributes: time stamp, object-ID (object identification number), object type (classification, e.g. fishing boat, cargo, etc.) and position (given by x-, y- and z-coordinates using the Swedish grid, RT90). There are some measurement errors associated with the objects positions, otherwise there are no uncertainties in the observations.

Figure 2. Scenario, southern coast of Sweden.

2.1.1. Preprocessing of the data

The training data set has been preprocessed by cutting out a region of interest, in this case a region south of Sweden (see figure 2). The selected area consist of observations (from unique objects). The original attributes have been preprocessed into the following attributes: **time stamp, type, x-coordinate, y-coordinate, z-coordinate, velocity and heading**. Nevertheless, the behavior of the different vessels varies from type to type, so they are treated separately. Therefore, the original data is divided regarding type of vessel in the following classes: F (Fartyg, vessel), FF (Fiskefartyg, fishing boat) and HF (Handelsfartyg, cargo ship).

In order to exemplify and demonstrate the approach, this section describes the implementation and results obtained for one of the vessel types, HF.

2.2. Evaluation and results

2.2.1. Implementation

For the first evaluation of the algorithm we have used the HF training data. Speed and heading were selected as the descriptive features. Like this, we are able to plot 3D probability density functions and the final GMM map (with more than two attributes it will be impossible for us to show examples of the final PDF and GMM map). Matlab 7.1 was used for the implementation and the SOM was implemented using the functions (with some minor modifications) included in the `somtoolbox` (provided by the Helsinki University of Technology). These are briefly the implementation steps of the anomaly detector:

1. Preprocessing of the training data:

   (a) Calculation of attributes from the training data, e.g heading.
   (b) Classification of the samples regarding vessel type: F, FF and HF.

2. Normalization of the training data.
3. SOM calculation. Every map unit will be characterized with a model vector containing the speed and heading average (μ_{speed}, $\mu_{heading}$) of the set of samples which has this map unit as the best matching unit.
4. Covariance matrix calculation. For each map unit we calculate the covariance matrix of all the samples which has this map unit as the best matching unit.
5. Prior probabilities calculation (see figures 4(a) and 4(b)). The figures show, for each map unit, how probable it is to be selected as the best matching unit.
6. GMM combining the Gaussian distributions of each map unit (see figure 5(a)) using the equation 2.
7. Calculation of the probability value using Bayes' theorem.

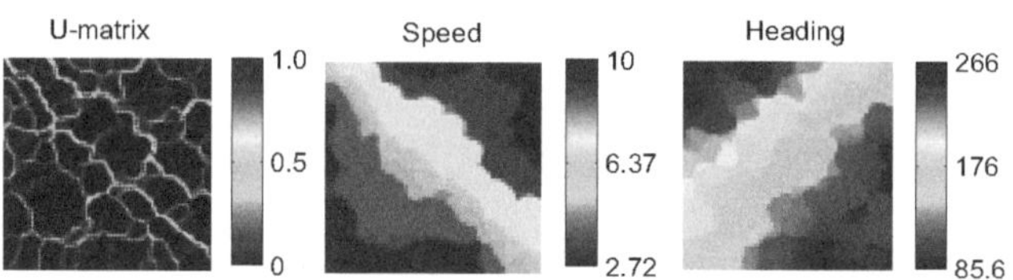

Figure 3. SOM for the HF (cargo ship) vessels. The maps have rectangular structure and the dimensions of the grid are 60 by 60 (D). The first map corresponds to the unified distance matrix (U-matrix) and then the individual feature maps, speed and heading. The U-matrix visualizes distances between neighboring map units, and thus shows the cluster structure of the map: high values of the U-matrix indicate a cluster border, uniform areas of low values (blue) indicate the clusters themselves [6]. The feature maps for speed and heading show clusters of data with similar values (a color identifies a cluster).

Normalization The different features (speed, heading, position) have different scales or ranges (for example, the speed can take values from 1 to 15, while the heading can vary between 0 to 359). Since we want a general algorithm that creates clusters given data from any distribution, the attributes must be normalized. Otherwise, some features will cause bias over others [7]. The attributes, in this case speed and heading, have been normalized independently between 0 and 1.

The Self-Organizing Map The SOM can be seen in figure 3. The map has a rectangular structure. The picture shows on the left the Unified distance matrix (U-matrix), calculated based on the speed and heading, followed by each component's SOM. The U-matrix visualizes distances between neighboring map units and displays the map's cluster structure: high values of the U-matrix indicate a cluster border and uniform values indicate clusters themselves [6].

Covariance matrix   One of the difficulties we have found in our implementation was on the calculus of Σ^{-1} in equation (2). Obviously, the features speed and heading are somehow related so independence between both cannot be assumed (therefore, the calculus of Σ is more complex given that it is not enough with the calculus of the variances). Σ was in many of the cases not stable, so its inverse could not be calculated. In order to solve this problem, white noise ($N\,(0,1)$) was added to the Σ's components.

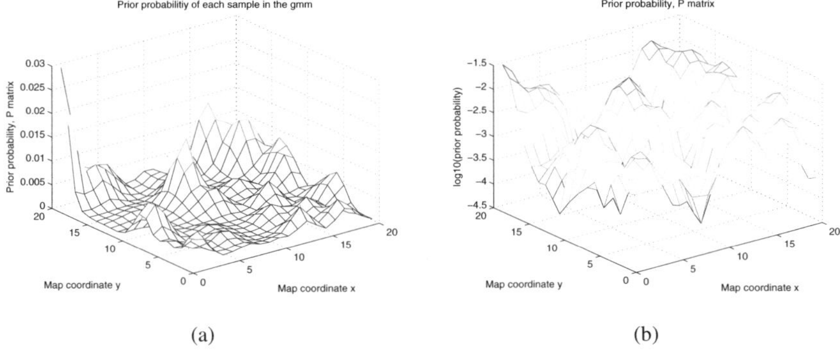

(a)   (b)

Figure 4. Mixing proportions (natural units (a) and logarithmic representation (b)).

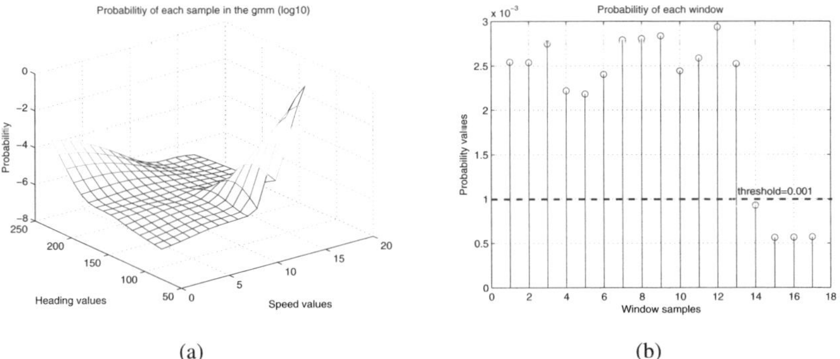

(a)   (b)

Figure 5. Figure (a) shows the final GMM model (in logarithmic units). Figure (b) depicts the accumulated probability values over a sliding window (*number samples* $= 50,\ overlap = 30$). The vessel presents anomalous speed values. Probability values lower than 0.001 (threshold) represent possible abnormal behavior.

2.2.2. Results

For testing our approach we have created a synthetic HF vessel that has an abnormal speed for its heading values, i.e., the sample pairs (*speed, heading*) are not considered normal compared to the training data. Therefore, we expect that the probability of having this behavior by exploiting the GMM model is low. The probability is accumulated over a time window. Both the length of the window and the alarm threshold can be specified by the operator. The abnormal behavior appears in the final samples of the trajectory, where the speed is higher than normal. Figure 5(b) shows the results. As we can see, the last window probabilities are clearly lower which indicates abnormal behavior. If we set an alarm threshold of 0.001, the operator will be notified in this case.

                    M. Riveiro et al. / Supporting Maritime Situation Awareness

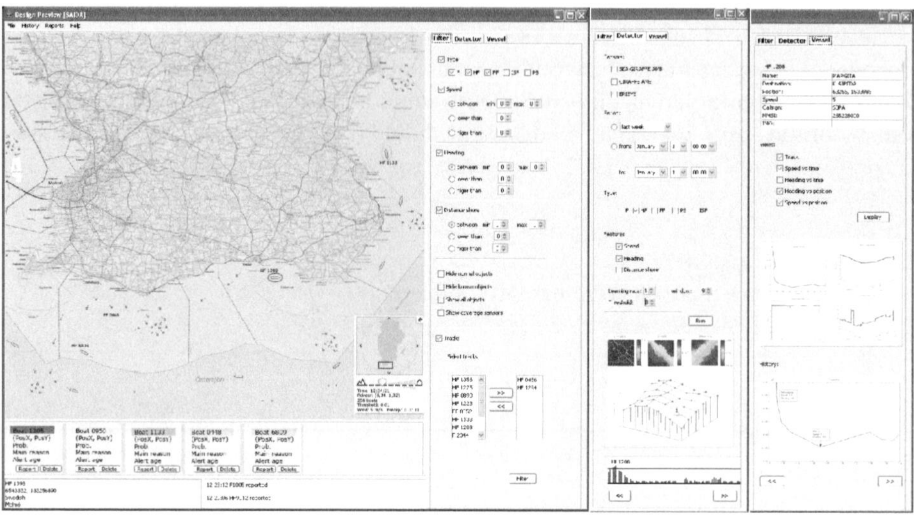

Figure 6. Graphical user interface: filter, detector and vessel module.

3. Future work and conclusions

Future improvements to this method involve the incorporation of geographical information (e.g. a new feature that can be considered is the distance from the shore to the vessel) or information regarding the relations with other vessels or objects in the environment (e.g distance to the closest vessel). The evaluation of this methodology will be complemented with tests on real world data. In this case, modifications or extensions to the methodology described here can be required, since the assumption of no abnormal behavior in the training data may not hold. We also intend to compare this method to existing ones, e.g. the work presented in [4] and [3].

Anomaly detection is a complex real life problem. Humans are often incapable of coping with the size of the data that must be analyzed in these cases. Nevertheless, we believe that the power of computational methods can be complemented with human background knowledge, imagination and flexible thinking. For example, human expert knowledge can be very valuable for the validation of the normal behavior model learned from the training data. In order to take advantage of expert knowledge, we have designed a graphical user interface that supports interaction and involves the user in the anomaly detection process. The prototype is presented in figure 6. Functions like selection of features for the SOM calculation, selection of data sources (sensors), filtering, adjustment of the threshold value and detailed information regarding the anomalies are included in the prototype.

To summarize, we have described an unsupervised approach to the problem of finding vessel anomalies, in order to enable a maritime situation awareness. Preliminary results show that this approach produces satisfactory and promising outcomes.

Acknowledgements

This work was supported by the Information Fusion Research Program (University of Skövde, Sweden) in partnership with the Swedish Knowledge Foundation under grant 2003/0104 and carried out in collaboration with Saab Microwave Systems (Gothenburg, Sweden). We would like to thank Håkan Warston, Martin Smedberg and Thomas Kronhamn (Saab Microwave Systems) for providing the data and for their valuable feedback. Thanks also to the other members of the ground situation awareness for their suggestions and fruitful discussions.

The SOM calculations were partially implemented using the Matlab SOM toolbox provided by Helsinki University of Technology [8].

References

[1] N. Bomberger, B. Rhodes, M. Seibert, and A. Waxman, "Associative learning of vessel motion patterns for maritime situation awareness," in *Proceedings of the 9th International Conference on Information Fusion*, July 2006.

[2] J. B. Kraiman, S. L. Arouh, and M. L. Webb, "Automated anomaly detection processor," in *Proceedings of SPIE: Enabling Technologies for Simulation Science VI*, A. F. Sisti and D. A. Trevisani, Eds., Jul 2002, pp. 128–137.

[3] A. Dahlbom and L. Niklasson, "Trajectory clustering for coastal surveillance," in *Proceedings of the 10th International Conference on Information Fusion*, 2007.

[4] F. Johansson and G. Falkman, "Detection of vessel anomlies - a bayesian network approach," in *Proceedings of the 3rd International Conference on Intelligent Sensors, Sensor Networks and Information Processing*, 2007.

[5] H. Warston and H. Persson, "Ground surveillance and fusion of ground target sensor data in a network based defense," in *Proceedings of the 7th International Conference on Information Fusion*, 2004, pp. 1195–1201.

[6] J. Vesanto, J. Himberg, E. Alhoniemi, and J. Parhankangas, "Self-organizing map in Matlab: the SOM Toolbox," in *Proceedings of the Matlab DSP Conference*, November 1999, pp. 35–40.

[7] L. Portnoy, E. Eskin, and S. J. Stolfo, "Intrusion detection with unlabeled data using clustering," in *Proceedings of ACM CSS Workshop on Data Mining Applied to Security (DMSA-2001)*, Nov 2001.

[8] J. Vesanto, J. Himberg, E. Alhoniemi, and J. Parhankangas, "SOM toolbox for matlab 5," Licentiate thesis, Helsinki University of Technology, 2000.

Tenth Scandinavian Conference on Artificial Intelligence
A. Holst et al. (Eds.)
IOS Press, 2008

Better Safe than Sorry

Optimal Troubleshooting through A Search with Efficiency-based Pruning*

THORSTEN J. OTTOSEN and FINN V. JENSEN

Department of Computer Science, Aalborg University, Denmark

Abstract. Decision theoretic troubleshooting combines Bayesian networks and cost estimates to obtain optimal or near optimal decisions in domains with inherent uncertainty. In this paper we use the well-known A* algorithm extended with pruning based on the efficiency of actions for finding optimal solutions in troubleshooting. In particular, we focus on models with dependent actions.

Keywords. Decision theoretic troubleshooting, Bayesian networks, A* search, dependent actions

Introduction

Decision theoretic troubleshooting combines Bayesian networks with cost estimates to obtain a probabilistic cost optimization problem. Solutions to such problems give us an optimal decision making procedure that takes into account all future ramifications of all decisions.

As an example of a troubleshooting task, consider the task of repairing a car that cannot start. We can take the following actions: put gas on the car, change the batteries, clean the spark plugs etc., and we may ask the following questions: what is the fuel meter standing?, how old is the car?, does the lights work? etc. We are then faced with the problem of finding the order of actions and questions that will *minimize* our effort to get the car working.

When actions in a model can remedy overlapping sets of faults, we say that the model has *dependent actions*. Finding an optimal solution in models with dependent actions is of great practical importance since dependent actions can be expected to occur in many non-trivial domains. However, all non-trivial troubleshooting scenarios have been shown to be NP-hard—this includes models with dependent actions [1].

Two different approaches has previously been used for finding optimal strategies: [2] describes a branch & bound algorithm whereas [3] describes an AO* algorithm. The AO* algorithm can be used for models with questions, but since a model without questions does not lead to OR-nodes in the search tree, we only need to consider the well-known and simpler A* algorithm [4] [5] for models with dependent actions.

The AO* (as well as the A*) algorithm requires the use of an admissible heuristic function. We reuse the admissible heuristic function from [3] and at the same time prune the search tree using a result about the efficiencies of actions from [2]. The result is that our method is 3-4 times as fast and uses 2-3 times less memory as state of the art.

1. Decision Theoretic Troubleshooting and Efficiency-based Pruning

You have a device which has been running well up to now, but suddenly it is malfunctioning. To fix the problem you have a set $\mathcal{A}$ of *actions*, which may fix the problem and a set $\mathcal{Q}$ of *questions*, which may help identifying the problem. Each action or question S has a positive *cost* $C_S(\varepsilon)$ possibly depending on evidence ε. Your task is to fix the problem as cheaply as possible.

A general troubleshooting model describes the probabilistic relation between the possible faults $\mathcal{F}$ and the outcomes of actions and questions. In this paper we deal with troubleshooting scenarios without questions. That is, the model provides for all $A \in \mathcal{A}$ and $F \in \mathcal{F}$ probabilities $P(F \mid \varepsilon)$ and $P(A \mid F, \varepsilon)$, where ε is evidence. In Figure 1 is shown a simple model.

When solving a troubleshooting problem, we have some initial evidence ε^0, and in the course of executing actions in the troubleshooting sequence we collect further evidence, namely that the actions have failed so far. We write ε^i to denote that the first i actions have failed and we have by assumption $P(\varepsilon^0) = 1$ because the device is faulty. We write that an action has failed by $A = n$ whereas $A = y$ means it has succeeded. The presence of the fault F is written $F = y$, and the set of faults that can be repaired by an action A is denoted $\mathrm{fa}(A)$. For example, in Figure 1 we have $\mathrm{fa}(A_2) = \{F_2, F_3\}$.

When there are no questions, a *troubleshooting strategy* is a sequence of actions $s = \langle A_1, \ldots, A_n \rangle$ prescribing the process of repeatedly performing the next action until an action fixes the problem or the last action has been performed. The standard criteria for comparing different sequences is the *expected cost of repair*:

Definition 1. *The expected cost of repair (ECR) of a troubleshooting sequence* $s = \langle A_1, \ldots, A_n \rangle$ *with costs* C_{A_i} *is the mean of the costs until an action succeeds or all actions have been performed:*

$$\mathrm{ECR}\,(s) = \sum_{i=1}^{n} C_{A_i}(\varepsilon^{i-1}) \cdot P(\varepsilon^{i-1}) \tag{1}$$

We then define an *optimal sequence* as a sequence with minimal ECR. Also, $\mathrm{ECR}^*(\varepsilon)$ is the ECR for an optimal sequence of actions not appearing in ε. As an example consider a sequence for the model in Figure 1:

$$\mathrm{ECR}\,(\langle A_2, A_1, A_3 \rangle) = C_{A_2} + P(A_2 = n) \cdot C_{A_1} + P(A_2 = n, A_1 = n) \cdot C_{A_3}$$

$$= C_{A_2} + P(A_2 = n) \cdot C_{A_1}$$

$$+ P(A_2 = n) \cdot P(A_1 = n \mid A_2 = n) \cdot C_{A_3}$$

$$= 1 + \frac{7}{20} \cdot 1 + \frac{7}{20} \cdot \frac{3}{7} \cdot 1 = 1.50$$

A crucial concept in troubleshooting is that of efficiency:

Definition 2. *The efficiency of an action* A *given evidence* ε *is*

$$\mathrm{ef}(A = y \mid \varepsilon) = \frac{P(A = y \mid \varepsilon)}{C_A(\varepsilon)} \tag{2}$$

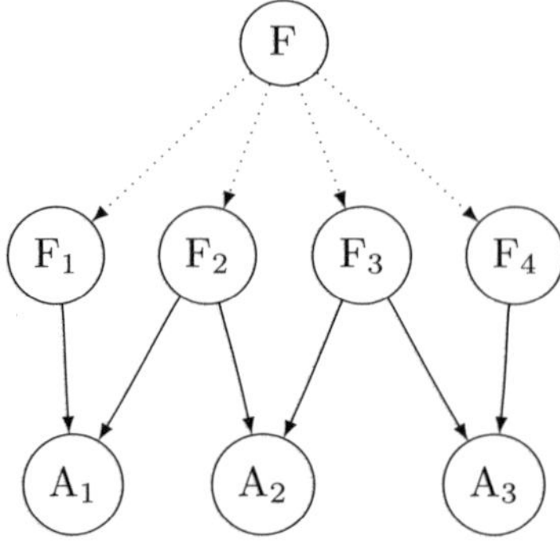

	$\mathcal{F}=F_1$	$\mathcal{F}=F_2$	$\mathcal{F}=F_3$	$\mathcal{F}=F_4$
$P(A_1 = y \mid \mathcal{F})$	1	1	0	0
$P(A_2 = y \mid \mathcal{F})$	0	1	1	0
$P(A_3 = y \mid \mathcal{F})$	0	0	1	1
$P(\mathcal{F})$	0.20	0.25	0.40	0.15
$C_{A_1} = C_{A_2} = C_{A_3} = 1$				

Figure 1. Left: a simple Bayesian network model for a troubleshooting scenario. The dotted lines indicate that the faults F_1 to F_4 are states in a single fault node F. A_1, A_2 and A_3 represent actions, and parents of an action node A are faults which may be fixed by A. Right: the quantitative part of the model.

It is a classical result [6] [7] that if the following *basic assumptions* hold

1. *single fault:* exactly one fault is present,
2. *independent actions:* actions have

    (a) *stable probabilities*:

$$P(A_i = y \mid \varepsilon \cup \{F_j = y\}) = P(A_i = y \mid F_j = y) \quad \forall i, j \tag{3}$$

    (b) *no overlapping*:

$$\mathrm{fa}(A_i) \cap \mathrm{fa}(A_j) = \emptyset \ \text{ whenever } i \neq j \tag{4}$$

3. *independent costs:* the cost of actions do not depend on other actions being performed,

then an optimal troubleshooting sequence can be found by ordering the actions after decreasing efficiency. Note that if assumption 2(b) is violated, we call that situation for troubleshooting with *dependent actions* (even though assumption 2(a) is not violated). It has also been shown that if any of the basic assumptions are relaxed, then the problem is NP-hard [1]. On the other hand, as pointed out in [2], we can say the following about the efficiency of subsequent actions in an optimal troubleshooting sequence:

Theorem 1. *Let* $s = \langle A_1, \ldots, A_n \rangle$ *be an optimal sequence of actions with independent costs. Then it must hold that*

$$\mathrm{ef}(A_i = y \mid \varepsilon^{i-1}) \geq \mathrm{ef}(A_{i+1} = y \mid \varepsilon^{i-1}) \ \forall i \in \{1, \ldots, n-1\} \tag{5}$$

The search problem for troubleshooting with dependent actions has been addressed by means of a branch & bound algorithm [2] and by means of an AO* algorithm [3]. The proposed AO* algorithm also works for scenarios with questions, but with no questions, the algorithm becomes an A* search.

In this paper we study whether efficiency-based pruning based on Theorem 1 can speed up the A* search. In particular, we study scenarios with a high degree of overlapping actions. However, applying the theorem requires two extensions to the search heuristic:

1. we need to perform a full propagation in the Bayesian network (compared to updating a single node), and
2. we need to pass information about the set of pruned actions from parent to child nodes in the search tree.

Therefore, it is not obvious whether the pruning is an advantage.

2. Optimal Sequences with A*

A* (and AO*) is a best-first search algorithm that works by continuously expanding a frontier node n for which the value of the *evaluation function*

$$f(n) = g(n) + h(n) \tag{6}$$

is minimal until finally a goal node t is expanded. The cost between two nodes n and m (m reachable from n) is denoted $c(n, m)$, and the function $g(n)$ is the cost from the start node s to n whereas $h(n)$ is the *heuristic function* that guides (or misguides) the search. If $h(n) \equiv 0$, A* degenerates to Dijkstra's algorithm. The cost of the shortest path from s to n is denoted $g^*(n)$, and from n to t it is denoted $h^*(n)$. The smallest cost between two nodes is $c^*(n, m)$ and we also write C^* for $c^*(s, t)$ (or ECR* in troubleshooting contexts).

Definition 3. *A heuristic function $h(n)$ is admissible if*

$$h(n) \leq h^*(n) \ \forall n \tag{7}$$

The importance of this definition stems from the following theorem [4]:

Theorem 2. *If the heuristic function $h(n)$ is admissible, then A* finds the optimal path from s to t.*

Finally, we note that in troubleshooting, $g(n)$ is given by

$$g(n) = \mathrm{ECR}\left(\langle A_1, \ldots, A_n \rangle\right) \tag{8}$$

where $\langle A_1, \ldots, A_n \rangle$ are the actions performed on the path from s to n.

3. The Admissible Heuristic Function

The AO* algorithm has been used for obtaining optimal troubleshooting strategies by means of an admissible heuristic function $\underline{\mathrm{ECR}}$ [3]:

Definition 4. *Let $\mathcal{E}$ denote the set containing all possible evidence. The function $\underline{\mathrm{ECR}}$: $\mathcal{E} \mapsto \mathcal{R}^+$ is defined for each $\varepsilon \in \mathcal{E}$ by*

$$\underline{\mathrm{ECR}}(\varepsilon) = \sum_{F \in \mathcal{F}} \mathrm{P}(F = y \,|\, \varepsilon) \cdot \mathrm{ECR}^*(\varepsilon \cup \{F = y\}) \tag{9}$$

A nice property of $\underline{\text{ECR}}(\varepsilon)$ is that it is rather inexpensive to compute because instantiating the fault node renders the child nodes independent: for each fault F, the optimal ECR given the presence of the fault, $\text{ECR}^*(\varepsilon \cup \{F = y\})$, is found by ordering the unperformed actions that can repair F according to decreasing efficiency (because the basic assumptions hold). We illustrate this with an example.

Consider the fault F_2 in Figure 1 which can be repaired by actions A_1 and A_2, but (for the sake of this example) let $P(A_1 = y \,|\, F_2) = 0.9$ and $P(A_2 = y \,|\, F_2) = 0.8$ instead. Since we have stable probabilities (assumption 2(a)), the efficiencies of the two actions are 0.9 and 0.8, respectively. We get

$$\text{ECR}^*(\varepsilon \cup F_2 = y) = \text{ECR}\left(\langle A_1, A_2 \rangle \,|\, F_2 = y\right)$$
$$= C_{A_1} + P(A_1 = n \,|\, F_2 = y) \cdot C_{A_2}$$
$$= 1 + 0.1 * 1 = 1.1$$

Finally we can justify the use of $\underline{\text{ECR}}$ [3]:

Theorem 3. *The function* $\underline{\text{ECR}}(\varepsilon)$ *is admissible, that is,*

$$\underline{\text{ECR}}(\varepsilon) \leq \text{ECR}^*(\varepsilon) \;\; \forall \varepsilon \in \mathcal{E} \tag{10}$$

4. Implementation

Our implementation of A^* is based on $\underline{\text{ECR}}$ and exploits two important optimizations:

1. it combines nodes with similar past into a single node (*coalescing*)
2. it prunes the tree by using a close-to-optimal upper bound $\overline{\text{ECR}}$ of ECR^*
   (let us call this *bounding*)

We believe an implementation with these two optimizations represent state of the art.

Whenever two nodes n and m are coalesced, we can throw the path to n away if $g(n) > g(m)$, and continue from m only. However, if the search has already grown a tree rooted at n, we can reuse this tree by updating the $f(\cdot)$ values of its leafs. Alternatively, this tree is just discarded and recalculated, but in either case we have to do some extra work. However, coalescing is still a big win since it effectively reduces the complexity of the search from $O(|\mathcal{A}|!)$ to $O(2^{|\mathcal{A}|})$ because we only have $\binom{|\mathcal{A}|}{d}$ sequences with different evidence at depth d in the tree.

Whether such a close bound $\overline{\text{ECR}}$ is easy to obtain depends somewhat on the model in question, but by choosing a close bound, we ensure a conservative comparison: any new method will be at least as effective as reported. In our case we were able to calculate this upper bound by performing a naive greedy search with recalculations. That is, always pick the action with highest efficiency followed by a propagation etc. In practice this gave us bounds that came within one percent from ECR^*. Like in a branch & bound algorithm we prune any node n if $f(n) \geq \overline{\text{ECR}}$.

Table 1. Experimental results for models with 15 to 24 actions. The average number of associated faults per action ranges from 2.2 to 3.42. "EP" means "efficiency-base pruning", "C" means "coalescing" and "B" means "bounding". Time is measures in seconds, the "Pruned" column indicates the number of pruned nodes, and the "Tree" column is the size of the search tree. "R. Time" is the time relative to the rightmost "Time" column.

Method	$A^* + EP$				$A^* + C + B$				$A^* + EP + C + B$		
Model / Dep.	Time	Pruned	Tree	R. Time	Time	Pruned	Tree	R. Time	Time	Pruned	Tree
15 / 2.2	0.58	69k	17k	1.41	1.44	89k	19k	3.51	0.41	63k	8k
16 / 2.5	1.89	189k	45k	1.24	3.41	188k	44k	2.23	1.53	131k	17k
17 / 2.88	3.77	267k	76k	3.04	4.16	246k	52K	3.35	1.24	168k	19k
18 / 2.22	19.19	2735k	467k	2.64	31.66	1616k	438k	4.35	7.28	1077k	128k
19 / 2.32	17.97	1614k	361k	1.88	30.27	1437k	295k	3.17	9.55	989k	109k
20 / 2.8	17.94	1219k	294k	2.26	28.94	1291k	261k	3.64	7.95	897k	87k
21 / 2.76	47.23	4768k	969k	2.06	77.17	3474k	650k	3.37	22.88	2490k	248k
22 / 2.82	-	-	-	-	246.2	9931k	1824k	3.56	69.17	7759k	708k
23 / 3.22	-	-	-	-	367.78	13485k	2387k	3.51	104.72	10343k	969k
24 / 3.42	-	-	-	-	646.28	20533k	4025k	6.73	96.02	12437k	977k

5. Results

We have compared three versions of A^* :

1. Basic A^* with efficiency-based pruning ($A^* + EP$)
2. A^* with coalescing and bounding ($A^* + C + B$)
3. A^* with coalescing, bounding, and efficiency-based pruning ($A^* + EP + C + B$).

The results are shown in Table 1. Our results show that method 1 is about twice as fast as method 2, but that it consumes memory more greedily and runs out of memory on larger models (the average relative time is 2.08). So efficiency-based pruning cannot stand alone.

Method 3 is about 3 to 4 times as fast as method 2, and at the same time method 3 uses the least memory. The average relative time is 3.74 and the average relative tree size is 2.86. That is, efficiency-based pruning reduces complexity with a factor of 3 to 4, although we had hoped for more.

References

[1] Marta Vomlelová. Complexity of decision-theoretic troubleshooting. *International Journal of Intelligent Systems, Volume 18, Issue*, pages 267–277, 2003.

[2] Finn V. Jensen, Uffe Kjærulff, Brian Kristiansen, Claus Skaanning, Jiri Vomlel, and Marta Vomlelová. The SACSO methodology for troubleshooting complex systems. *Artificial Intelligence for Engineering Design, Analysis and Manufacturing*, 15:321–333, 2001.

[3] M. Vomlelová and J. Vomlel. Troubleshooting: NP-hardness and solution methods. *Soft Computing Journal, Volume 7, Number 5*, pages 357–368, 2003.

[4] P. E. Hart, N. J. Nilsson, and B. Raphael. A formal basis for the heuristic determination of minimum cost paths. *IEEE Trans. Systems Science and Cybernetics*, SSC-4(2):100–7, 1968.

[5] Rina Dechter and Judea Pearl. Generalized best-first search strategies and the optimality af A^*. *J. ACM*, 32(3):505–536, 1985.

[6] Kadane. J. and Simon. H. Optimal strategies for a class of constrained sequential problems. *The Annals of Statistics*, 5:237–255, 1977.

[7] Jayant Kalagnanam and Max Henrion. A comparison of decision analysis and expert rules for sequential diagnosis. In *UAI '88: Proceedings of the Fourth Annual Conference on Uncertainty in Artificial Intelligence*, pages 271–282, Amsterdam, The Netherlands, 1990. North-Holland Publishing Co.

Tenth Scandinavian Conference on Artificial Intelligence
A. Holst et al. (Eds.)
IOS Press, 2008

Combining Measurement Data and Erlang-B Formula for Blocking Prediction in GSM Networks

Pasi LEHTIMÄKI [a,1], Kimmo RAIVIO [a]

[a] *Adaptive Informatics Research Centre, Helsinki University of Technology, Finland*

Abstract. In cellular network performance optimization, it is important to be able to predict the amount of user-experienced quality problems such as call blocking with alternative modifications to the network configuration. In this paper, a method based on mathematical optimization and knowledge representation to predict the amount of blocking in GSM networks is presented. The method is based on exploiting the available statistical measurement information describing the individual characteristics of the network elements. In addition, application domain knowledge about blocking is included to the model by using the well known Erlang-B formula to establish a mapping between blocking and existing network measurements. The results of the experiments show that the proposed method performs better than the comparison method based on basic Erlang-B formula and raw measurement data.

Keywords. Blocking prediction, Erlang-B formula, GSM network, measurement data, radio resource optimization.

Introduction

In cellular networks, the optimization of radio resources becomes necessary when the number of subscribers increase while the amount or resources remain limited. When optimizing the radio resource usage, the number of subscribers for which the quality of service requirements are met is maximized in order to gain maximal profit for the operators with minimum costs [6]. One of the most important quality of service indicators in GSM networks is service (call) blocking. The maximization of the number of subscribers that can be served corresponds to the minimization of service blocking, meaning that as many subscribers as possible should be able to access the network without service denial.

The amount of blocking can be reduced by changing the capacity of the network in a way that more communication channels are available in locations with higher user density. In addition, it is possible to adjust the size of the Base Transceiver Station (BTS) coverage areas (cells) and therefore, to control the amount of input traffic in the cells. In both cases, it would be appropriate to be able to predict the amount of blocking if the cell sizes (the amount of input traffic) or the number of communication channels are modified.

---

[1] Corresponding Author: Pasi Lehtimäki, Adaptive Informatics Research Centre, Helsinki University of Technology, P.O. Box 5400, FIN-02015 HUT, Finland; E-mail: Pasi.Lehtimaki@hut.fi

In this paper, an artificial intelligence (AI) based approach to predict the amount of blocking is presented. The proposed approach combines the benefits of data analysis methods and knowledge representation techniques. Past measurements made from the BTSs are an important source of information describing the unique properties of the BTSs such as the propagation environment and network configuration. In order to make predictions in cells without past capacity problems, the well-known Erlang-B formula is included to the model that allows the establishment of mapping between blocking, number of channel requests and the number of busy communication channels for which good statistical data records are available.

Next, the use of traditional Erlang-B formula in blocking prediction is presented and its drawbacks are demonstrated. In Section 2, the proposed method combining the Erlang-B formula with the measurement data is presented. Finally, the results of the experiments with artificial and real data sets are presented in Section 3.

1. Traditional Blocking Modeling

1.1. Erlang's loss system

Traditionally, the Erlang-B formula is used as a model when computing the amount of blocking with different number of channels and demand [2]. When the incoming transactions follow the Poisson arrival process with arrival rate λ, transaction length is exponentially distributed with mean $1/\mu$ and the number of channels N_c is finite, the probability that n channels are busy at random point of time can be computed using the Erlang-distribution

$$p(n|\lambda, \mu, N_c) = \frac{(\lambda/\mu)^n/n}{\sum_{k=0}^{N_c}(\lambda/\mu)^k/k}. \tag{1}$$

Using this formula, the expected value for the number of blocked requests is obtained by multiplying the number of arriving requests with the blocking probability, leading to $B = \lambda p(N_c|\lambda, \mu, N_c)$. The expected value for the congestion time is $C = p(N_c|\lambda, \mu, N_c)$ and the expected value for the number of busy channels is $M = \sum_{n=0}^{N_c} np(n|\lambda, \mu, N_c)$.

The Erlang-B formula can be applied in long-term blocking prediction if reasonable predictions for the number of requests, average channel hold time and number of channels are available. The most straightforward method would be based on hourly averages of number of requests and channel hold time in past observations. More precisely, the average value $\mu_{R,h}$ for the number of requests R at hour h could be estimated from N past observations from hour h using $\mu_{R,h} = \frac{1}{N}\sum_i^N R_{h,i}$ and similarly, the mean $\mu_{T,h}$ for the channel hold time T at hour h is estimated using $\mu_{T,h} = \frac{1}{N}\sum_i^N T_{h,i}$.

1.2. Drawbacks of using Erlang-B formula in long-term prediction

The main problem with the use of the previously discussed approach in capacity optimization is that the theoretical predictions for the number of blocked requests are not well describing the blocking measurements made in operative GSM networks. The reason may be in stochastic nature of the capacity due to the different priorities of the transactions [5] or variating propagation conditions [3]. In addition, each BTS has unique software and hardware configuration as well as resource allocation algorithms having an influence on blocking behavior.

The amount of variation in transaction arrival rate during the measurement period has a strong impact on blocking. Figure 1 demonstrates the connection between the number of requests R in hour, the number of blocked requests in hour and the blocking percentage. The number of requests R per hour takes values from 500 to 8000. The time period of one hour was divided into 180 segments of length 20 seconds. For each value of R, different distributions for the number of channel requests per segment were simulated. Then, the Erlang-B formula was used to compute the segmentwise values for the number of blocked requests, and finally, the sum of the segmentwise values were obtained. The number of channels was 16 and the average channel hold time was 5 seconds. Therefore, this is a typical setting for the analysis of the capacity of a BTS with 16 Standalone Dedicated Control CHannels (SDCCHs).

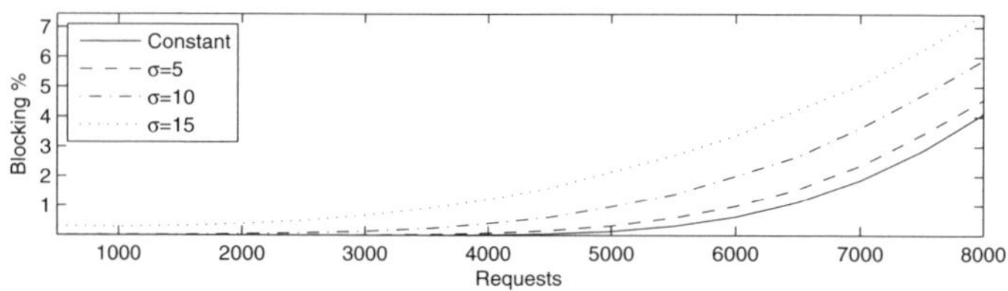

Figure 1. The effect of variability in arrival rate to blocking. Clearly, the more variation in arrival rate is present, the more blocking occurs.

The solid line shows the cumulative values over one hour for the number of requests and blocked requests when the arrival rate of incoming channel requests during the segment i of each hour is $\lambda(i) = R/180$. In other words, this means that the arrival rate is constant during the one hour time period. The dashed line shows the corresponding results in the case when the arrival rate during the segments is Normally distributed around the mean $\lambda(i) \sim N(\mu = R/180, \sigma = 5)$. This leads to the approximately same number of requests in hour, but now, there are also segments during which the arrival rate exceeds the mean of the arrival rate and are more likely generating also blocked requests. The dot-dashed line and the dotted lines show the results for the cases when the arrival rate during segments are Normally distributed with standard deviations $\sigma = 10$ and $\sigma = 15$. It is clear, that the more variation exists in arrival rates between segments, the more blocking can be expected to occur. The typical target value for SDCCH blocking probability is usually 0.2%.

2. Extended Blocking Model

2.1. The model

Now, suppose that the time period of one hour is divided into N_s segments of equal length. Also, assume that we have a vector $\Lambda = [0 \; 1\Delta_\lambda \; 2\Delta_\lambda \; \ldots \; (N_\lambda - 1)\Delta_\lambda]$ of N_λ possible arrival rates per segment with discretization step Δ_λ Let us denote the number of blocked requests during a segment with arrival rate Λ_i with $B_i =$

$p(N_c|\Lambda_i, \mu, N_c)\Lambda_i$, where $p(N_c|\Lambda_i, \mu, N_c)$ is the blocking probability given by the Erlang-distribution. Also, the congestion time and the average number of busy channels during a segment with arrival rate Λ_i are denoted with $C_i = p(N_c|\Lambda_i, \mu, N_c)$ and $M_i = \sum_{n=0}^{N_c} np(n|\Lambda_i, \mu, N_c)$. In other words, the segment-wise values for blocked requests, congestion time and average number of busy channels are based on basic Erlang-B formula. For short time segments, the assumptions related to Erlang-B formula can be said to hold.

Now, assume that the number of segments with arrival rate Λ_i is a_i and $\sum_i a_i = N_s$. Then, predictions for the cumulative values over one hour for the number of requests R, blocked requests B, congestion time C and average number of busy channels M can be computed with

$$
\begin{bmatrix}
\Lambda_1 & \Lambda_2 & \dots & \Lambda_{N_\lambda} \\
B_1 & B_2 & \dots & B_{N_\lambda} \\
C_1/N_s & C_2/N_s & \dots & C_{N_\lambda}/N_s \\
M_1/N_s & M_2/N_s & \dots & M_{N_\lambda}/N_s
\end{bmatrix}
\begin{bmatrix}
a_1 \\ a_2 \\ \vdots \\ a_{N_\lambda}
\end{bmatrix}
=
\begin{bmatrix}
\hat{R} \\ \hat{B} \\ \hat{C} \\ \hat{M}
\end{bmatrix}
\tag{2}
$$

or in matrix notation $\mathbf{X}\mathbf{a} = \hat{\mathbf{Y}}$. Note, that it is necessary to divide the last two rows of matrix $\mathbf{X}$ with N_s, since the congestion time calculation in matrix $\mathbf{X}$ is based on time unit corresponding to the length of the segment instead of the whole time period consisting of N_s segments. Similarly, M denotes the average number of busy channels during the whole time period of N_s segments, while $\sum_i M_i a_i$ would indicate the sum of segment-wise averages of number of busy channels.

2.2. Estimation

Now, the problem is that the vector $\mathbf{a}$ is unknown and it must be estimated from data using the observations of $\mathbf{Y}$ and matrix $\mathbf{X}$ which can be constructed by applying the Erlang-B formula to the number of channels N_c, observed average channel hold time μ and the selected Λ vector. The most common procedure for parameter estimation in regression problems is the minimization of prediction error. Let us denote the prediction error between the observed output vector $\mathbf{Y}$ and the corresponding predictions $\hat{\mathbf{Y}}$ with $\mathbf{e} = \mathbf{Y} - \hat{\mathbf{Y}} = \mathbf{Y} - \mathbf{X}\mathbf{a}$. Since the output vector $\mathbf{Y}$ includes variables that are measured in different scales, it is necessary to include weighting of variables into the cost function. Now, the error vector becomes

$$
\mathbf{e}_w =
\begin{bmatrix}
w_1 & 0 & \dots & 0 \\
0 & w_2 & \dots & 0 \\
\vdots & \vdots & \ddots & \vdots \\
0 & 0 & \dots & w_n
\end{bmatrix}
\left[\mathbf{Y} - \hat{\mathbf{Y}} \right] = \mathbf{W}\mathbf{e}
\tag{3}
$$

and the cost function to be minimized is

$$
E_w = \frac{1}{2}\mathbf{e}_w^T \mathbf{e}_w = \frac{1}{2}\mathbf{Y}^T \mathbf{W}^T \mathbf{W}\mathbf{Y} - \mathbf{Y}^T \mathbf{W}^T \mathbf{W}\mathbf{X}\mathbf{a} + \frac{1}{2}\mathbf{a}^T \mathbf{X}^T \mathbf{W}^T \mathbf{W}\mathbf{X}\mathbf{a}.
\tag{4}
$$

Since the first term does not depend on variable $\mathbf{a}$ to be estimated, it can be ignored from the cost function. Denoting $\mathbf{f} = -\mathbf{X}^T\mathbf{W}^T\mathbf{W}\mathbf{Y}$ and $\mathbf{H} = \mathbf{X}^T\mathbf{W}^T\mathbf{W}\mathbf{X}$, the optimization problem can be represented in the form

$$\min_{\mathbf{a}}\left\{\frac{1}{2}\mathbf{a}^T\mathbf{H}\mathbf{a} + \mathbf{f}^T\mathbf{a}\right\}, \quad w.r.t \;\; 0 \leq \mathbf{a}_i \leq N_s, \;\; \sum_i \mathbf{a}_i = N_s. \tag{5}$$

In other words, the goal is to find the vector $\mathbf{a}$ that provides the smallest prediction errors for variables R, B, C and M. This is the form of standard quadratic programming problem and there are several algorithms and programming packages that can be used to solve the parameter estimate [1].

2.3. A probabilistic model for arrival rate

Suppose that we have N_d observations for variables R, B, C and M, all measured at hour h during different days. The optimization problem described in the previous section could be solved for each of the N_d observation vectors separately, leading to N_d solution vectors $\mathbf{a}$ for hour h. Let us denote the ith solution vector for hour h with $\mathbf{a}_h^{(i)}$ and the jth element of the corresponding solution vector with $\mathbf{a}_{jh}^{(i)}$. Since $\mathbf{a}_{jh}^{(i)}$ described the number of segments with arrival rate Λ_j during ith observation vector at hour h, the probability for a random segment during ith observation period to have an arrival rate Λ_j can be computed from $\mathbf{a}_{jh}^{(i)}$ with $p_{jh}^{(i)} = \mathbf{a}_{jh}^{(i)}/N_s$, where N_s is the number of segments.

Now, if we are interested in occurrences of Λ_j at hour h in the long run, it would be straightforward to sum the occurrences of the Λ_j during the N_d observations. In other words, the probability for observing a segment with arrival rate Λ_j at hour h would become $p_{jh} = \frac{1}{N_d N_s}\sum_{i=1}^{N_d}\mathbf{a}_{jh}^{(i)}$. Now, the probabilities for each arrival rate Λ_j at hour h form a probabilistic model for arrival rate.

The above probabilistic model can be used to compute the elements of the average model $\bar{\mathbf{a}}$ using $\bar{\mathbf{a}}_{jh} = p_{jh}N_s$. In other words, the average model includes the expected number of occurrences of Λ_j at hour h during N_s segments. Now, this average model can directly be used in prediction of the output variables of $\mathbf{Y}$ given the selected $\mathbf{X}$ matrix. In particular, we are interested in prediction of number of blocked requests B in the output vector $\mathbf{Y}$. From now on, we refer to this method as the Erlang-B with variating arrival rate (EBV_λ) and the method presented in Section 1.1 as the Erlang-B with constant arrival rate (EBC_λ).

3. Experiments

3.1. Artificial data sets

In order to study the performance of the proposed method, four different data sets were generated. The number of channel requests per hour takes values $R = [1000, 8000]$, the number of channels is 16 and the average channel hold time was 5 seconds. In the first data set, all the requests appeared with constant arrival rate during each of the $N_s = 180$ segments for all values of R. In the remaining three data sets, the arrival rates of the segments are drawn from Normal distributions with mean $\mu_\lambda = R/N_s$ and standard de-

Table 1. The prediction errors of the EBC$_\lambda$ and EBV$_\lambda$ methods with the artificial data sets.

$p(\lambda)$	EBC$_\lambda$	EBV$_\lambda$ $N_\lambda = 5$	EBV$_\lambda$ $N_\lambda = 10$	EBV$_\lambda$ $N_\lambda = 15$	EBV$_\lambda$ $N_\lambda = 20$	EBV$_\lambda$ $N_\lambda = 25$	EBV$_\lambda$ $N_\lambda = 30$
Constant	0	2.54	0.436	0.201	0.126	0.124	0.0949
N(R/N_s, 1)	0.739	2.50	0.411	0.182	0.114	0.100	0.0785
N(R/N_s, 3)	5.41	1.92	0.12	0.0668	0.0666	0.066	0.0661
N(R/N_s, 5)	14.9	1.07	0.0751	0.0739	0.072	0.0725	0.0732

viations $\sigma = 1, 3, 5$. Then, the Erlang-B formula was used to compute the segmentwise values of B, C and M. Finally, the sum of the segmentwise values for R, B, C and M were obtained to correspond data from one hour time periods. This hourwise data was used as input data for the EBV$_\lambda$ method. The predictions for B of the EBV$_\lambda$ were compared with the corresponding predictions given by the EBC$_\lambda$ method for which the total number of requests R during N_s segments was used as the only input.

Table 1 demonstrates the performance of EBC$_\lambda$ as well the EBV$_\lambda$ method with different values of N_λ. Clearly, the prediction errors of the EBC$_\lambda$ method that assumes constant arrival rate get worse as the amount of variation in arrival rate increases. Secondly, the prediction errors of the EBV$_\lambda$ method assuming varying arrival rate performs better as the number of values for arrival rate N_λ increases. Although, no significant improvements for $N_\lambda \geq 15$ are achieved. Thirdly, the prediction accuracies of the EBV$_\lambda$ for certain value of N_λ become better as the amount of deviation in arrival rate increases. In other words, data with small variation in arrival rate seems to be difficult to model for the EBV$_\lambda$ method. Most likely, this is a result of bad matching between the true arrival rate in the data and the closest candidate Λ_j in the arrival rate vector Λ.

3.2. Real GSM network data

In addition to the self-generated data sets, we have made experiments with measurement data from an operational GSM network consisting of hundreds of measurements over 40 day time period in 2500 BTSs. For this study, we have chosen BTSs with different capacities that include the most serious blocking problems. Before the raw data can be used in model estimation, some preprocessing was performed in order to prevent the use of data from abnormal operational conditions. The preprocessed data set was divided into two proportions. The first half of the data was used as a training data for model estimation. The second half of the data was used as a validation data.

3.3. Error measures

In this section, the performance measures used to compare the EBC$_\lambda$ and EBV$_\lambda$ methods in long-term prediction of blocking are introduced. Let us assume, that we have the observations of R, B, C and M from a single time period of one hour. The quadratic programming techniques can be used to find the instantaneous parameter estimate $\mathbf{a}$ that provides the smallest prediction error with the selected $\mathbf{X}$ matrix.

The ability of the proposed method to explain the instantaneous values of the output variable B in vector $\mathbf{Y}$ in the training data with $24 \times N_d$ samples can be measured with $E^{trn}_{\mathbf{a}_h^{(i)}} = \frac{1}{24N_d} \sum_{h=0}^{23} \sum_{i=1}^{N_d} \left| B_h^{(i)} - \hat{B}_{\mathbf{a}_h^{(i)}} \right|$, where the subscript $\mathbf{a}_h^{(i)}$ of the error measure is used to denote that the prediction $\hat{B}$ is obtained with $\mathbf{a}$ estimated from the ith observation from hour h using the EBV_λ method. E^{trn}_{ebc} indicates the performance of the EBC_λ method in which the Erlang-B formula is directly applied to the observations of number of requests and average channel hold time in the training data. In other words, it is similar to the above error measure given that the number of blocked requests is given by $\hat{B}^{(i)}_{ebc}$.

Since we are interested in long-term prediction and the cumulative behavior of the prediction errors, the hourwise validation error $H^{val}_{\bar{\mathbf{a}}_h} = \frac{1}{24N_d} \sum_{h=0}^{23} \left| \sum_{i=1}^{N_d} B_h^{(i)} - N_d \hat{B}_{\bar{\mathbf{a}}_h} \right|$ was also computed. This error measure allows the analysis of how the prediction $\hat{B}$ fits the sum of blocked requests given the hour h. The same measure can be used with EBC_λ by replacing the output variable predictions with $\hat{B}_{h,ebc}$ and is denoted with H^{val}_{ebc}.

Finally, the total prediction error of the EBV_λ in the whole validation set can be measured with $T^{val}_{\bar{\mathbf{a}}_h} = \frac{1}{24N_d} \left| \sum_{h=0}^{23} \sum_{i=1}^{N_d} B_h^{(i)} - N_d \sum_{h=0}^{23} \hat{B}_{\bar{\mathbf{a}}_h} \right|$. The corresponding measure for EBC_λ is denoted by T^{val}_{ebc}.

3.4. Prediction of SDCCH and TCH blocking

Table 2. The prediction errors of the EBC_λ and the EBV_λ methods with real GSM network data.

Type	Id	N_c	$P_{B>0}$	$\bar{B}_{B>0}$	$E^{trn}_{\mathbf{a}_h^{(i)}}$	E^{trn}_{ebc}	$H^{val}_{\bar{\mathbf{a}}_h}$	H^{val}_{ebc}	$T^{val}_{\bar{\mathbf{a}}_h}$	T^{val}_{ebc}
SDCCH	052	16	0.1071	28.14	1.34	2.06	3.25	3.96	3.22	3.96
SDCCH	053	16	0.1007	23.89	1.50	2.93	0.82	1.87	0.37	1.87
SDCCH	011	32	0.0357	36.36	1.02	1.62	1.14	0.96	0.43	0.96
SDCCH	032	32	0.0903	26.30	0.42	1.01	3.24	3.73	3.23	3.73
TCH	002	11	0.4647	105.11	3.17	9.88	12.00	26.19	5.48	26.19
TCH	018	11	0.5719	262.71	4.86	14.28	35.49	56.95	21.60	56.93
TCH	007	25	0.4562	443.78	6.14	23.54	40.85	61.41	21.01	60.88
TCH	063	70	0.1433	312.77	2.12	13.24	15.58	44.59	13.06	44.59

In the experiments with real GSM network data, we have experienced that the number of possible arrival rate values $N_\lambda = 7$ provides good results. However, one of the λ values was always selected to be $\lambda' = \bar{R}_h/N_s$, i.e the hourly average of number of requests divided by the number of segments, in order have at least one arrival rate value that is close to the most expected value. Also, the weights for the output variables were $w_i = 1/\sigma_{Y_i}$, i.e the greater the standard deviation σ_{Y_i} of the variable Y_i in the measurement data, the smaller weight was used in order to avoid them to dominate in parameter estimation.

In Table 2, the results of the experiments with SDCCH and TCH (Traffic CHannel) data are shown. We have selected four BTSs with serious SDCCH blocking problems and four BTSs with serious TCH blocking problems. In the table, the number of channels N_c, the frequency of observations with blocking $P_{B>0}$ and average size of the blocking peak $\bar{B}_{B>0}$ are shown. Then, the instantaneous prediction errors E^{trn} for the number of blocked requests B in the training data are shown for the EBV_λ (left) and EBC_λ (right) methods. Also, the hourwise prediction errors H^{val} and the total prediction errors T^{val} over the validation data are shown.

According to the table, the proposed EBV_λ method provides smaller instantaneous prediction errors than the EBC_λ method for each of the analyzed BTSs. In other words, the flexibility of the EBV_λ method allows more accurate explanation of the training data.

Also, the EBV_λ provides better hourwise prediction errors for all BTSs except one (BTS 011). In this BTS, blocking is more rare than in the other analyzed BTSs. It is likely that there are some differences in blocking patterns between the training and validation sets of this BTS, and therefore, more data should be used in estimation and validation when comparing these two methods with this data.

However, the most important comparison is the one in which the prediction errors for the sum of blocked requests during a time period of approximately 20 days are analyzed. As can be seen from the table, the proposed EBV_λ provides clearly smaller total prediction errors than the EBC_λ method. These results indicate that a more flexible method that is able to characterize cell-specific traffic patterns is able to provide better predictions of blocking in operative GSM networks.

4. Conclusions

In this paper, a method that exploits the GSM network measurement data and Erlang-B formula in blocking prediction is presented. The results of the experiments show that the proposed EBV_λ method is able to give better predictions than the use of the basic Erlang-B formula. This is due to the fact that the sampling frequency used in BTS level data collection is too low in order to be directly applicable to the Erlang-B formula. During a time period of one hour, the arrival rate of the incoming transactions most likely faces some variation, causing the basic Erlang-B formula to give underestimated blocking predictions. We used the measurement data to estimate the distribution for the hourly arrival rates during short time segments and applied the Erlang-B formula for the different segmentwise arrival rates. The proposed method can be used to predict the amount of blocking if traffic balancing or cell size adjustments must be made in operative GSM networks [4]. The proposed method can also be easily modified to prediction of blocking in other types of communication channels if the Erlang-B formula with suitable modifications or extensions are used in the model.

References

[1] S. Mokhtar Bazaraa, D. Hanif Sherali, and C. M. Shetty. *Nonlinear Programming: theory and algorithms.* John Wiley and Sons, Inc., 1993.

[2] R. B. Cooper. *Introduction to Queueing Theory.* Elsevier, 2nd edition, 1981.

[3] Di Huo. Generalized Erlang-B formula for mobile and wireless radio channels. In *Proceedings of the Global Telecommunications Conference, Communication Theory Mini-Conference (GLOBECOM 95),* November 1995.

[4] Pasi Lehtimäki. A model for optimisation of signal level thresholds in GSM networks. *International Journal of Mobile Network Design and Innovation.* (accepted).

[5] Hongxia Sun and Carey Williamson. Simulation evaluation of call dropping policies for stochastic capacity networks. In *Proceedings of the SCS Symposium on the Performance Evaluation of Computer and Telecommunication Systems (SPECTS),* July 2005.

[6] Jens Zander and Seong-Lyun Kim. *Radio Resource Management for Wireless Networks.* Artech House, Inc., 2001.

Tenth Scandinavian Conference on Artificial Intelligence
A. Holst et al. (Eds.)
IOS Press, 2008

Load Prediction Using Combination
of Neural Networks and Simple Strategies

Maciej GRZENDA
Warsaw University of Technology,
Faculty of Mathematics and Information Science,
Pl. Politechniki 1, 00-661 Warszawa, POLAND
e-mail: M.Grzenda@mini.pw.edu.pl

Abstract. Numerous techniques of artificial intelligence have been used for building prediction models. One of such tasks is the prediction of heat consumption in a district heating system. Not only is it required for ensuring sufficient heat production, but also it is necessary to avoid substantial heat loss due to overestimated demand for heat. The work presents the use of multilayer perceptrons for building prediction models. However, instead of building prediction models based on artificial neural networks only, hybrid approach is considered and evaluated. Evolutionary approach used to combine neural networks and a number of simple methods into hybrid prediction models is presented. Such models are developed for groups of consumers sharing similar thermal properties identified by self-organising map. It has been shown that by combining neural networks with simple predictive strategies lower prediction error rates can be achieved than in case of using neural networks only.

Keywords. Multilayer perceptron, Evolutionary Programming, Load prediction, District Heating System, Self-Organising Maps

Introduction

District heating systems (DHS) [1,2,10] are used in many cities throughout the world to distribute the heat from heat sources to heat consumers through a pipeline system. The consumers fall into different categories like family houses, commercial buildings, hotels and hospitals. The time required for hot water to reach its consumer may be several hours. At the same time the volume of heat required by a building depends on a number of factors, including weather conditions with ambient air temperature being the most important contributor to the overall demand for heat used for space heating. In addition, the heat is used for hot tap water supply. Thus its consumption significantly depends on the time of the day and type of a consumer. Moreover, there is a need to predict the total demand for heat in the system in order to control the heat production and minimise the cost of operation of a DHS. A prediction module can be seen as a part of automated control system for DHS and its heat sources. For an overview of problems that need to be solved when developing the control system for DHS, see [1].

Most of the researchers have concentrated until now on the prediction of the total volume of heat required in the DHS during each hour. A number of methods have been used for this purpose. One of the first approaches was to use neural networks model with a two-layer associative memory using Learning Vector Quantisation (LVQ) to predict the load of the system [8]. A strongly related problem of cooling load prediction in a district heating and cooling system has been discussed in [11], where the results of load prediction using nonlinear auto regressive moving average (NARMA) and different filtering methods have been compared. Another approach is to apply superposition of Box-Jenkins models based on the correlation analysis of time series [1]. Still, the problem of load prediction in a DHS remains an open issue, as most studies assume that consumers' demands are given and perfectly known [10]. The latter assumption allows to largely simplify the development of control strategies. Unfortunately, any errors made when predicting the load of the system cause significant problems in managing it [10].

At the same time, thanks to the growing availability of Supervisory Control and Data Acquisition (SCADA) systems detailed time series data of actual heat consumption at selected consumers gradually becomes available. The work concentrates on one of the aspects of developing a prediction model basing on detailed real data coming from one of the companies in Poland operating a DHS in a popular holiday resort. With a new state of the art SCADA system installed, the actual heat consumption is constantly collected at selected consumers and transmitted to a central server. As a consequence, a novel approach has been attempted i.e. to develop a prediction model that can take into account detailed time series obtained at selected consumers and predict heat consumption for different categories of consumers separately. The results of previous works aiming to guide the selection of monitored consumers [5] and predict demand for heat [6] have provided basis for the construction of hybrid prediction models described in this work.

The remainder of this paper is organised as follows:

- real heat consumption data available for modelling purposes is described,
- general overview of SOM-based identification of consumer groups sharing similar heat demand profiles is presented,
- the way evolutionary construction of multilayer perceptrons is used to predict demand for heat at individual consumers is described. Standard approach using models based on Multilayer Perceptrons (MLP) [7] is compared with a construction of hybrid models using both MLP and a combination of simple methods.
- simulation results showing the advantages of hybrid models constructed through the evolution process are presented.

1. Data set and problem description

The problem analysis is based on the data set from one of the Polish DHS utilities. The challenges faced by this company include proper response to substantial changes in heat demand. This demand can be expected to be different for different consumers. Detailed analysis of the consumer groups identified in the DHS can be found in [5].

Monthly sales information from the billing system for the period of last four years has been used. Unlike other data sets describing consumers, the billing data provides complete information for virtually every consumer $c_i \in C, C = \{c_i : i = 1, ..., N\}$. $N = 1109$ sales profiles have been obtained. Every sales profile of a consumer $c_i, i = 1, ..., N$ is represented by a vector $S_i = (s_{i,1}, ..., s_{i,12})$, where $s_{i,m}$ denotes the average heat sale to consumer i during month m.

Furthermore, each sales profile has been normalised so as to obtain average demand profile $\tilde{S}_i = (\tilde{s}_{i,1}, \tilde{s}_{i,2}, ..., \tilde{s}_{i,12})$ out of original consumer profile S_i as follows:

$$s_{\tilde{i},k} = \frac{s_{i,k}}{\sum_{m=1}^{m=12} s_{i,m}}, k = 1, ..., 12 \tag{1}$$

What is of outstanding importance even normalised monthly heat sales can differ as much as 300% among consumers This clearly shows that heat consumers have diverse demand profiles, thus any prediction model attempting to predict demand for heat of an individual consumer can not rely on weather conditions and time of the day and week only. Moreover, in order to calculate the dynamic state of DHS using hydraulic and thermodynamical model, demand for heat at each consumer at each hour is needed.

To tackle these problems, an advanced SCADA system has been implemented by the DHS to constantly monitor selected heat consumers. As a consequence detailed time series has been acquired. This contains the actual total consumption of heat d_h^i at consumer i, where h denotes the index of a day and hour i.e. the number of hours that have elapsed since the SCADA system installation. Still, detailed consumption data d_h^i is available for selected periods of time only, which are likely to be different for each consumer. Thus, the normalised load of consumer i has been calculated $\tilde{d}_h^i = \frac{d_h^i \cdot 365}{\sum_{m=1}^{m=12} s_{i,m}}$ In other words, it is normalised against average daily consumption of a consumer.

2. Prediction models for consumer groups

While a separate demand profile $\tilde{S}_i$ for each consumer can be calculated, the problem remains to address the diversity of consumers' needs. In general, two approaches could be attempted. First of all, detailed attributes describing each consumer including but not limited to the thermal properties of a building, the space to be heated and the number of inhabitants could be collected. Moreover, this data would need to be regularly updated. Still, in spite of significant cost required to collect detailed consumer description, some crucial factors affecting heat consumption would remain unknown. Among these factors, dynamic changes in the number of inhabitants and subjective notion of heat comfort are of greatest importance. Especially, in case of hotels this would inevitably cause limited accuracy of prediction. Therefore, another approach has been considered. Groups of consumers with similar demand profiles have been identified using self-organising maps [6]. Prediction models for individual groups of consumers can be constructed using multilayer perceptrons then.

2.1. Demand profiles and SOM-based approach

2.1.1. Algorithm overview

Different approaches could be proposed to determine possible groupings of demand profiles. Among them numerous clustering algorithms can be listed. Both agglomerative and partitioning algorithms like complete linkage or k-means algorithm could be applied. However, significant drawbacks of this approach would be the lack of straightforward visualisation for multidimensional data groupings and limited potential for the identification of natural modality of the set.

Therefore, in order to answer the problem of demand profiles identification, self-organising neural networks have been applied. The purpose of using self-organising neural networks, namely Self-Organising Maps (SOMs) [7], is to provide measure of locating demand pattern groupings i.e. typical profiles $\hat{S}_k, k << N$ that would explain diversity in the population of $\tilde{S}_i, i = 1, .., N$ demand profiles. Thus, two-dimensional square lattice of J neurons was created and demand profiles $\tilde{S}_i, i = 1, .., N$ were used as input patterns. A number of computation series have been performed, using different weight update algorithms.

2.1.2. Consumer groupings

To illustrate the results of computations, the computations performed using NGAS method have been selected. In all cases, for each neuron $j, j = 1, ..., J$ in the lattice, at the end of tuning phase, the winning count Y_j has been calculated: $Y_j = \sum_{i=1}^{N} eval(i, j)$, while

$$eval(i, j) = \begin{cases} 1 & \text{if } \| \tilde{S}_i - w_j \| = min_{k=1,...,J} \| \tilde{S}_i - w_k \| \\ 0 & \text{otherwise} \end{cases} \tag{2}$$

Thus $Y_j : j = 1, ..., J$ denotes the number of demand patterns $\tilde{S}_i$ that are the most similar to the weight vector w_j in terms of Euclidean distance. Obtained results show that a number of distinctive demand profiles providing centroids of input consumer's profiles have been identified. This suggests that observed diversity in the input patterns can be explained by underlying typical demand profiles. In addition, some 40% of neurones remain virtually inactive i.e. $Y_j \leq 2$, in spite of using NGAS algorithm that promotes diversity among neurones. In other words, when dealing with heat demand prediction, it is enough to concentrate on a limited number of consumers demand patterns. Thus, it is justified to develop prediction models dealing with a limited number of consumer groups each. Detailed presentation of this approach and identified groups can be found in [6].

3. Prediction models

3.1. Evolutionary construction of MLP

Standard prediction models are constructed using MLP networks. For each non-empty group of consumers $C_j, j = 1, ..., J$ identified by SOM, a single MLP network is constructed. To train the neural networks, evolutionary construction of multilayer perceptrons ($ECoMLP$) [4,6] has been applied. The method follows evolutionary programming paradigm and evolves a population of MLP networks to minimise the prediction error measured on a learning set and obtain networks with generalisation abilities. The primary features of the method are as follows:

- the number of networks in each layer is set through the process of mutation and selection, the network connection weights are also mutated,
- self-adaptive control of weight update mutation is applied, each individual in the population can be affected by the mutation operator based on uniform or normal distribution. In other words, the weight mutation probabilities are evolved together with the genotype of each individual.

The remaining details describing the algorithm and the way it has been applied for time series prediction can be found in [4,6]. In this case, the ECoMLP algorithm has been used to predict heat demand at selected consumers belonging to the same group C_j. Detailed time series available for selected consumers of the C_j group has been used to construct both learning and testing set. The motivation for using evolutionary method is as follows:

- The problem requires numerous multilayer perceptrons to be constructed, as there is a need for a separate MLP network for each group C_i,
- Because of the number of networks involved, no trial-and-error or human expert intervention in architecture selection can be accepted.
- The objective function is not a standard mean square error. The problem may require non-differentiable and even non-continuous error measure for the reasons listed below.

3.2. Data preparation

In order to compare ECoMLP and its modified counterpart training and validation data sets have been prepared for one of the consumer groups C_j. The group contains 8 monitored consumers. Out of all data patterns in detailed time series available for consumers of C_j group, learning set L and validation set V have been created, containing 1537 and 506 data patterns, respectively. $\hat{A}_h = avg_{i=1,...,N}(\tilde{d}_h^i)$ and $\hat{D}_h^j = avg_{i \in C_j}(\tilde{d}_h^i)$ stand for average heat consumption of all consumers and consumers of C_j group during the hour h.

Each data pattern p_h contains the following values:

- average consumption among group members of a learning or validation set $\hat{G}_{h-6}^j, \hat{G}_{h-7}^j, \hat{G}_{h-8}^j, \hat{G}_{h-24}^j,$
- average consumption of all consumers $\hat{A}_{h-6}, \hat{A}_{h-7}, \hat{A}_{h-8}, \hat{A}_{h-24},$

- time and weather data: hour h, ambient temperature $temp$, day of week index, time of the day status for annotating peak hours of hot tap water demand,
- the value to be predicted $\hat{G}_h$.

The group of consumers C_j has been divided into two subsets $C_{j,L}$ and $C_{j,V}$ such that $C_j = C_{j,L} \cup C_{j,V}$ and $C_{j,L} \cap C_{j,V} = \phi$. The data coming from the consumers belonging to these two subsets has been used for building learning and validation set. Other attributes e.g. $\hat{G}^j_{h-9}$ can be also included. However, the number of attributes should be limited to avoid poor generalisation due to insufficient number of data patterns.

3.3. Combination of MLP and simple strategies

In standard ECoMLP method the fitness function used to drive the evolution process is based on the transformation of error rate calculated for MLP. A modification of this approach will be considered. In the modified method, the prediction model combines the signal produced by MLP with a combination of simple strategies. Thus, instead of the $\phi(p_h)$ representing the output signal of MLP produced basing on the pattern p_h described above, the following function is used:

$$\widehat{\phi(p_h)} = a_0 \cdot \phi(p_h) + \frac{a_1 - temp_h}{tcmp_h \mid 30} \cdot a_2 + a_3 \cdot G_{h-24} + \tag{3}$$

$$a_4 \cdot \frac{G_{h-6} + G_{h-7} + G_{h-8} + G_{h-24}}{4} + \tag{4}$$

$$a_5 \cdot \frac{A_{h-6} + A_{h-7} + A_{h-8} + A_{h-24}}{4} \tag{5}$$

The covariates $a_i : i = 1, ..., 5$ are a part of genotype of each individual evolved using ECoMLP. The mutation operator affects both the genotype part representing MLP and the part of the genotype containing the vector a. Therefore, the hybrid model is evolved as a whole and optimal combination of the listed above input data and MLP is searched for. The method combining the MLP-based prediction model and simple strategies described above, will be referred to as MECoMLP method in the remainder of this work.

4. Results

To ensure unbiased evaluation of the methods 50 runs of the algorithm have been executed for each method. The fitness function took into account desired form of predicted heat demand profile. A priori knowledge regarding acceptable error rate from the point of view of prospective heat supply optimisation has been applied. Therefore, the following fitness function has been devised to drive evolutionary process:

$$F(\phi^g_i) = \frac{\sum_{j=1}^{card(L)} \theta(\phi^g_i, j)}{card(L)} \tag{6}$$

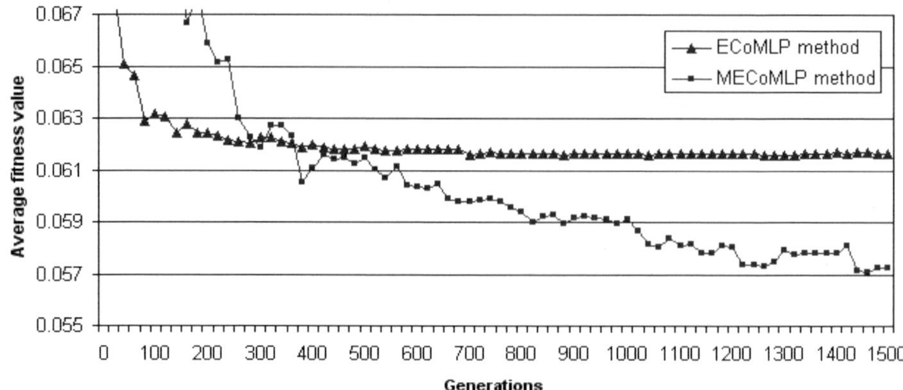

Figure 1. Average value of fitness function for the best individual in the population calculated on the validation set

where $\theta(\phi_i^g, j)$ stands for an error rate of prediction for pattern j by neural network ϕ_i^g i.e. multilayer perceptron i in generation g. The error rate takes into account the following information regarding acceptable errors in heat demand prediction. In particular, it is acceptable to some extent to underestimate demand for heat during a single hour, as long as the predicted demand for both preceding and succeeding hour is not underestimated. Therefore,

$$\xi(x) = \begin{cases} 0.9 \ when \ x > 0.9 \\ x \quad otherwise \end{cases} \tag{7}$$

and

$$\theta(\phi_i^g, j) = \begin{cases} 0 & when \ (\xi(\phi_i^g(l_j)) \geq 0.85 \times \xi(d_j)) \\ & \wedge(\xi(\phi_i^g(l_j)) \leq \xi(d_j)) \\ & \wedge(\phi_i^g(l_{j-1}) \geq (d_{j-1})) \wedge (\phi_i^g(l_{j+1}) \geq (d_{j+1})) \\ |\ \phi_i^g(l_j) - d_j\ |\ otherwise \end{cases} \tag{8}$$

For clarity purposes $d_0 = d_{card(L)+1} = \phi_i^g(l_0) = \phi_i^g(l_{card(L)+1}) = 0$ for $i = 1, ..., card(\Phi)$, l_j denotes learning pattern j. By using this or similar fitness function $F()$ expectations regarding heat demand prediction can be expressed. In case of fitness function defined above, the average value of $F()$ measured on a learning set after $G = 1500$ generations for the average best individual ϕ_b^G was equal to 0.0191 and 0.0186 for ECoMLP and MECoMLP methods, respectively.

The results of the calculations on the validation set are presented on the fig. 1. The figure depicts the average value of $F()$ obtained in each generation by the best individual of each of the 50 populations associated with different algorithm runs. The MECoMLP method has resulted in a decreased value of error rate comparing to the error rates achieved by ECoMLP models. Because of introducing $a_i : i = 1, ..., 5$ additional attributes, the MECoMLP method has to evolve more complex genotype than the original method. In spite of this fact, the results measured both on the learning and validation set show the supremacy of the modified approach. Moreover, generalisation has been achieved by the networks.

5. Conclusions and future works

Heating load prediction is an important aspect of control strategy for DHS. Traditionally, total demand at heat source is predicted or even the heat consumption is assumed to be known. It has been proposed to utilise the data describing individual heat consumption. This data has become available with the advent of widely available low-cost monitoring systems.

Prediction models used to forecast heat consumption at individual consumers have been constructed. In order to address diverse thermal properties of buildings and consumption profiles, SOM networks have been applied first. For different consumer groups, MLP networks can be constructed. The latter method has been compared with hybrid prediction models combining MLP and simple strategies. Not only did it allow to decrease prediction error, but also premature convergence of the original method has been avoided. Therefore, by exploiting the potential of evolutionary computation neural networks have been coupled with a linear combination of pattern attributes.

In the future, the method can be even further extended to accommodate some other prediction techniques. Moreover, the use of numerous prediction models applied at different periods of time can be attempted.

References

[1]   J. Balate et al., Strategy evolution of control of extensive district heating systems, *International Conference on Power Engineering, Energy and Electrical Drives, POWERENG 2007*, 12-14 April 2007, 678 –683

[2]   P. Davidsson, F. Wernstedt, Embedded Agents for District Heating Management, *Proceedings of Third International Joint Conference on Autonomous Agents and Multi-Agent Systems*, 2004, July 19-23, 2004, 1148 – 1155

[3]   D.B. Fogel, An Overview of Evolutionary Programming. *The IMA Volumes in Mathematics and its Applications*, **Vol. 111**, 1999, 89–109

[4]   M. Grzenda, B. Macukow, Evolutionary Neural Network-Based Optimisation for Short-Term Load Forecasting, Control and Cybernetics, **vol. 31**, 2002, 371–382

[5]   M. Grzenda, The Use of Neural Networks to Control Data Acquisition Process, *Artificial Intelligence and Soft Computing*, ed. A. Cader et al., EXIT Publishers, 2006, 34–41

[6]   M. Grzenda, B. Macukow, Demand Prediction with Multi-Stage Neural Processing, *Advances in Natural Computation and Data Mining*, ed. L. Jiao et al., Xidian University Press, 2006, 131–141

[7]   S. Haykin, *Neural Networks: a Comprehensive Foundation*, Prentice-Hall Inc., 1999

[8]   N. Kashiwagi, T. Tobi, Heating and cooling load prediction using a neural network system, *Proceedings of 1993 International Joint Conference on Neural Networks, IJCNN '93-Nagoya*, 1993, **Vol. 1**, 939 – 942

[9]   M. Martinetz, S. Berkovich, K. Schulten, "Neural-gas" Network for Vector Quantization and Its Application to Time Series Prediction, *IEEE Trans. on Neural Networks*, **Vol.4**, 1993, 558–569

[10] G. Sandou et al., Predictive Control of a Complex District Heating Network, *44th IEEE Conference on Decision and Control, 2005 European Control Conference. CDC-ECC '05.*, 12-15 Dec. 2005, 7372 – 7377

[11] M. Sakawa et al., Cooling load prediction in a district heating and cooling system through simplified robust filter and multi-layered neural network, IEEE International Conference on Systems, Man, and Cybernetics, *IEEE SMC '99 Conference Proceedings*, 1999, **Vol. 3**, 995–1000

Tenth Scandinavian Conference on Artificial Intelligence
A. Holst et al. (Eds.)
IOS Press, 2008

Towards Automatic Model Generation by Optimization

Per NYBLOM [a] and Patrick DOHERTY [a]

[a] *Department of Computer Science, Linköping, {perny, patdo}@ida.liu.se*

Abstract.

The problem of automatically selecting simulation models for autonomous agents depending on their current intentions and beliefs is considered in this paper. The intended use of the models is for prediction, filtering, planning and other types of reasoning that can be performed with simulation models. The parameters and model fragments of the resulting model are selected by formulating and solving a hybrid constrained optimization problem that captures the intuition of the preferred model when relevance information about the elements of the world being modelled is taken into consideration. A specialized version of the original optimization problem is developed that makes it possible to solve the continuous subproblem analytically in linear time. A practical model selection problem is discussed where the aim is to select suitable parameters and models for tracking dynamic objects. Experiments with randomly generated problem instances indicate that a hillclimbing search approach might be both efficient and provides reasonably good solutions compared to simulated annealing and hillclimbing with random restarts.

Keywords. Automatic model generation

1. Introduction

Simulation models are commonly used in many disciplines for various purposes. In Artificial Intelligence, such models can e.g. be used to support prediction and decision making capabilities for autonomous agents. Agents that operate in complex environments can typically not use highly detailed models of all parts of their surroundings, especially when such models are used for task planning where the effects of many possible alternative action choices have to be predicted. Lack of computational resources often limit both the model and the planning horizon when a timely response is of importance. Traditionally, anytime algorithms [2] are often used to handle the need for a timely response where a reasonably good solution can be found quickly and if possible, the solution quality increases with time.

Another complementary approach to deal with the problem of limited computational resources and the need for a timely response is to try to vary the models and reason on several abstraction levels. In this paper we will consider an approach where the models are generated dynamically depending on the current beliefs and intentions at hand. This is very much related to the call for dynamic abstraction techniques within hierarchical reinforcement learning [1] and the automatic generation of simulation models to answer queries about physical dynamic systems [9].

The focus of this approach is to find a good tradeoff between the resulting model's accuracy and feasibility for the current situation in order to get as good expected performance of the agent as possible given the computational limitations. A part of that tradeoff is in this paper formulated as an optimization problem that captures the limitations and how good the resulting model will be given the agent's available model fragments and relevance information. A motivating example is also presented where the problem is to find the parameters of a set of model fragments that can be used to represent dynamic objects (such as vehicles) for tracking applications. These objects can be more or less relevant for different reasons and the relevance can change depending on the situation. The agent must therefore adapt its models to be able to get the most out of its computational resources. We are not aware of any previous work where this particular approach is taken to generate models.

We believe that automatic model generation in general has the possibility of making autonomous agents more robust when faced with unexpected situations because it can be used to focus the agents' attention by generating models of different complexity when e.g. their default assumptions turn out to be invalid [11].

2. Motivating Example

This section introduces a practical model generation/selection problem which motivates the dynamic change of models and other parameters depending on situation and relevance information. The context will be simulation model generation for particle filters with the purpose of tracking dynamic objects in e.g. traffic situations.

Particle filters [4] are often used in tracking applications where it is important to model nonlinear or multimodal phenomenons. When constructing a particle filter, it is often not clear what type of information to use in each particle and how many particles to use in total. A good choice must be a reasonable tradeoff that takes the available computational resources and the accuracy of the resulting filter into account.

When several objects or relations between objecs are important for the tracking agent, another complication arises. The agent must then be able to dynamically prioritize between the different parts of its environment and change its models accordingly. The relevance of these parts may change rapidly depending on the situation and this should be reflected in the way the agent uses its resources.

To make this method work, a metamodel that predicts the performance and computational cost of the different generated models must be available. This requires that a large empirical study must be performed where the performance of the models are measured for the different filter parameter settings. For particle filters in general, the performance increases with the number of particles and update frequency and we expect that this trend can be modelled by suitable mathematical functions.

When such a metamodel is available, it is possible to use optimization methods to maximize the performance of the filter sets given the relevance of the objects and relations between them. The optimization problem must also be constrained with the available computational resources.

This paper presents a method to select model types and settings by formulating such an optimization problem that can take relevance information and available computational resources into consideration.

3. The Model Selection Problem

This section describes how to use optimization for model selection where the input is the possibly relevant elements E (such as vehicles, other objects and features such as distances between objects), a set of possible representations REP (model fragments such as models of vehicles and pedestrians) for these elements together with representation value. Intuitively, the representation value describes how "good" it is to represent the elements E in the agent's current context with the different representations which is supposed to be extracted empirically as described in Section 2. This information is only considered in isolation in the metamodel and the task of the model selection is to find a good tradeoff between the representations when all these elements must be represented in some way *together in the same model* with limited computational resources. The output from the model selection is the representation to use for each element together with the update frequencies for the different model fragments.

Model fragments that include derivatives of state variables can be simulated with different update frequencies and the accuracy of the result often increases with the frequency. The quality of the result does not increase linearly with the frequency though. For example, if there is a large quality difference between 1 Hz and 10 Hz update frequency for a particle filter, there is typically not the same increase in quality for a difference between 1000 Hz and 1009 Hz (although there is some increase). It is important that this model quality increase is captured in the optimization problem formulation (see the frequency value function v_F below).

The optimization problem, which attempts to formulate the preferred simulation model parameters in terms of update frequencies and choice of model fragments, contains the objective function $g : \mathbb{R}^n \times REP^n \to \mathbb{R}$ which is assumed to have the following format:

$$(1) \qquad g(f, r) = \sum_{e \in E} v_R(e, r) v_F(r_e, f_e)$$

where E is the set of elements $\{e_1, \cdots e_n\}$, r is the vector $[r_{e_1} \cdots r_{e_n}]$ of discrete variables that determine the representation r_e for each element $e \in E$ and f is the vector $[f_{e_1} \cdots f_{e_n}]$ of continuous variables that specifies the update frequencies. The *frequency value function* $v_F : REP \times \mathbb{R} \to \mathbb{R}$ captures the non-linear increase in quality of the resulting model with the frequency when a certain representation r_e with frequency f_e is used. The purpose of the *representation value function* $v_R : E \times REP^n \to \mathbb{R}$ is to represent both the relevance of an element and the suitability of representing it with a representation r_e in the context of all other elements' representations.

The resulting model takes a certain amount of time for each step depending on the set of model fragments used, and since the computational resources are limited, it is important to choose the model fragments wisely depending on how computationally intensive they are to simulate. The function $t_{step} : E \times REP^n \to \mathbb{R}$ specifies the amount of time it takes to make one step with a model fragment representation $r_e \in REP$ in the context of the other elements' representations. The constant T_{max} specifies the maximum amount of real world time that the simulation model can take per simulated time.

The update frequencies of the different representations then determine the following constraint:

$$(2) \qquad c(r, f) = \sum_{e \in E} t_{step}(e, r) f_e - T_{max} \leq 0$$

If the frequency value function $v_F(r_e, f_e)$ is strictly increasing for a fixed representation r_e (which seems to be a safe assumption), then the inequality in equation 2 can be replaced by an equality because it will always be active in an optimal solution.

The limit of the coarseness of the simulation updates can be modelled as follows:

$$(3) \qquad \forall e \in E[f_e \geq f_{min}(r_e)]$$

where the function $f_{min} : REP \rightarrow \mathbb{R}$ determines the minimum update frequency for each representation to increase the possiblity of a better resulting simulation model.

The *continuous subproblem* is defined as the constrained optimization problem in equations 1, 2 and 3 when r is fixed. Similarly, the *discrete subproblem* is defined as the optimization problem where f is fixed. Note that both of these subproblems have to be solved simultaneously, the only reason to divide them into two subproblems is that the continuous one can be solved separately by pure continuous methods.

4. Problem Specialization

The optimization problem defined by the Equations 1, 2 and 3 are supposed to be used in autonomous agents that may not have much computational resources. This means that the problem must be solved very quickly, which typically means that a reasonably good solution must be ready within few seconds or fractions of a second depending on the situation.

We have specialized the original optimization problem by selecting a particulary suitable frequency value function $v_F(r_e, f_e)$ that both approximately captures the constraints in equation 3 and makes the continuous subproblem very easy to solve. This makes it possible to use a search strategy where the discrete variables in r are first set to a value and then the global optimum of the continuous subproblem is found.

Several options for choosing the frequency value function $v_F(r_e, f_e)$ are possible but it is important that $v'_F(r_e, f_e)$ is a strictly decreasing function for a fixed r_e (due to the decrease in quality increase with frequency. See the discussion in Section 3). Our choice of the continuous function $v_{F,c}(f_e)$ (which denotes $v_F(r_e, f_e)$ when r is fixed) is a variant of the natural logarithmic function:

$$(4) \qquad v_{F,c}(f_e) = log(1 + f_e - f_{min,e})$$

This choice of frequency value function has the following consequences:

- If $f_e < f_{min,e}$, the element e provides a negative contribution to the objective function which can either be seen as a penalty for the quality decrease of e's simulation result or as a way to filter out elements that are irrelevant

- f_e can never be less than $f_{min,e} - 1$ ($v_{F,c}$ is not defined otherwise)

The derivative of $v_{F,c}(f_e)$ wrt f_e is a positive and strictly decreasing function which means that it fits the description of a frequency value function in Section 3. We are not certain that this particular choice of frequency function is suitable for selecting the update frequency of particle filters without any empirical investigation, but any concave, increasing function will make the approach described in this paper feasible.

5. The Continuous Subproblem

One important key to solving the reformulated problem is to take advantage of the fact that for every choice of representation r, the optimization problem transforms into a continuous optimization subproblem that can be solved in linear time in terms of the number of elements $|E|$.

The continuous variant of the objective function $g_c(f)$ and constraint $c_c(f)$ becomes the following:

$$(5) \qquad g_c(f) = \sum_{e \in E} v_{R,e} log(1 + f_e - f_{e,min})$$

$$(6) \qquad c_c(f) = \sum_{e \in E} t_e f_e - T_{max} = 0$$

where $v_{R,e} = v_R(e, r)$ and $t_e = t_{step}(e, r)$ for a fixed value r.

The objective function $g_c(f)$ is concave and the linear constraint is convex, which means that an optimal solution exist. The KKT conditions [8] for the continuous subproblem then shows that there exists a scalar λ in all local optimal solutions such that the following condition holds [1]:

$$(7) \qquad -\lambda \nabla g_c(f) = \nabla c_c(f)$$

$\nabla g_c(f)$ and $\nabla c_c(f)$ are the gradients of $g_c(f)$ and $c_c(f)$ wrt f.
For our choice of $v_{F,c}(f_e)$ (see Equation 5), this condition is equivalent to:

$$(8) \qquad \lambda \frac{-v_{R,e}}{1 + f_e - f_{e,min}} = t_e$$

for all elements $e \in E$, which defines a system of $|E|$ linear equations with $|E| + 1$ unknowns. The constraint in Equation 6 fills in the missing equation which in total gives the following system of equations:

---

[1] The negative sign on the left hand side in Equation 7 is due to the formulation of the KKT conditions for a minimization problem which in our case means that $-g_c(f)$ is minimized.

$$(9) \qquad \begin{bmatrix} t_{e_1} & & v_{R,e_1} \\ & \ddots & \vdots \\ & t_{e_n} & v_{R,e_n} \\ t_{e_1} & \cdots\ t_{e_n} & 0 \end{bmatrix} \begin{bmatrix} f_{e_1} \\ \vdots \\ f_{e_n} \\ \lambda \end{bmatrix} = \begin{bmatrix} t_{e_1}(f_{e_1,min} - 1) \\ \vdots \\ t_{e_n}(f_{e_n,min} - 1) \\ T_{max} \end{bmatrix}$$

where $n = |E|$.

This system of equations can be solved in linear time ($\Theta(n)$) by first solving λ:

$$(10) \qquad \lambda = \frac{T_{max} - \sum_e t_e(f_{e,min} - 1)}{-\sum_e v_{R,e}}$$

and then finding the solution for f:

$$(11) \qquad f_e = f_{e,min} - 1 - \frac{v_{R,e}}{t_e}\lambda$$

f_e will become less than $f_{e,min} - 1$ if $\lambda \geq 0$ ($v_{R,e}$ and t_e are always strictly positive constants), which would make $g_c(f)$ undefined for that solution. It is possible to avoid this problem by noting that λ can only become positive if $T_{max} - \sum_e t_e(f_{e,min} - 1) \leq 0$, which in practice means that the agent is unable to simulate the model fragments even if all frequencies are set to the lowest possible.

Since there is a unique solution by directly applying the KKT conditions and at least one optimal solution exists, the solution found by solving Equation 9 is the global optimizer if $T_{max} - \sum_e t_e(f_{e,min} - 1) > 0$. If $T_{max} - \sum_e t_e(f_{e,min} - 1) \leq 0$, there is no solution.

If the choice of frequency value function turns out to be a bad one, it is still possible to solve the continuous subproblem by convex optimization methods due to the nature of frequency value function.

6. The Discrete Subproblem

We have shown that the optimal solution to the continuous subproblem can be calculated in linear time. In this section we show that the *0-1-knapsack optimization problem* can be transformed into the discrete subproblem in polynomial time, which means that the discrete subproblem is NP-hard [5].

The 0-1-knapsack optimization problem is defined as follows:

$$(12) \qquad \text{maximize } \sum_{i=1}^{n} p_i x_i$$

$$(13) \qquad \text{subject to } \sum_{i=1}^{n} w_i x_i \leq c$$

where $x_i = 0$ or 1.

If $REP = \{0, 1\}$, $v_F(r_e, f_e) = 1$ for all $r_e \in r$ when $f_e = 1$, $v_R(e_i, r) = p_i r_i$ and $t_{step}(e_i, r) = w_i$, then any 0-1-knapsack optimization problem can be transformed into a discrete subproblem in polynomial time. Due to the NP-hardness of the 0-1-knapsack optimization problem, the discrete subproblem is NP-hard as well.

7. Experiments

We have performed a set of experiments where the focus was to find an efficient method that delivers reasonably good solutions quickly, which is useful when a timely response is of importance. The strategy for solving the complete specialized hybrid optimization problem is to use a separate search for the discrete variables which are then evaluated by solving the continuous subproblem quickly. Our method of choice for the search in the discrete variables was hillclimbing (HC) local search which was compared to simulated annealing [6] and random restart hillclimbing (RRHC).

HC and RRHC used a neighbourhood function that returns $|E|(|REP| - 1)$ neighbour states in which every single element $e \in E$ was set to all its possible representations REP. All states in the neighbourhood are valued by solving the continuous subproblem. The simulated annealing implementation used a random neighbourhood function N_{sa} where two elements' representations were changed randomly and the temperature was decreased as $t \leftarrow 0.98t$ where t is the current temperature. The temperature level was changed when 50 state changes had been performed or when the maximum number of steps (1000) had been taken. SA terminated when 5 temperature levels had passed in a row without any state change and then HC was performed on the best solution found so far (in order to at least get a local optimal solution).

Each test used randomly generated problem instances where the representation value function $v_R(e, r) = v_R(e, r_e)$ and $t_{step}(e, r) = t_{step}(e, r_e)$ which made it feasible to represent v_R and t_{step} with matrices. This simplification does not change the NP-hardness of the discrete subproblem. There were two possible starting states available: One was called the *greedy start state* r_g and it maximized $\frac{v_R(e, r_e)}{t_{step}(r_e)}$ (most value per simulation step time). The other one was called the *cheap start state* r_c which minimized $t_{step}(r_e)(f_{min}(r_e) - 1)$ (cheapest representation for all elements). The cheap start state is always a valid state if any solution exists.

When an invalid state s was encountered (happens when $\lambda \geq 0$), the value for s was set to $-\gamma(\lambda + 1)$ where γ is set to a large constant (10^9 in our implementation) to penalize invalid solutions hard. This solution seemed to work very well for this problem type and is related to the use of penalty functions in constrained optimization problems [10].

7.1. Problem Difficulty

We are not able to predict at this stage what characteristics the problem instances will have that will occur in practical situations when models are to be generated. We do believe that for the environment described in Section 2, the relevance function will take many possible values depending on the situation and that no particular pattern will exist that persist over all problem instances that we will consider. We initially performed an experiment with completely random problem instances and the result indicated that the simple hillclimbing approach were able to seriously compete with RRHC and SA. This result might be a good sign for practical applications due to the low cost of HC but we wanted to perform tests with more difficult problem instances. One possible measure of the difficulty of problems can be identified by varying T_{max}. A low T_{max} makes a fewer set of representations possible to use, which leads to a smaller set of valid solutions. When T_{max} increases, the set of solutions increase until all representations are possible for all elements. Somewhere between the smallest and very large T_{max}, we expect to find the most problem instances that have non-trivial solutions, which could possibly indicate a phase transition.

In the randomly generated problem instances, a constant $\alpha > 1$ is used to approximately vary the number of valid states and problem difficulty. T_{max} is set to $\alpha \sum_{e \in E} t_{step}(r_c)(f_{min}(r_c) - 1)$ where r_c is the cheap start state.

7.2. Cheap VS Greedy

When α is rather low, the set of possible states is reduced and it might seem natural to start the search in the cheap start state. If α is high, it might be better to start in the greedy start state instead. In one experiment, we compared the solution found by HC to SA and RRHC when HC started in the greedy, cheap and a random start state. α was varied between 1.1 and 10000 and 2000 randomly problems were generated for each setting with 30 elements and 20 representations. The result of this experiment is shown in Figure 1 where the upper subplot shows the fraction of the states when RRHC or SA finds a better solution than HC and the middle subplot shows the relative difference $\frac{|V_{best} - V_{hc}|}{|V_{best}|}$ between the best value found V_{best} and the result after HC V_{hc}. The lower plot shows the number of states visited by the hillclimbing search for the different start state types.

From the results it seems like the cheap state is the best singleton start state for this class of problem instances if one only considers the quality of the result. If, on the other hand, the time it takes to find a local optimum is more important than the solution quality, the greedy start state performs better than the cheap one for $\alpha \gtrsim 5$. The best result is received when both the greedy and the cheap start state are used. It is also interresting to note that the random start state provides as good solution quality as the greedy start state but it takes much longer time to find a local optimum.

For a much larger α, we expected that the greedy start state would outperform the cheap one due to the advantage of starting closer to a local optimum. The results in Figure 1 indicate on the other hand that the cheap start state is better to use even for a large α if the solution quality is very important. However, when HC starts at the greedy start state the time until a local optimum is found is much less than for the cheap and random states.

8. Conclusion and Future Work

The paper investigated a particular type of optimization problem that aims to capture the intuition of how the relavance of elements in an environment should be reflected in an automatically generated model that can be used for reasoning by autonomous agents. It was argued that a particular specialized version of the original optimization problem was suitable for the task due to the possibility of solving the continuous subproblem exactly in linear time. It remains to show that the logarithmic function used in the specialized version can model the performance increase wrt update frequency, but if this is not possi-

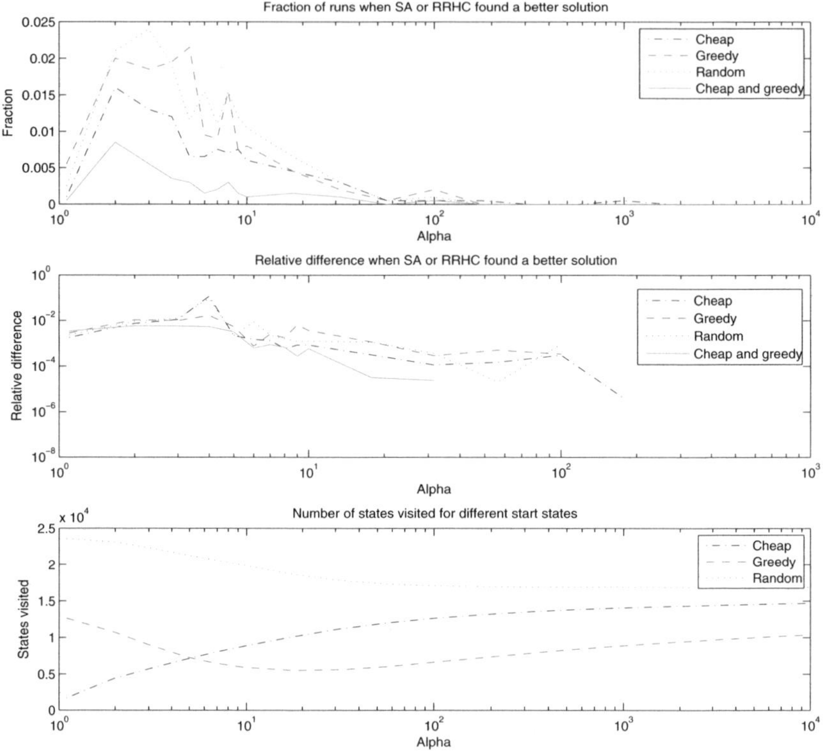

Figure 1. The experimental results when α was varied between 1.1 and 10000.

ble we might have to use convex optimization methods instead. The discrete subproblem was shown to be NP-hard.

The complete hybrid reformulated problem was solved with hillclimbing (HC) search with a simple neighbourhood function and compared to simulated annealing and random restart hillclimbing. Within the limitations of the experiment, the results indicated that informed starting states were better than randomly generated ones if the time to find a local optimum is of importance. The solution quality was best when HC was started in a so called "cheap" state which is always a valid state if a solution exists at all.

As future work, we will work towards actually using the model generation in a context where settings for particle filters are selected during vehicle tracking missions with our real autonomous helicopter system [3]. We also plan to use the method to select models for other tasks such as planning and extraction of the most likely sequence. Methods for such tasks that are more suitable for use with simulation models will be prioritized such as forward search, sequence estimation with particle filters [7] and reinforcement learning [13]. Some of these methods have already been used in context of task planning where simulation models are used to generated tractable discrete planning models [12] [11].

A future issue is also the representation of the function $v_R(e, r)$ which can be used to express the suitability of element representation combinations. We expect that constraints such as $r_{e_i} = a \Rightarrow r_{e_k} = b_1 \vee \cdots \vee r_{e_k} = b_m$ will be common in problem domains where a choice of representation for an element constrain other elements' representations. The main problem with these "extra constraints" is that we then have to deal with satisfiability of these constraints as well.

Acknowledgements

Many thanks to Martin Magnusson who has given a lot of useful comments to earlier versions of this paper.

References

[1]   A. G. Barto and S. Mahadevan, 'Recent advances in hierarchical reinforcement learning.', *Discrete Event Dynamic Systems*, **13**(4), 341–379, (2003).

[2]   T. L. Dean and M. Boddy, 'An analysis of time-dependent planning', in *Proceedings of the Seventh National Conference on Artificial Intelligence*, pp. 49–54, (1988).

[3]   P. Doherty, 'Advanced research with autonomous unmanned aerial vehicles', *Proceedings on the 9th International Conference on Principles of Knowledge Representation and Reasoning*, (2004).

[4]   A. Doucet, N. Freitas, and N. Gordon, *Sequential Monte Carlo Methods in Practice.*, Springer Verlag New York, 2001.

[5]   M. R. Garey and D. S. Johnson, *Computers and Intractability: A Guide to the Theory of NP-Completeness*, W. H. Freeman, 1979.

[6]   S. Kirkpatrick, C. D. Gelatt, and M. P. Vecchi, 'Optimization by simulated annealing', *Science*, **220**(4598), 671–680, (1983).

[7]   M. Klaas, D. Lang, and N. Freitas, 'Fast maximum a posteriori inference in monte carlo state spaces', in *Tenth International Workshop on Artificial Intelligence and Statistics*, (2005).

[8]   H. W. Kuhn and A. W. Tucker, 'Nonlinear programming', in *Proceedings of the Second Berkeley Symposium on Mathematical Statistics and Probability*, pp. 481–492, (1951).

[9]   A. Y. Levy, Y. Iwasaki, and R. Fikes, 'Automated model selection for simulation based on relevance reasoning', *Artificial Intelligence*, **96**(2), 351–394, (1997).

[10]   J. Nocedal and S. J. Wright, *Numerical Optimization*, Springer Verlag, 2006.

[11]   P. Nyblom, 'Dynamic abstraction for hierarchical problem solving and execution in stochastic dynamic environments', in *Starting AI Researcher Symposium (STAIRS)*, (2006).

[12]   P. Nyblom, 'Dynamic planning problem generation in a uav domain', *6th IFAC Symposium on Intelligent Autonomous Vehicles (IAV)*, (2007).

[13]   R. S. Sutton and A. G. Barto, *Reinforcement Learning An Introduction*, The MIT Press, 1998.

Tenth Scandinavian Conference on Artificial Intelligence
A. Holst et al. (Eds.)
IOS Press, 2008

A Heuristic-Based Approach for a Betting Strategy in Texas Hold'em Poker

Teemu SAUKONOJA [a] Tomi A. PASANEN [a]

[a] *Gamics Laboratory, Department of Computer Science, University of Helsinki, Finland*

Abstract. Artificial intelligence research in Texas Hold'em poker has recently mainly focused on heads-up fixed-limit games. Game theoretic methods used in the poker agents capable of playing at the very best level are not easily generalized to other forms of Texas Hold'em poker. In this paper we present a general heuristic-based approach to build a poker agent, where the betting strategy is defined by estimating the expected values of the actions. The approach is well suited for a larger number of players and it is also easily modified to suite no limit games.

Keywords. Texas Hold'em, betting strategy, evaluation function

Introduction

The popularity of poker games and especially the popularity of Texas Hold'em poker have significantly grown in the last few years. Nowadays, Texas Hold'em poker is also a very popular testbed for artificial-intelligence research and recently made poker agents are already capable of playing at world-class level in some forms of Texas Hold'em poker.

Texas Hold'em poker is well suited for artificial-intelligence research because of its nature: imperfect information and randomness that cause uncertainty in decision-making. It also provides a well-abstracted field allowing the use of different methods while trying to build a poker agent. We assume that the reader knows the rules and general tactics of Texas Hold'em. If the game is not familiar or additional information about the game, the problem field or the strategies is needed, we recommend [9] for background reading.

Lately, the artificial-intelligence research in Texas Hold'em poker has mainly focused on fixed-limit heads-up games where the results have been very promising. Methods used in the agents are based on approximation of the game-theoretic equilibrium strategy [6]. Even if the methods are very suitable for two-player fixed-limit Texas Hold'em, there is no guarantee that the methods could be used in any other form of Texas Hold'em poker.

For example, no-limit Texas Hold'em poker is strategically much more complex: a single error can be a crucial which is not true when betting is limited. It is also easy to notice that adding a new attribute to the game, the betting amount, the number of states in the game increases exponentially. Moreover, even if multiplayer Texas Hold'em is considered strategically less complex than the heads-up game (at least for human players), the grown number of players also increases the number of the game states exponentially. These are the reasons why the experimental results in no-limit or multiplayer Texas Hold'em poker are not as good as they are in the fixed-limit heads-up game.

Heuristic expert knowledge or simulation-based methods have been used in some agents, mainly focused on playing full-table fixed-limit Texas Hold'em poker. Systems based on these methods, like Poki [2], are still the best choice when building an agent that is capable of playing at the decent level in tables having more than two players. If the betting strategy is not based on the simulations, the evaluation function is a critical part.

In Sections 1 and 2 we present a heuristic approach for building a betting strategy in a poker agent by defining the structure of the evaluation function. The approach has some advantages over methods mainly used to build poker agents. Firstly, it is very simple and flexible so it can be used to build poker agents capable of varying its playing level. Secondly, it is easy to generalize into different amounts of players and even into the no-limit games. The approach needs some minor modifications for being able to play at its best possible level in the other forms of the game, but the framework still remains the same. In Section 3 we describe some experimental results in heads-up games and conclude with final remarks in Section 4.

1. Defining the Evaluation Function

To build a poker agent based on a heuristic betting strategy we need a way to estimate the expected values of the actions. Estimation can be done by an evaluation function that will calculate the expected values from the given parameters. The parameters can be derived by an opponent modelling system or they can be defined by expert knowledge. Estimation can also be done by using simulations to define the expected values of the actions directly. With these two estimation methods the rest of the structure of the agent can be similar or they can also be used together [2].

A heuristic evaluation function in a poker agent has a role to unify all the information given by an opponent modelling system or expert knowledge that has been used to build an agent. The role the evaluation function has is quite different compared to classical two-player perfect information games, like chess, where the evaluation function is used to estimate the goodness of a game state, and it is usually used with the game-tree search where the search is cut at some level of the tree. Next we present two possible evaluation functions for Texas Hold'em poker: *strategic method* and *direct estimation*. Strategic method is more expert-knowledge-derived while in the direct estimation method opponent modelling is more important.

1.1. Strategic Method

The method is based on expert knowledge which defines the possible different scenarios of how the particular hand could end up. Let $\mathcal{S}$ be the set of possible scenarios. If we have "good cards" in the beginning we can have the following example scenarios $s_1, s_2, s_3, s_4 \in \mathcal{S}$:

- s_1: the agent bets/raises from beginning to showdown;
- s_2: the agent bets/raises until all the others have folded their hands;

- s_3: the agent bets/raises in the beginning until some other player raises after which the agent folds; and
- s_4: the agent only calls all the time if some other player bets/raises.

Similarly we can list detailed scenarios for other classes of hands. (In practice we need about 10 classes for different hands [8].) Straight combination of hand classes and scenarios introduces tens or hundreds of different cases. To reduce the number of cases we can group similar scenarios together keeping two scenarios different only if the outcome is highly different. For the final scenarios we could end up with the following five $s_1, s_2, s_3, s_4, s_5 \in \mathcal{S}$:

- s_1: games, where the agent first bets/raises and continues to bet/raise or call to the end;
- s_2: games, where the agent bets/raises and eventually all the opponents fold their hands;
- s_3: games, where the agent bets/raises and at least one or several of the opponents raise, when the agent folds at some point of the hand;
- s_4: games, where the agent checks or calls first and checks, calls or raises later in the hand that ends up in a showdown; and
- s_5: games, where the agent checks or calls first and folds later at some point of the hand.

As we see, it is possible to define very different scenarios. The more scenarios you have, the easier is the task to derive the estimated pot sizes and amount of bets. The flaw of having a great number of different scenarios is that the overall structure of the evaluation function becomes more incoherent and it is more difficult to test or maintain the system. Even if the number of different scenarios is not fixed, the expected values $E()$ to win or to lose expressed as bets of all the possible scenarios can be calculated with only three formulas presented here.

For scenarios $S_1 \subseteq \mathcal{S}$ that will end at the showdown the expected value can be calculated as follows:

$$(s_i \in S_1): E(s_i) = P_w \times ES - EB$$

where P_w is the agents probability to win the hand, ES is the estimated total pot size and EB is the estimated total amount of bets the agent will invest in this particular hand. Similarly the expected value for the scenarios $S_2 \subseteq \mathcal{S}$ that will end in every other player folding their hands can be calculated:

$$(s_i \in S_2): E(s_i) = P_{vf} \times (ES - EB)$$

where P_{vf} is the probability of the situation, where every other player folds their hands. For the scenarios $S_3 \subseteq \mathcal{S}$ where the poker agent itself folds its hand, the expected value can be calculated:

$$(s_i \in S_3): E(s_i) = P_{hf} \times (-EB)$$

where P_h is the probability that the agent itself folds its hand. Now we can calculate the overall expected value of the action a as follows:

$$E(a) = \sum_j \sum_{s_i \in S_j} P(s_i)E(s_i)$$

where $P(s)$ is the probability of scenario s to occur.

The defining of the attributes can be done by expert knowledge or opponent modelling, usually a combination is the best choice; the balance between methods depends on the accuracy of the opponent modelling system. If the agent includes a very developed opponent modelling system, there is no need to use the expert knowledge so much. Instead, if the opponent modelling system is very simple, expert-knowledge-based functions are needed to make the system able to use this opponent modelling data to define the parameters.

If we use a lot of scenarios, the opponent modelling has to be able to give the probabilities of different scenarios or these should be able to calculate by the heuristic functions with an aim of fixing some assumption probabilities in the beginning.

1.2. Direct Estimation

The direct estimation method is more straightforward than the presented strategic method. Now the ground of the evaluation function is the formula to calculate the overall expected value of the action to be taken next check/call/bet/raise. As we saw in the strategic method, the less scenarios we have, the more difficult it is to derive the estimated size of the bets and total pot.

The overall expected value for an action a is calculated as

$$E(a) = P_w \times ES_w - EB_w + P_{vf} \times (ES_{vf} - EB_{vf}) - P_{hf} \times EB_{hf}.$$

The needed attributes are the same as in the strategic method, but now we should be able to estimate them directly. The methods that can be used to define the attributes are pretty much the same as those presented with the strategic method, but advanced opponent modelling techniques guarantee a better outcome. We can do that by heuristic functions that are based on expert knowledge or we can use opponent modelling to define these attributes. If we use expert-knowledge-based functions, the functions can be made to fit against average opponents, but they do not fit very well against an opponent that uses an unorthodox strategy. It can also lead to a situation where the opponent has an easy task to exploit the flaws in the game if we do not use randomness while choosing actions.

It is noticeable that even if we are calculating the overall expected value of the action, it is just the overall expected value of the action in that particular hand. There is no guarantee that the overall expected value of the action in that particular hand would be the overall expected value in the whole game. Without noticing this fact we give too much information to the opponent about our hand strength and possible actions.

2. Building a System

When building a poker bot, we have to understand that always simply choosing the best action, i.e., the action that maximizes the positive expected value in the current hand, is not the best way to play; it gives too much information to an opponent. Because we did not implement this strategy level in the evaluation function, we used randomized strategy outside the evaluation function; here a probability distribution defines the action to choose [7]. In the system we use an action selector to choose the right action based on the randomized strategy and the estimated expected values.

In addition to methods defining the betting strategy, a classical model of building a poker agent includes an opponent modeller and a hand evaluator. Evaluating the strength of our own hand is a straightforward part of the artificial intelligence system. The hand strength can be seen as a probability to win the current hand. It includes the current strength of a hand and the estimated change of the strength in other stages of the game. An opponent modeller can be used e.g. to infer the probability distribution of the opponent's possible hands or actions.

2.1. Opponent Modelling

As we already touched on in the last chapter, the opponent modelling plays a major role in this kind of solution. Depending on which method we use as an evaluation function and how expert-knowledge-independent we would like the agent to be, there are different ways to execute the opponent modelling. An orthodox way to do the opponent modelling is to use some statistical parameters and use expert knowledge with them. Also the system can calculate the probability distribution of the opponent's possible hands, based on an opponent's actions, and the probability to win the current hand can be derived from that.

In addition to statistical methods, other methods can also be used to execute opponent modelling. For example neural networks suit this task well [5]. Unifying two or more of these methods is also possible. The different methods can vote for the answer given by the opponent modeller, weighted by the past accuracy of these methods.

2.2. Description of the System

Our experimental system includes the main components as follows:

- Evaluation function.
- Action selector.
- Opponent modeller.
- Hand evaluator.
- Rule-based expert system for the pre-flop betting strategy.

In the post-flop betting strategy, we used the direct estimation technique as an evaluation function. For each action with an estimated positive expected value a probability defined by the expected value of the action was attached. The action selector used the attached probabilities while choosing randomly the action to be done: The action that provides a greater expected value is more likely to be chosen. In addition to that, we used a method that we called *continued aggression*, where the aggressive action (bet/raise) in the previous betting round implied greater probabilities than was actually estimated for the actions continuing aggression.

We used simple hand-strength evaluation to evaluate the effective hand strength EHS that includes the current hand strength HS and the positive $PPOT$ and negative potential $NPOT$ of the hand with the upcoming card at the next stage of the game presented in [2]:

$$EHS = HS \times (1 - NPOT) + (1 - HS) \times PPOT .$$

The current hand strength is the probability to have the best hand at the moment. The positive potential is the percentage of the hands we are behind at the moment, but expected to be ahead after the next card. The negative potential is the percentage of the hands we are ahead at the moment, but expected to be behind after the next card. The current hand strength HS is computed by

$$HS = \frac{h_s + h_e/2}{h}$$

where h_s denotes the number of hands that are weaker than the current hand, h_e denotes the number of hands that are equal to the current hand, and h denotes the number of hands used in estimation. Positive potential $PPOT$ and negative potential $NPOT$ are computed by

$$PPOT = \frac{h_{gs} + h_{ge}/2 + h_{es}/2}{h_g + h_e/2}$$

$$NPOT = \frac{h_{sg} + h_{se}/2 + h_{eg}/2}{h_s + h_e/2}$$

where h_g denotes the number of hands that are stronger than the current hand, and a value h_{xy} denotes the number of hands h_x that are weaker ($x = s$), equal ($x = e$), or stronger ($x = g$) and that are expected to be weaker ($y = s$), equal ($y = e$), or stronger ($y = g$) after the next card.

As an opponent-modelling system we used our own two-stage method. Firstly, the system gathers up some basic information about the actions made by the opponents and use these with simple heuristic functions to define the parameters needed by the evaluation function. Alongside with that, the system saves the complete *betting chain* of every hand played in the game. With betting chain we mean every action made in the current hand chained together. When enough similar chains to the current point of the hand are collected, the parameters needed by the evaluation function are used directly. The evaluation function together with the opponent-modelling system use is depicted in Fig. 1.

The heuristic functions used in the system are very simple and the values returned are not even meant to be very accurate. They only give a rough approximation used before enough data is collected. The pre-flop betting strategy used is made by a probabilistic rule-based expert system. The total effect of the pre-flop play is so insignificant that there was no need to use advanced methods.

3. Experimental Results

Even if the approach is mainly focused on multiplayer games, we decided to test the approach against several other poker agents in fixed limit heads-up Texas Hold'em. The reason to choose the fixed limit heads-up game was that in that form of Texas Hold'em poker, there are already some benchmark programs that are suitable for testing.

We tested our system against three different systems that are all based on very different kinds of methods. Sparbot [1] is a game theoretic pseudo-optimal player, Vexbot [3] is a learning player, based on game-tree searches and Pokibrat is a heads-up variant

```
function calcEV(act)
  ch <- current betting chain + act
  Cx <- chains similar to ch
  nx <- number of chains in Cx
  hs <- player's hand strength
  if (nx > set condition)
    Cs <- chains in Cx ending
          showdown
    oh <- average opponent's hand
          strength in Cs
    pw <- calculated probability to
          win by heuristic function
          given hs and oh
    sw <- average pot size in Cs
    bw <- average bets in Cs
    Cv <- chains in Cx ending
          opponent to fold
    nv <- number of chains in Cv
    pv <- nv/nx
    sv <- average pot size in Cv
    bv <- average bets in Cv
    Ch <- chains in Cx ending
          player to fold
    nh <- number of chains in Ch
    ph <- nh/nx
    bh <- average bets in Ch
  else calculate needed parameters
       by heuristic functions
  return (pw * sw - bw)
         + pv * (sv - bv) - ph * bh
```

Figure 1. Calculation of evaluation function

Table 1. Test results against the opponents.

Opponent	Result (SB/h)
Sparbot	−0.023
Vexbot	−0.242
Pokibrat	+0.015

of the Poki system. More information about the test process and methods can be found at [8].

Results shown in table 1 are only indicative of the real game level of the system. However, it is noticeable that against the Sparbot and Poki systems our system is quite competitive, while against the Vexbot system there can be seen Vexbot's good adaptation skills, where it can exploit the flaws of the opponent after a period of played hands. In this case the period was about 1000 hands.

There are some flaws in the betting strategy of the system that are possible to exploit for a learning opponent. Firstly, avoiding exploitation could be done by increasing randomness in the action selector. Secondly, a better opponent modelling could lead to better adaptation through which it is possible to learn counter-strategies against the opponent's strategy to exploit the flaws of an agent.

There is also possibility to develop the evaluation function and other heuristic functions. The interesting part would be trying to find an evaluation function that takes into account the whole game, not just the current hand. Fixing these flaws and developing the system for a better level is not an easy task to do. Testing and developing the system through exploited flaws is a very time-consuming process because of the randomness. In [10] is presented some methods to help this process.

4. Conclusion

The presented heuristic approach offers a general way to execute the betting strategy in Texas Hold'em poker. The experimental test shows that there are some flaws in the system, but they are not crucial. The system fits right away, even better, for multiplayer fixed limit games, where opponents are not able to exploit the flaws of the system as easily as in the heads-up game. The method is also worth trying in no-limit games.

However, we have to remember that if we want to build a system that is capable of playing at the world-class level in no-limit Texas Hold'em poker, there are some features that make the task much more challenging; now an agent is able to lose its whole current stack in one particular hand. Usually the amount can be something like 100 big blinds, but it can be even more. It is noticeable that losing can occur by only one mistake, when in a fixed-limit game one mistake in a game is not as crucial when you can lose a maximum of one big bet, which is only two big blinds. So in a no-limit game the cost of one mistake can be 50 times the cost of one mistake in a fixed-limit game. On the other hand, avoiding errors can lead to suboptimal play.

The important role of errors in decision-making in no-limit games increases the importance of opponent modelling from before. It also makes it possible to use new methods in the systems. The opponent modelling system for example can make observations about the reasons that led to errors in the decision-making process [4].

References

[1]   Darse Billings, Neil Burch, Aaron Davidson, Robert Holte, Jonathan Schaeffer, Terence Schauenberg, and Duane Szafron, 'Approximating game-theoretic optimal strategies for full-scale poker', in *Proceedings of the Eighteenth International Joint Conference on Artificial Intelligence*, (2003).

[2]   Darse Billings, Aaron Davidson, Jonathan Schaeffer, and Duane Szafron, 'The challenge of poker', *Artificial Intelligence*, **134**(1-2), 201–240, (2002).

[3]   Darse Billings, Aaron Davidson, Terence Schauenberg, Neil Burch, Michael Bowling, Robert Holte, Jonathan Schaeffer, and Duane Szafron, 'Game tree search with adaptation in stochastic imperfect information games', in *Proceedings of the Computers and Games: 4th International Conference (CG'04)*, (2004).

[4]   Gabe Chaddock, Marc Pickett, Tom Armstrong, and Tim Oates, 'Models of strategic deficiency and poker', in *Working Notes of the AAAI Workshop on Plan, Activity, and Intent Recognition (PAIR)*, pp. 31–36, (2007).

[5]   Aaron Davidson, Darse Billings, Jonathan Schaeffer, and Duane Szafron, 'Improved opponent modeling in poker', in *Proceedings of the 2000 International Conference on Artificial Intelligence (ICAI'2000)*, pp. 1467–1473, (2000).

[6]   Michael Johanson, *Robust Strategies and Counter-Strategies: Building a Champion Level Computer Poker Player*, Master's thesis, University of Alberta, October 2007.

[7]   Daphne Koller and Avi Pfeffer, 'Generating and solving imperfect information games', in *Proceedings of the 14th International Joint Conference on Artificial Intelligence (IJCAI)*, pp. 1185–1192, Montreal, Canada, (August 1995).

[8]   Teemu Saukonoja, *Heuristisen panostusstrategian toteuttaminen pokerin tekoälysovelluksissa*, Master's thesis, University of Helsinki, November 2007.

[9]   David Sklansky, *Theory of Poker*, Two Plus Two Publishing, 1994.

[10] Martin Zinkevich, Michael Bowling, Nolan Bard, Morgan Kan, and Darse Billings, 'Optimal unbiased estimators for evaluating agent performance', in *Proceedings of the Twenty-First National Conference on Artificial Intelligence (AAAI)*, pp. 573–578, (2006).

Chipper – A Novel Algorithm for Concept Description

Ulf JOHANSSON[a,1], Cecilia SÖNSTRÖD[a], Tuve LÖFSTRÖM[a,b], Henrik BOSTRÖM[b]
[a]*University of Borås, School of Business and Informatics, Borås, Sweden*
[b]*University of Skövde, School of Humanities and Informatics, Skövde, Sweden*

Abstract. In this paper, several demands placed on concept description algorithms are identified and discussed. The most important criterion is the ability to produce compact rule sets that, in a natural and accurate way, describe the most important relationships in the underlying domain. An algorithm based on the identified criteria is presented and evaluated. The algorithm, named Chipper, produces decision lists, where each rule covers a maximum number of remaining instances while meeting requested accuracy requirements. In the experiments, Chipper is evaluated on nine UCI data sets. The main result is that Chipper produces compact and understandable rule sets, clearly fulfilling the overall goal of concept description. In the experiments, Chipper's accuracy is similar to standard decision tree and rule induction algorithms, while rule sets have superior comprehensibility.

1. Introduction

In most cases, a data mining project has its origin in a business problem, where a decision-maker or an executive requests improved support for their decisions. Depending on the type of business problem, different data mining tasks or problem types can be identified. Several taxonomies of data mining problems exist and they agree upon the most important problem types. The problem type *concept description* does not, however, appear in all taxonomies and when it is included, the definitions differ. The CRISP-DM [1] framework identifies six basic problem types in data mining:

- **Data description and summarization**, aimed at concise description of data characteristics, typically in elementary and aggregated form.
- **Segmentation**, aimed at separating data into interesting and meaningful subgroups or classes.
- **Concept descriptions**, aimed at understandable descriptions of concepts or classes.
- **Classification**, aimed at building models which assign correct class labels to previously unseen and unlabeled data items.
- **Prediction**, which differs from classification only in that the target attribute or class is continuous. Prediction is normally referred to as regression.
- **Dependency analysis**, aimed at finding a model that describes significant dependencies or associations between data items or events.

---

[1] Corresponding author: Ulf Johansson and Cecilia Sönströd are equal contributors to this work. Email: {ulf.johansson, cecilia.sonstrod }@hb.se.

We have earlier, see [2] and [3], argued that the CRISP-DM definition of concept description captures the essential properties of this task, since it states that the purpose of concept description "is not to develop complete models with high prediction accuracy, but to gain insights". As noted in [3], an important implication of this is that models need not be capable of describing the whole data set. The statement that high predictive accuracy is not required is somewhat deceptive, though, since it refers only to the purpose of the model. To obtain the goal of bringing insights, models should only include relationships between data items that represent meaningful relations in the underlying domain. This entails that concept description models should have the ability to generalize well to new data from the same domain. Obviously, the model must also represent the relationships it contains in a manner that is easily interpretable. To conclude, it follows from the CRISP-DM definition and discussion of concept description that models should describe the targeted concept in an accurate and comprehensible way.

For each of the above problem types, CRISP-DM suggests several appropriate techniques. For concept description, the only two techniques mentioned are rule induction methods and conceptual clustering. Obviously, many rule induction algorithms exist, although none is specifically aimed at concept description. Examining the demands placed on a concept description model, it is clear that rule induction techniques maximizing an information gain measure for every split do not favor good concept description models. Typically, accurate decision trees tend to be fairly complex.

2. Background and related work

We have previously explored the possibility of using predictive modeling techniques for concept description, see e.g. [4][5]. The method of first building an opaque model with high predictive accuracy, typically using some sort of ensemble technique, and then using a powerful rule extraction tool to produce rules was seen to yield models that are comprehensible and have high accuracy. As mentioned above, high accuracy is not important for the purpose of producing accurate predictions, but to guarantee that the model captures general and important relationships in the data, and hence in the underlying domain.

However, when examining the rules/trees obtained in this manner, it became clear that, in the context of concept description, the hitherto used simplistic view of comprehensibility (interpreted as transparent and fairly small models) should be refined. For example, a decision tree containing a root split immediately singling out a large number of instances based on one attribute, is clearly a better description than one where the same instances are classified further down in the tree, possibly with several different splits. In [2], this discussion lead to the following break-down of comprehensibility:

- **Brevity**: The model should classify as many instances as possible using few and simple rules.
- **Interpretability**: The model should express conditions in a way that humans tend to use, i.e. without Boolean conditions or closed intervals.
- **Relevance**: Only those relationships that are general (i.e. have high accuracy) and interesting should be included in the model. What constitutes an interesting relationship is clearly domain and/or problem specific.

Using this refined view of comprehensibility as a basis, it is natural to look for alternative ways of producing rules for concept description, both regarding representation and search strategy. As far as representation is concerned, decision lists seem like an obvious alternative, since they capture the intuitive notion that once a set of instances is explained, those instances can be disregarded when considering the rest. Algorithms producing decision lists are also known as sequential covering algorithms [6], since rules are learnt one at a time. For each rule, all instances covered by this rule are removed from the data set and the next rule is learnt from the remaining instances. Several sophisticated algorithms for producing decision lists exist, and they typically use some information gain measure to decide how to refine rules in each step. Early examples of decision list algorithms include AQ [7] and CN2 [8]. More recent is RIPPER [9], based on IREP [10]. In short, RIPPER constructs its rule sets in three phases, called growing, pruning and optimization. In the growing phase, conditions are added to a rule as long as no negative examples are covered. In the pruning phase, conditions are removed based on performance on a validation set. Pruning may result in the rule covering negative examples. Furthermore, for binary problems, the majority class is the default class and all rules describe the minority class. An instance not covered by any rule is thus assigned the majority class. RIPPER is reported to be well suited to problems with uneven class distributions and scale up well to large data sets, see [9] and [11].

3. Method

In this section, the proposed algorithm, named Chipper, is first presented in detail and then the experiments are described. Chipper is a deterministic algorithm for generating decision lists consisting of simple rules. In its current state, it handles only binary problems and can thus be used for concept descriptions where the aim is to obtain a description of one class in relation to one or several others.

The basic idea is to, in every step, search for the rule that classifies the maximum number of instances using a split on one attribute. For continuous attributes, this means a single comparison using a relational operator. For nominal attributes, this is translated to a set of instances having identical values for that attribute.

Two main parameters, called *ignore* and *stop*, are used to control the rule generation process. The *ignore* parameter specifies the misclassification rate that is acceptable for each rule and can have different values for each output class. The motivation for the *ignore* parameter is that it can be used to view the data set at different levels of detail, with higher values prioritizing the really broad discriminating features of data items and with low values trying to capture more specific rules. The *stop* parameter specifies the proportion of all instances that should be covered by rules before terminating. The motivation for this parameter is that it can be used to find only the most general relationships in the data, instead of trying to find rules to cover particular instances. This parameter is also motivated by the observation in CRISP-DM that concept description models may well be partial. In effect, these two parameters control the level of "granularity" for the decision list.

When building rule sets, Chipper can be made to prioritize rules with high accuracy instead of simply maximizing the number of covered instances, by using the *prefer_accuracy* flag. If used, then for each possible rule, a score is calculated using (1) below.

$$\text{score} = \#\text{instances\_covered} \times \text{rule\_accuracy} \qquad (1)$$

Consequently, when *prefer_accuracy* is true, the candidate rule fulfilling the *ignore* criterion with highest score is chosen. When no more rules can be constructed, the class with the largest remaining number of instances is taken as the default class; this means that different parameter settings can produce rule sets with different default classes. The main operation of Chipper is given in pseudo code below.

```
Input: a data set with two classes
Output: a decision list
Parameters: a stop value S. For each class c, an ignore parameter I_c
while proportion of instances classified is smaller than S
  for each attribute a
    find best_split_a;
  select the best_split covering most instances
  formulate a rule using this split
  remove all instances covered by this rule from the data set
```

The sub-procedure *find best_split$_a$* greedily compares possible splits using one attribute and a single relational operator; i.e. for continuous attributes '<' or '>', and for categorical '='. The *ignore* parameter determines the acceptable number of misclassified instances, either as an absolute number of instances or as a proportion of remaining instances.

3.1. Data sets

Nine publicly available data sets from the UCI machine learning repository [12] were chosen for the experiments, mainly on the basis of having interpretable attributes. A summary of the characteristics of the data sets used is given in Table 1 below, where *Instances* is the total number of instances, *Cont.* is the number of continuous variables and *Cat.* is the number of categorical input variables.

Table 1: Data set characteristics

Data set	Instances	Cont.	Cat.
BUPA	345	6	0
Cleve	303	6	7
Diabetes (Pima)	768	8	0
German	1000	7	13
Hepatitis	155	6	13
Iono	351	34	0
Labor	57	8	8
Sick	3772	22	7
Votes	435	0	16

3.2. Experiments

Two main experiments were carried out to evaluate Chipper for concept description. In all experiments, standard 10-fold cross validation was used. In the first experiment, Chipper was used with parameter settings to optimize predictive power; with *ignore* at 4.5% for both classes, *stop* at 95% and *prefer_accuracy* set to true. Comparisons were carried out against the J48 tree inducer, which is based on C4.5 [13], as implemented in the data mining tool WEKA [14] and against JRIP, the WEKA implementation of RIPPER. For both these techniques, the default settings in WEKA were used.

Using the refined comprehensibility criteria above, the only aspect that is feasible to measure numerically is brevity. It is not, however, obvious how this measure should be constructed. With this is mind, the following three brevity measures were used:

- **Classification complexity** (CC), which measures the average number of tests needed to classify an instance. A low value thus signifies good brevity.
- **Top rule classification rate** (TR), which measures the proportion of instances classified by the top rule in the rule set. For this measure, a high value is desirable from a brevity perspective.
- **Brevity index** (BI_x), as an index capturing how much the x first tests in the rule set classify. This index takes values in [0, 1], where 0 indicates that all instances are classified with the first rule and 1 indicates that all instances are classified after rule number x. The index is calculated using (2) below:

$$BI_x = \frac{\left(\sum_{i=1}^{x} 2^{i-1} p_i\right) + 2^x p_{rest} - 1}{2^x - 1} \tag{2}$$

where p_i is the proportion of instances classified in rule (or test) i. p_{rest} is the proportion of instances not classified by the x first rules.

An inherent problem when comparing Chipper against RIPPER is that RIPPER rules contain conjunctions and that no natural translation to the Chipper representation language exists; this is handled by choosing to count either the number of tests or the number of rules, whichever is most natural for the measure at hand. For BI_x, the choice was made to use two different versions, one using number of tests and one using number of rules.

The CC measure represents the choice of evaluating the whole model, i.e. every classification made. For RIPPER, a conjunctive rule is taken to classify at the last conjunct, meaning that a top rule classifying 50 instances with a single AND is taken to classify all those 50 instances with two tests. It should be noted that using such a high stop parameter as 95 in Chipper gives a disadvantage for CC. For the TR measure, a RIPPER top rule with conjunctions is counted as a single rule, which is a rather charitable interpretation. On the other hand, this is a measure that Chipper aims to optimize, and so would be expected to perform well on. Arguably, neither CC nor TR manages to capture brevity in a satisfactory way. CC is too detailed, taking the whole model into account and making distinctions between classification by, say, rule number 10 and rule number 15. TR, on the other hand, is too blunt, since it ignores the possibility that several of the top rules together classify a large proportion of instances. Brevity index is an attempt at a more balanced measure, with the possibility of using a different level of detail. In this study, we opted for BI_3 with the simple motivation that three conditions are quite easy to grasp to a human trying to interpret a rule set, but can still capture several important relationships in the data set.

In the second experiment, the effect of different parameter settings was studied in detail for the Hepatitis data set, with the intention of illustrating how Chipper can be used for different data mining purposes. This also serves as an evaluation of Chipper's ability to fulfill the interpretability and relevance aspects of comprehensibility.

4. Results

The main results from Experiment 1 are shown below. Although the main purpose is to investigate how Chipper performs regarding accuracy compared to standard decision trees and RIPPER, the size of trees/rules produced are also reported, see Table 2. The size measure given is the number of tests in the rule set.

Table 2: Accuracy results from Experiment 1. Chipper set at 4.5-4.5-95

	J48			RIPPER			Chipper		
Data set	size	acc.	rank	size	acc.	rank	size	acc.	rank
BUPA	25	68.7%	1	4	64.6%	3	16	66.2%	2
Cleve	25	77.6%	2	6	81.5%	1	19	72.7%	3
Diabetes (Pima)	38	73.8%	3	9	76.0%	2	15	77.6%	1
German	139	70.5%	3	5	71.7%	1	19	71.1%	2
Hepatitis	20	83.9%	1	5	78.1%	3	9	80.0%	2
Iono	34	91.5%	1	2	89.7%	2	4	84.6%	3
Labor	2	73.7%	3	4	77.1%	2	4	90.0%	1
Sick	60	98.8%	1	10	98.2%	2	1	94.6%	3
Votes	5	96.3%	2	3	95.4%	3	4	96.5%	1
Average rank			1.89			2.11			2.00

As can be seen from the table, all three techniques perform similarly regarding accuracy over a number of data sets. It is, however, interesting to note that, although Chipper does not explicitly optimize overall accuracy, it still performs slightly better than RIPPER. Since the ultimate goal is comprehensibility in the context of concept description, the measures on brevity defined above are used to compare RIPPER and Chipper. In Table 3 below, all brevity measures are shown. Bold type indicates the best value for that brevity measure.

Table 3: Comprehensibility results from Experiment 1

Data set	Chipper					RIPPER				
	#tests	CC	TR	BI_3Test	BI_3Rule	#tests	CC	TR	BI_3Test	BI_3Rule
BUPA	16	6.21	0.13	**0.70**	0.70	4	**3.51**	**0.25**	0.79	**0.11**
Cleve	19	5.40	0.22	**0.54**	0.54	6	**4.75**	**0.26**	0.78	**0.29**
Diabetes (Pima)	15	**4.16**	**0.36**	**0.44**	0.44	9	7.24	0.23	0.80	**0.32**
German	19	6.18	**0.18**	**0.65**	0.65	5	**4.48**	0.17	0.85	**0.12**
Hepatitis	9	**2.51**	0.57	**0.31**	**0.31**	5	4.55	0.08	0.87	0.36
Iono	4	1.98	0.26	0.20	0.20	2	**1.74**	0.25	**0.10**	**0.11**
Labor	4	**1.75**	0.52	**0.17**	**0.17**	4	3.12	0.26	0.69	0.64
Sick	**1**	**1.00**	**1.00**	**0.00**	**0.00**	10	8.54	0.06	0.95	0.40
Votes	4	1.59	0.57	**0.13**	**0.13**	3	4.64	0.32	0.73	0.28
#Wins	1	5	7	8	4	8	4	2	1	5
Average	10.1	**3.4**	**0.42**	**0.35**	0.35	5.3	4.7	0.21	0.73	**0.29**

Regarding rule set size, RIPPER produces more compact rule sets, having the smallest rule set on all but one data set. However, Chipper is explicitly set at classifying at least 95% of all instances, leading to large rule sets. Looking at the different brevity measures, the overall picture is that Chipper clearly outperforms RIPPER. For CC, Chipper obtains the best brevity on 5 out of 9 data sets. For the data sets where Chipper has worse CC the difference is usually quite small, and Chipper also has the best average CC. Regarding TR, Chipper is substantially better than RIPPER, winning 7 data sets and averaging 42% of instances being classified by the top test in the rule set.

The BI$_3$ measure shows a similar trend when number of tests is used, with Chipper showing the best results. When using number of rules, RIPPER unsurprisingly obtains a lower BI$_3$ value. The results from Experiment 2 on the Hepatitis data set are shown in Table 4 below, as a summary of rule set size and accuracy.

Table 4: Results from Experiment 2. Rule set size and accuracy for Chipper on Hepatitis

	Ignore					
	2%		4.5%		6%	
Stop	acc.	#tests	acc.	#tests	acc.	#tests
65	78.7%	3	75.3%	3	78.7%	1
80	82.0%	6	78.0%	5	78.0%	3
95	81.3%	12	80.0%	9	79.3%	6

In the design of Chipper, the *Stop* parameter is meant to allow the user to set the level of detail contained in the rule set. From Table 4, it is clear that an increased *Stop* value will produce longer decision lists, which, of course, is in accordance with how this parameter is supposed to work. The *Ignore* parameter is intended as a way of controlling accuracy requirement; however, it cannot be expected to directly correlate to overall accuracy. Especially when using a low *Stop* value, and thus having quite a large proportion of instances classified by the default rule, overall accuracy does not, to a large extent, depend on individual rule accuracy. In Table 4, this is seen by comparing, for example, the accuracies obtained for *Stop* 65. Finally, it is reassuring to note that Chipper is quite consistent regarding accuracy over different parameter settings, meaning that descriptions produced overall have high generality. Figures 1 and 2 below show some sample rules obtained using different parameter settings.

```
if BILIRUBIN  <= 1.3 -> DIE   105/9      if BILIRUBIN  <= 1.3 -> DIE   105/9
if ASCITES    == 1   -> LIVE  11/1       if ASCITES    == 1   -> LIVE  11/1
if SGOT       <= 69  -> DIE   16/2       if SGOT       <= 69  -> DIE   16/2
Default: DIE                             if SPLEEN PAL == 1   -> LIVE  7/1
                                         if STEROID    == 2   -> DIE   7/0
                                         if AGE        >= 56  -> LIVE  3/0
                                         Default: DIE
```

Fig. 1. Chipper rule for Hepatitis with parameters 0.06-0.06-80 (left) and 0.06-0.06-95 (right)

```
if ALBUMIN    >= 3.9 -> DIE 83/3         if ALBUMIN    >= 3.9  -> DIE   83/3
if FATIGUE    == 2   -> DIE 14/1         if FATIGUE    == 2    -> DIE   14/1
if ALK PHOSPH >= 168 -> DIE 9/1          if ALK PHOSPH >= 168  -> DIE   9/1
Default: LIVE                            if ALBUMIN    <= 2.8  -> LIVE  11/0
                                         if PROTIME    >= 63   -> DIE   5/0
                                         if BILIRUBIN  >= 3.9  -> LIVE  5/0
                                         Default: DIE
```

Fig. 2. Chipper rule for Hepatitis with parameters 0.02-0.02-65 (left) and 0.02-0.02-80 (right)

One important observation from these rules is that the *Stop* parameter provides a tool for controlling model granularity. Specifically, the left hand side rule in Fig. 2 is a high-level description of the underlying relationship. On this data set, Chipper seldom uses the same attribute twice. One can also note that for the same Ignore value, each rule set starts in the same way; a direct consequence of Chipper's deterministic search strategy. Regarding comprehensibility, the rules are all fairly short and have good brevity measures. Each rule is very simple, making the models highly interpretable.

Regarding relevance, this clearly depends on whether one class is deemed more interesting than the other and also on which attributes a decision-maker would be interested in.

5. Conclusions

In this paper, the Chipper algorithm producing decision lists for concept description has been presented and evaluated. For a concept description model, the important properties are accuracy (to ensure that the model describes general relationships in the underlying domain) and comprehensibility (to ensure that the model presents these relationships as clearly as possible). Comprehensibility can be further broken down into the three properties of brevity, interpretability and relevance. In this study, three different brevity measures were suggested; classification complexity, top rule classification rate and brevity index.

In the experimentation, Chipper was found to perform very well. More specifically, when compared against the standard decision tree technique J48 and the decision list algorithm RIPPER on a number of publicly available data sets, Chipper obtained comparable accuracies and is thus seen to describe general relationships in the data. Additionally, Chipper rule sets were in general more comprehensible than RIPPER rule sets, especially regarding brevity. In more thorough experimentation on one data set, this high accuracy was seen to be stable over different parameter settings, meaning that generality was retained even for very high-level descriptions. To conclude, the proposed Chipper algorithm clearly fulfills the concept description aim of bringing insights into the relationships and properties of a data set.

References

[1]   The CRISP-DM Consortium, CRISP-DM 1.0, www.crisp-dm.org, 2000.
[2]   C. Sönströd, U. Johansson and R. König, Towards a Unified View on Concept Description, *The 2007 International Conference on Data Mining (DMIN07)*, Las Vegas, NV, 2007.
[3]   C. Sönströd and U. Johansson, Concept Description – A Fresh Look, *Proceedings of the 2007 International Joint Conference on Neural Networks*, IEEE Press, Orlando, FL, 2007.
[4]   U. Johansson, C. Sönströd and L. Niklasson, Why Rule Extraction Matters, *8th IASTED International Conference on Software Engineering and Applications*, p. 47-42, Cambridge, MA, 2004.
[5]   U. Johansson, C. Sönströd and L. Niklasson, Explaining Winning Poker – A Data Mining Approach, *5th International Conference on Machine Learning and Applications*, p. 129 – 134, Orlando, FL, 2006.
[6]   J. Han and M. Kamber, *Data Mining – Concepts and Techniques 2nd ed.*, Morgan Kaufman, 2006.
[7]   R. S. Michalski, On the quasi-minimal solution of the general covering problem, *Proceedings of the Fifth International Symposium on Information Processing*, p.125-128, Bled, Yugoslavia, 1969.
[8]   P. Clark and T.Niblett, *The CN2 induction algorithm*, Machine Learning, 3: 261-283, 1989.
[9]   W. Cohen, Fast Effective Rule Induction, *Proceeding of 12th International Conference on Machine Learning (ICML '95)*, p. 115-123, Tahoe City, CA, 1995.
[10] J. Fürnkrantz and G.Widmer, Incremental Reduced Error Pruning, *11th International Conference on Machine Learning (ICML '94)*, p. 70-77, San Mateo, CA, 1994.
[11] T. G. Dietterich, *Machine Learning Research: Four Current Directions*, AI Magazine '18, 97-136, 1997.
[12] C. L. Blake and C. J. Merz, *UCI Repository of Machine Learning Databases*, University of California, Department of Information and Computer Science, 1998.
[13] J. R. Quinlan, *C4.5: Programs for Machine Learning*, Morgan Kaufman, 1993.
[14] I. H. Witten and E. Frank, *Data Mining: Practical Machine Learning Tools and Techniques 2nd ed.*, Morgan Kaufman, 2005.

Tenth Scandinavian Conference on Artificial Intelligence
A. Holst et al. (Eds.)
IOS Press, 2008

141

A Novel Framework for Case-Based Decision Analysis

Ning XIONG[1] and Peter FUNK[2]
School of Innovation, Design and Engineering
Mälardalen University, Västerås, Sweden

Abstract. Case-based reasoning (CBR) and decision analysis have been two separate research areas aiming to solve problems from different perspectives. CBR is powerful to offer solutions to problems by reusing previous experiences, while decision theory exhibits its strength in dealing with uncertain, nondeterministic situations subject to likelihoods, risks, and probable consequences. In this paper, we present a novel framework of integrating CBR and decision analysis for the purpose of case-based decision analysis. CBR is employed as a methodology to reason from previous cases for building a decision model given the current situation, while decision theory is applied to the decision model learnt from previous cases to identify the most promising, secured, and rational choices. In such a way, we take advantage of both the ability of CBR to learn without domain knowledge and the strength of decision theory to analyze under uncertainty.

Keywords. case-based reasoning, decision analysis, decision tree, utility

Introduction

Theory for decision analysis has shown great importance for intelligent agent systems. Aiming to provide powerful methodologies and tools for agents to analyze uncertain scenarios, decision theory [1-2] concentrates on identifying, among available alternatives, the "best" course of actions from a reasonable perspective for promoting the satisfaction of the agent objective. However, practical applications of decision theory entail formulating a real world problem into an exact decision model, which may be hard in many situations due to complexity, uncertainty, poor domain knowledge, and incomplete information.

A more pragmatic way for decision analysis is to look at previous similar situations and their solutions when facing a new situation to make choice. By doing this, we require no fully understood domain knowledge and avoid efforts to build a precise decision model. The research into this realm is strongly supported by the methodology of case-based reasoning (CBR) [3] from artificial intelligence. The fundamental tenet followed is the rule that similar situations have similar solutions such that the decision made to a past similar case can be largely reused for dealing with the new situation. On the other hand, as the case-based approach simplifies problems by mainly recalling and reusing, it dose not take into account the stochastic property of occurrences of outcomes and related benefits and risks when a decision is to be made.

---

[1] ning.xiong@mdh.se
[2] peter.funk@mdh.se

In this paper we propose a novel framework of integrating CBR and decision analysis. Our point is that CBR and decision theory have merits in different aspects and can complement each other in a unified paradigm. The ability of CBR is utilized to learn from previous experiences for creating a situation dependent decision model, while information in the decision model learnt from cases is further analyzed using decision theory to find out optimal, rational, and low risk solutions. We deem such integration beneficial in taking advantage of both the ability of CBR to learn without domain knowledge and the strength of decision theory to analyze under uncertainty.

Two previous papers [4-5] deserve mentioning here as relevant works. Decision theory was applied to support case retrieval in a practical CBR system [4]. The paper [5] proposed using CBR to facilitate model building in Bayesian-network based decision support systems.

1. Background Knowledge

1.1. Case-based reasoning for problem solving

An overview of the procedure for case-based problem solving is depicted in Fig. 1. Given a new target situation Q, we look for its similar cases in the case library which are assumed relevant for solving Q. The matching between target Q and a known case C in the case library is guided by a similarity function. After similarity matching, a subset of cases is retrieved from the case library in terms of the rule of *KNN* (*k* nearest neighborhoods) or a specified similarity threshold [6]. The retrieved cases are then delivered along with their similarity scores to the block "decision fusion" for finalizing the solution to the new situation Q.

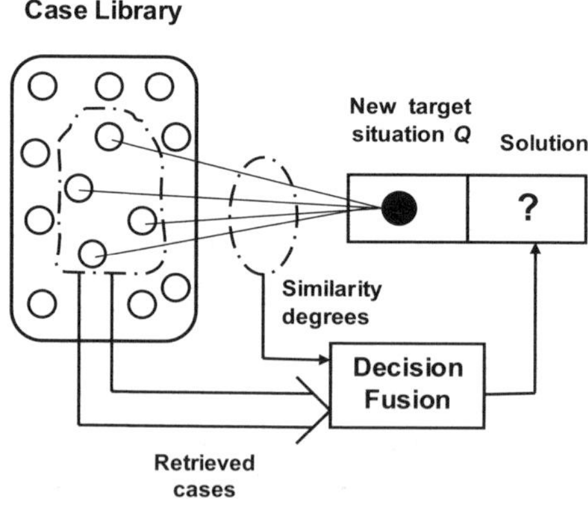

Figure 1. An overview of case-based problem solving

In the step of decision fusion we consider every retrieved case as an influential source that recommends its own solution as a candidate to treat the new situation. If all retrieved cases have an identical solution, consensus is immediately reached regarding the final decision. Otherwise we have to launch a voting procedure to choose the most plausible alternative from given candidates. Since similarity of a case can be considered as an estimate of the appropriateness of its solution to the new circumstance, the values of similarity of the retrieved cases that have an identical solution are accumulated into a voting score for the associated candidate. In general, the voting score for a candidate solution S is calculated by

$$VS(S) = \sum_{\forall C \in Retrieved} \begin{cases} Sim(C,Q), & if \quad Solution(C) = S \\ 0, & otherwise \end{cases} \tag{1}$$

Finally we select the solution S^* that has the largest voting score as the solution for the target situation Q, i.e.,

$$S^* = \arg \max_{\forall S}[VS(S)] \tag{2}$$

From the above we can see that the CBR approach produces a deterministic mapping from situations to solutions by voting upon the subset of retrieved cases. The belief behind voting is the assumption that the appropriateness of a case solution is uniquely determined by the similarity of that case. This would be an over-simplified hypothesis, leading to ignorance of probable outcomes and consequences under alternative solutions.

1.2. Decision model for decision analysis

The decision problem for an agent can be abstracted as follows. Given an environment with possible states s_1, s_2, …,s_n, the agent has to make a choice from a set of alternative actions $\{a_1, a_2, …, a_m\}$. The outcome or consequence of an action is dependent on the real state of the environment. A general utility function has been defined for all possible outcomes regarding actions and states. By u_{ij} we denote the general utility of performing action a_i when state s_j is true, i.e., $u_{ij} = U(a_i \mid s_j)$. But the agent has no exact knowledge about the state of the environment, only a probability distribution of the states is available for decision analysis.

This (decision) problem can also be modelled as a decision tree as shown in Fig. 2, where p_i refers to the probability of state s_i ($i=1…n$). The availability of such a model is prerequisite to apply well founded decision analysis methods such as Bayesian decision theory [1] and the principle of general risk constraints [7] for making profitable, secured, and rational choices.

However, constructing a perfect decision tree to abstract an underlying situation is not trivial. It requires thorough understanding of the circumstance and detailed domain knowledge for elicitation of all relevant information. In many cases it is hard to define accurate values for probabilities concerning states of the environment and general utilities regarding actions and states in a decision tree. First of all, estimates for probabilities of states are very likely to be subjective or imprecise. Shapira [8] observed that most people usually can not distinguish between probabilities roughly ranging from 0.3 to 0.7. Moreover, general utilities regarding actions and states correspond to a sort of generalized information which is hard to explicate without deep domain knowledge. Instead of giving utility in a general meaning, users in real life would feel more natural and confident to specify individual utility scores associated with specific cases by evaluation of concrete results therein. Next we will show how both the state probabilities and the (general) utilities in the decision tree can be estimated from previous cases for a new situation by using a case-based approach.

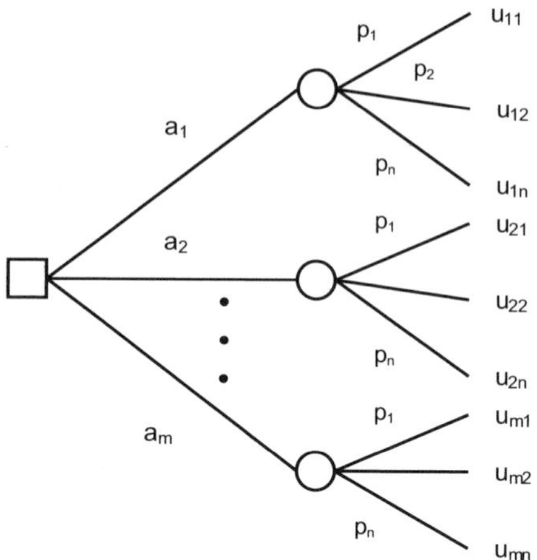

Figure 2. A decision problem modelled as a decision tree

2. Case-Based Modelling of Decision Trees

We consider decision tree as a vehicle carrying knowledge and information about candidate actions and their probable consequences. The content of the vehicle is situation dependent. In different situations we may have different alternatives, varying probabilities and different consequences. Here we propose a case-based approach to creating situation dependent decision trees. The basic idea is to derive the right content of the decision model by resorting to previous similar cases with respect to a given new situation. This approach is different from the one described in subsection 1.1 where CBR aims to directly finalize solutions based on a subset of retrieved cases. Contrarily, in this paper, we apply CBR in an intermediate stage for the creation of a qualified decision model, which can then be utilized by various decision analysis methods to find out rational, justified choices.

A procedure for case-based modelling of decision trees is shown in Fig. 3. It starts with similarity matching between a new situation and previous cases in the case library. Every case in the case library receives a similarity score according to a similarity metric. We will not detail the issue of similarity measurements due to the scope of this paper, but interesting readers can refer to the references [9-10] for more information. After similarity matching, a subset of cases that get the highest similarity scores or pass a specified similarity threshold are selected and retrieved. In the next step, we perform probability and utility derivation based on the subset of retrieved cases and the case library. The purpose is to exploit the information residing in the cases to acquire probabilities of environment states in the current situation as well as (general) utility estimates of alternative actions given different states. Finally, the derived probability and utility values are entered into the decision tree for decision analysis.

As basic notation, we assume that a case C_j in the case library is indexed by a 4-tuple $C_j=(B_j, E_j, A_j, U_j)$, where

• B_j is the description of the situation associated with the case. It can, for instance, consist of a set of observed or informed attribute values.

• $E_j = (P_j(s_1), P_j(s_2), …, P_j(s_n))$ represents the known probability distribution for states s_1, s_2, …, s_n in the situation associated with the case. States are usually not observable but reflect internal properties of the environment. Sometimes the probability of a state in a case is also notated as $P_j(s_i) = P(s_i \mid C_j)$.

• A_j denotes an action that was performed in the situation associated with the case.

• U_j is an individual utility score evaluating the outcome of performing action A_j in the situation associated with the case. Hence it is also notated as $U(A_j|C_j)$ later in the paper.

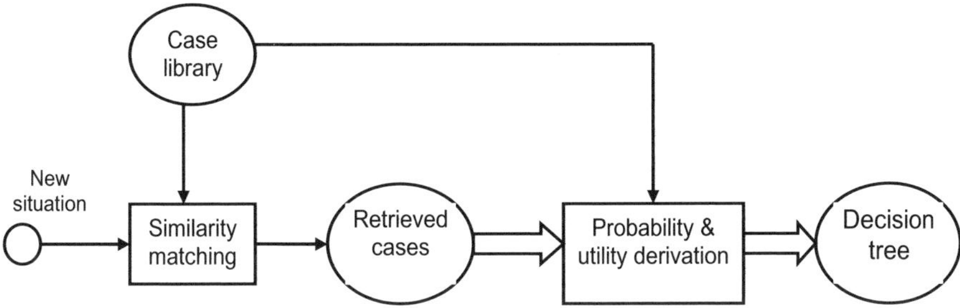

Figure 3. Case-based modelling of decision trees

2.1. Derivation of states probabilities based on retrieved cases

Suppose a set of cases have been retrieved after similarity matching, we now want to derive probabilities of states to build a decision tree for the current new situation Q. Without loss of generality, we denote the retrieved cases as $\{C_1, C_2, …, C_{Nr}\}$ where Nr is the number of cases retrieved. As a probability distribution is available in every retrieved case, we first attempt to aggregate these probability distributions to obtain an initial estimate about the probabilities of states. The similarity of a case can be considered as an indicator of the confidence of its probability distribution in the new situation. Hence the prior probability of a state s_i $(i=1…n)$ is calculated as a weighted average of its known probabilities in the retrieved cases by

$$P(s_i) = \frac{\sum_{j=1}^{Nr} Sim(C_j, Q) \cdot P_j(s_i)}{\sum_{j=1}^{Nr} Sim(C_j, Q)} \tag{3}$$

The degree of similarity, $Sim(C_j, Q)$, between case C_j and situation Q is used as a weight in the aggregation.

Next, the prior probabilities concerning states are further refined using the Bayes theorem. Assuming that cases are independent of each other, every similar case retrieved can be utilized as an independent evidence to update the prior probabilities according the Bayes theorem. We apply the evidences (retrieved cases) in a sequential manner such that the probability of state s_i is updated as follows:

$$P(s_i \mid C_1) = \frac{P(s_i) \cdot P(C_1 \mid s_i)}{\sum_{k=1}^{n} P(C_1 \mid s_k) P(s_k)} \tag{4}$$

$$P(s_i \mid C_1, C_2) = \frac{P(s_i \mid C_1) \cdot P(C_2 \mid s_i)}{\sum_{k=1}^{n} P(C_2 \mid s_k) P(s_k \mid C_1)} \tag{5}$$

$$\cdots\cdots\cdots\cdots\cdots\cdots\cdots\cdots\cdots\cdots$$

$$P(s_i \mid C_1, C_2, \cdots, C_{Nr}) = \frac{P(s_i \mid C_1, C_2, \cdots, C_{Nr-1}) \cdot P(C_{Nr} \mid s_i)}{\sum_{k=1}^{n} P(C_{Nr} \mid s_k) P(s_k \mid C_1, C_2, \cdots, C_{Nr-1})} \tag{6}$$

The probability updated in Eq. (4) represents the probability for state s_i given similar case C_1, which is further updated in Eq. (5) by the second similar case C_2. Generally, the probability $P(s_i \mid C_1, C_2, \cdots, C_t)$ is yielded by updating the prior probability $P(s_i \mid C_1, C_2, \cdots, C_{t-1})$ with the additional evidence C_t. Finally we obtain the ultimate probability assessment incorporating all the similar cases by Eq. (6).

It can be seen from Eqs. (4-6) that the values of conditional probabilities $P(C_j|s_i)$ are needed for all retrieved cases C_j ($j=1\ldots Nr$) to refine probabilities of states. To this end, we apply the Bayes theorem and transform the probability $P(C_j|s_i)$ to the following form:

$$P(C_j \mid s_i) = \frac{P(C_j) \cdot P(s_i \mid C_j)}{\sum_{C_k \in CL} P(s_i \mid C_k) \cdot P(C_k)} \tag{7}$$

where *CL* refers to the case library. Since we assume all cases in the case library are equally probable, Eq. (7) is simplified to

$$P(C_j \mid s_i) = \frac{P(s_i \mid C_j)}{\sum_{C_k \in CL} P(s_i \mid C_k)} = \frac{P_j(s_i)}{\sum_{\forall k} P_k(s_i)} \tag{8}$$

At this point it becomes easy to calculate the probability $P(C_j|s_i)$ by using probabilistic information stored in individual cases in the case library, which further enables updating state probabilities in terms of Eqs. from (4) to (6).

2.2. Derivation of general utilities of actions given states

The basic idea is to derive the general utility of performing one action under a given state by using information from the case library. However, owing to the fact that no exact information is known about states in cases, case specific utilities recorded can not provide direct answers to our inquiries. As an alternative, we here attempt to estimate this utility with an expected value by considering all those cases in which the underlying action was performed. By *Sub*(*a*) we denote a subset of cases in the case library in which the action *a* was performed. Then the expected value of the general utility of performing action *a* given state s_i can be given by:

$$U(a \mid s_i) = \sum_{C_t \in Sub(a)} U(a \mid C_t) \cdot P_a(C_t \mid s_i) \tag{9}$$

As $U(a|C_t)$ represents the known utility recorded in case C_t, what remains to resolve is the probability $P_a(C_t|s_i)$. By employing the Bayes theorem, this probability is reformulated as

$$P_a(C_t \mid s_i) = \frac{P_a(C_t) \cdot P(s_i \mid C_t)}{\sum\limits_{C_k \in Sub(a)} P_a(C_k) \cdot P(s_i \mid C_k)} \tag{10}$$

Considering that cases in the subset $Sub(a)$ are equally probable, Eq. (10) is reduced to

$$P_a(C_t \mid s_i) = \frac{P(s_i \mid C_t)}{\sum\limits_{C_k \in Sub(a)} P(s_i \mid C_k)} \tag{11}$$

Since $P(s_i|C_k)$ is available as the probability of state s_i in case C_k, we easily resolve Eq. (11), leading to acquirement of expected value of the general utility according to Eq. (9). This expected value then enters the decision tree as estimation of the (general) utility of action a given state s_i.

3. Decision Analysis Using Case-Based Decision Model

Once a decision model is constructed from cases, it can be applied to analyse and evaluate alternative actions in the current situation, taking into account both likelihoods and probable consequences. We introduce here a well established principle for doing such analysis of decisions. Further this basic principle can be extended for circumstances with fuzzy or imprecise utility values in specific cases, yet this issue will not be discussed in the paper due to the size limitation.

With complete information in the decision tree derived, we can now compute the expected utility of the various alternative actions. The expected utility of action a_j is defined as

$$EU(a_j) = P(s_1) \cdot U(a_j \mid s_1) + P(s_2) \cdot U(a_j \mid s_2) + \cdots + P(s_n) \cdot U(a_j \mid s_n) \tag{12}$$

where $P(s_i)$ and $U(a_j|s_i)$ represent the probabilities and (general) utility values derived from the retrieved cases and the case library respectively. Then a choice should be made among the alternatives according to the principle of maximizing the expected utility [1], which is formulated as follows:

The principle of maximizing expected utility (MEU): In a given decision situation the deciding agent should prefer the alternative with maximal expected utility. That means that alternative a_1 is preferred to a_2 if and only if $EU(a_1) > EU(a_2)$.

The expected utility of an action approximates the mean utility score that will be obtained if an agent meets the situation many times and chooses and conducts the same action constantly. In view of this, the significance of the MEU principle is to optimize the long term performance of decision making under uncertainty.

The merit of doing decision analysis after CBR can be illustrated with an example in the following. Assume that, given a target situation, two cases C_1 and C_2 are retrieved from the case base and they have actions a_1 and a_2 respectively. Both cases are assigned with good utility values as evaluations of their outcomes, but case C_1 is more similar to the target situation. Then, according to CBR alone, action a_1 associated with case C_1 will be judged more suitable as solution to the new situation. Nevertheless, if we further consider more information in the decision tree, we might change our preference after decision analysis. For instance, suppose that the state probabilities and utilities of actions under possible states (s_1 and s_2) are derived from previous cases as follows:

$$P(s_1 \mid C_1, C_2) = 0.6 \qquad U(a_1 \mid s_1) = 70 \qquad U(a_2 \mid s_1) = 40$$
$$P(s_2 \mid C_1, C_2) = 0.4 \qquad U(a_1 \mid s_2) = -90 \qquad U(a_2 \mid s_2) = 60$$

The expected utilities of a_1 and a_2 are $EU(a_1)$=6 and $EU(a_2)$=48 respectively in the current situation. Hence we will prefer action a_2 according to the MEU principle. We believe that a_2 is a more rational choice considering the high risk of action a_1 under state s_2. This rational choice is achieved by taking advantage of the case-based decision tree which accommodates more information than case similarity alone.

4. Conclusion

This paper presents a new framework for performing case-based decision analysis. We claim that case-based reasoning and decision theory can complement each other in a coherent, hybrid system. The contribution of case-based reasoning lies in the creation of a situation dependent decision model. This is achieved by deriving states probabilities and general utility estimates from the subset of retrieved cases and the case library. It follows that more accurate and objective data will be available in the decision model, promoting more reliable results of decision analysis. On the other hand, decision theory helps case-based reasoning with better evaluations of candidate solutions by considering all probable consequences, risks, and likelihoods rather than similarity of cases alone. This provides agents with more complete awareness of the situation and environment for making predictive, secured and rational choices.

References

[1]   P. Gärdenfors, and N. E. Sahlin, Introduction: Bayesian decision theory – Foundations and problems, in: *Decision, Probability, and Utility*, Cambridge University Press, 1997, 1-15.

[2]   H. Raiffa, *Decision Analysis: Introductory Readings on Choices under Uncertainty*, McGraw Hill, 1997.

[3]   A. Aamodt, and E. Plaza, Case-based reasoning: Foundational issues, methodological variations, and system approaches, Artificial Intelligence Com. **7** (1994), 39-59.

[4]   C. Tsatsoulis, Q. Cheng, and H.-Y. Wei, Integrating case-Based reasoning and decision theory, IEEE Expert: Intelligent Systems and Their Applications **12** (1997), 46-55.

[5]   H. Langseth, A. Aamodt, and O. Winnem, Learning retrieval knowledge from data, in: Proceedings of the Workshop ML-5 of the International Joint Conference on Artificial Intelligence, 1999, 77-82.

[6]   N. Xiong, and P. Funk, Learning similarity metric reflecting utility in case-based reasoning, Journal of Intelligent and Fuzzy Systems **17** (2006), 407-416.

[7]   L. Ekenberg, M. Boman, and J. Linneroth-Bayer, General risk constraints, Journal of Risk Research **4** (2001), 31-47.

[8]   Z. Shapira, Risk Taking: A managerial perspective, Russel Sage Foundation, 1995.

[9]   D. Wettschereck, and D. Aha, Weighting features, in: Proceedings of the 1st International Conference on Case-based Reasoning, 1995, 347-358.

[10] R. Kohavi, P. Langley, and Y. Yun, The utility of feature weighting in nearest neighbor algorithms, in: Proceedings of The European Conference on Machine Learning (ECML-97), 1997.

2. Poster Presentations

Tenth Scandinavian Conference on Artificial Intelligence
A. Holst et al. (Eds.)
IOS Press, 2008

Bayesian Inference Under Probability Constraints

Anna Pernestål[1] and Mattias Nyberg
Scania CV AB, Södertälje, Sweden
and
Dept. of Electrical Engineering, Linköping University, Sweden

Abstract. Inspired by the problem of fault isolation we consider Bayesian inference from training data and background knowledge. We discuss how the background knowledge can be translated to equality constraints and show how it is introduced in the computations. The main advantage of combining data and background knowledge is achieved when the amount of data is limited.

Keywords. Bayesian Inference, Background Knowledge, Probability

1. Introduction

We consider fault isolation, i.e. the problem of determining if there are any faults present in a process and if so, determine which. The fault isolation problem can be considered as a classification problem where the class (or fault) is to be determined. We apply Bayesian inference to compute the probability of a class variable C, given an observation vector $\mathbf{X}$, training data $\mathcal{D}$, and background knowledge $\mathbf{I}$,

$$p(C = c_i | \mathbf{X} = \mathbf{x}_k, \mathcal{D}, \mathbf{I}). \tag{1}$$

Bayesian inference from training data only has been frequently studied in the literature, see e.g. [1,3,4,6,9,10,11,12]. However, inspired by the fault isolation application, we note that there is also background knowledge available. For example, it may be known that one element in the observation vector is equally distributed under different values of the class variable. If there is a lot of data available, such relations are hopefully learned from training data. However, in many practical applications, and indeed in the fault isolation problem, there is only a limited amount of data available. The background knowledge must therefore be handled explicitly.

In the current work we show how inference can be improved by combining background knowledge and training data. We study a general type of background knowledge that appears in many applications as constraints on the underlying probability distributions [8,9]. This kind of background knowledge is previously studied in [8], with focus on parameter learning. Here we focus on inference, and we show how the background knowledge can be expressed as equality constraints in the computations.

2. Preliminaries

Before going into the computational details, we introduce the notation used, and present a previous result on inference based on training data only. Let C be a scalar class variable

---

[1]Corresponding Author. Email: annap@isy.liu.se

with domain $\mathbb{C} = \{c_1, \ldots, c_L\}$. The variable C describes the status of the system we are studying, and a value c_i is referred to as a *class*. Generally, we will use the convention that random variables are denoted by capital letters, and their values with lower case letters. The observations from the system is described by an observation vector $\mathbf{X} = (X_1, \ldots, X_R)$. Element X_l in the observation vector has domain $\mathbb{X}_l = \{x_{l1}, \ldots, x_{lK_l}\}$. Consequently, the observation vector $\mathbf{X}$ has domain $\mathbb{X} = \mathbb{X}_1 \times \mathbb{X}_2 \times \ldots \times \mathbb{X}_R$. To denote an assignment of the observation vector we write $\mathbf{X} = \mathbf{x}_k$, $k = 1, \ldots, K$, where $K = \prod_{l=1}^{R} K_l$. Each value $\mathbf{x}_k$ is a vector, and we write $\mathbf{x}_k = (\mathbf{x}_k[1], \ldots, \mathbf{x}_k[R])$ to denote the elements explicitly. With this notation $\mathbf{x}_k[i]$ is the value of X_i, when $\mathbf{X} = \mathbf{x}_k$.

Furthermore, there is training data available. Training data consists of N simultaneous values of the class variable C and the observation vector $\mathbf{X}$. A realization of training data is denoted $\mathcal{D}$. The underlying system is assumed to be such that samples in training data are independent. In practice this means that there is no memory in the underlying system, and it is valid (at least approximately) in most systems we want to inference about. For a detailed discussion on the meaning of the independence assumption, see [10].

To denote discrete probability distributions we use $p(Y = y|\mathbf{I})$, and for continuous probability density functions we use the notation $f(y|\mathbf{I})$. Here, $\mathbf{I}$ denotes the background information. In this work we have adopted the view of probability as described for example in [5,12], where the probability is uniquely determined by the information given behind the |-sign.

To formalize the problem, we start by rewriting (1) as

$$p(C = c_i|\mathbf{X} = \mathbf{x}_k, \mathbf{I}) = \frac{p(C = c_i, \mathbf{X} = \mathbf{x}_k|\mathcal{D}, \mathbf{I})}{p(\mathbf{X} = \mathbf{x}_k|\mathcal{D}, \mathbf{I})}. \tag{2}$$

The denominator is independent of C and is thus a constant for a given value of the observation vector. Thus it is sufficient to study the joint probability of C and $\mathbf{X}$. Inspired by this, we introduce a variable $\mathbf{Z} = (C, \mathbf{X})$ with values $\mathbf{z}_{ik} = (c_i, \mathbf{x}_k)$. The domain of $\mathbf{Z}$ is $\mathbb{Z} = \mathbb{X} \times \mathbb{C}$, and $\mathbf{z}_{ik}$ can take $M = RL$ different values. Often it is more convenient to enumerate the values of $\mathbf{Z}$ as $\mathbf{z}_1, \ldots, \mathbf{z}_M$. There is a unique transformation from the double subscript $\mathbf{z}_{ik}$ to the single subscript $\mathbf{z}_q$. However, the exact representation of this transformation is not important and will not be discussed in detail. We now summarize previous results on the computations of $p(\mathbf{Z} = \mathbf{z}_i|\mathcal{D}, \mathbf{I})$ using training data only. The computations are given in detail in for example [4,10].

Theorem 1
Let $\mathbf{Z}$ be a discrete variable with M possible values. Introduce parameters $\boldsymbol{\Theta} = (\Theta_1, \ldots, \Theta_M)^T$ with values $\theta = (\theta_1, \ldots, \theta_M)^T$ such that

$$p(\mathbf{Z} = \mathbf{z}_q|\boldsymbol{\Theta} = \theta, \mathbf{I}) = \theta_q, \quad q = 1, \ldots, M, \quad \theta_q > 0, \quad \sum_{q=1}^{M} \theta_q = 1. \tag{3}$$

Assume that $\boldsymbol{\Theta}$ is Dirichlet distributed with parameters $\alpha = (\alpha_1, \ldots, \alpha_M)$. Furhtermore, assume that there is a (possibly empty) set $\mathcal{D}$ of previous samples of $\mathbf{Z}$, and that the samples in the training data are independent. Let n_q be the count of samples in $\mathcal{D}$ where $\mathbf{Z} = \mathbf{z}_q$, and let $N = \sum_{q=1}^{M} n_q$ and $A = \sum_{q=1}^{M} \alpha_q$. Then it holds that

$$p(\mathbf{Z} = \mathbf{z}_q|\mathcal{D}, \mathbf{I}) = \frac{n_q + \alpha_q}{N + A}. \tag{4}$$

3. Problem Formulation

We will now extend the results in the previous section to also take background knowledge into account. We consider constraints on the parameters Θ defined by (3) of the form

$$E\Theta = F, \tag{5}$$

where $E \in \mathbb{R}^{l \times M}$, $F \in \mathbb{R}^l$, and l is the number of constraints. Constraints of the type (5) are very general, and several types of background knowledge can be represented in this form. Before going into the computations, let us see how the constraints may appear.

The following example from fault isolation can be found in [9]. The task is to draw conclusions about which faults that are present in a system, i.e. which class c_i that is present, given the current observations $\mathbf{X}$. For the isolation there is training data available. However, there is only training data available for some of the faults but not from all. Additionally, it is known that the fault F_1 does not affect observation X_3. This means that X_3 is equally distributed under fault F_1 and the fault free case. Different problems that lead to similar constraints can be found in e.g. [2,8].

Formally, knowledge of the type expressed in the isolation example can be written

$$p(X_i = x_{ik}|C = c_j, \Theta = \theta, \mathbf{I}_{\mathcal{E}}) = p(X_i = x_{ik}|C = c_l, \Theta = \theta, \mathbf{I}_{\mathcal{E}}), \tag{6}$$

where we have used $\mathbf{I}_{\mathcal{E}}$ to denote explicitly that constraint information of the type (5) is given by the background knowledge. If the constraints (6) holds for *all* values of Xe_i and C, the expression means that X_i and C are independent. However, the constraints considered here are more general and allow the variables to be independent only for some values of C. The prior probabilities for the classes are assumed to be given, and let $p(C = c_j|\mathbf{I}_{\mathcal{E}}) = \rho_{jl}p(C = c_l|\mathbf{I}_{\mathcal{E}})$. By applying the product rule of probabilities we can then write (6) as

$$p(C = c_j, X_i = x_{ik}|\Theta = \theta, \mathbf{I}_{\mathcal{E}}) = \rho_{jl}p(C = c_l, X_i = x_{ik}|\Theta = \theta, \mathbf{I}_{\mathcal{E}}). \tag{7}$$

To relate the distributions in (7) to the distribution of $\mathbf{Z}$, we marginalize over all possible values of the elements in $\mathbf{X}$ except X_i. Let $\mathbf{X}_{-i} = (X_1, \ldots, X_{i-1}, X_{i+1}, \ldots, X_R)$, and let $\mathbb{X}_{-i}$ be the domain of $\mathbf{X}_{-i}$. Then we can write

$$p(C = c_j, X_i = x_{ik}|\Theta = \theta, \mathbf{I}_{\mathcal{E}}) =$$

$$= \sum_{\mathbf{x}_{-i} \in \mathbb{X}_{-i}} p(C = c_j, X_i = x_{ik}, \mathbf{X}_{-i} = \mathbf{x}_{-i}|\Theta = \theta, \mathbf{I}_{\mathcal{E}}) =$$

$$= \sum_{\mathbf{z}_q \in \mathbb{Z}_{x_{ik},c_j}} p(\mathbf{Z} = \mathbf{z}_q|\Theta = \theta, \mathbf{I}_{\mathcal{E}}) = \sum_{\mathbf{z}_q \in \mathbb{Z}_{x_{ik},c_j}} \theta_q \tag{8}$$

where $\mathbb{Z}_{x_{ik},c_j} = \{\mathbf{z}_q \in \mathbb{Z} : \mathbf{z}_q = (\mathbf{x}_m, c_j), \mathbf{x}_m[i] = x_{ik}\}$, i.e. the set of all possible values of $\mathbf{Z}$ where $X_i = x_{ik}$ and $C = c_j$, regardless of the values of the other elements in the observation vector. By using (8) we can write the requirement (7) in the form

$$\sum_{\mathbf{z}_q \in \mathbb{Z}_{\mathbf{x}_{ik},c_j}} \theta_q = \rho_{jl} \sum_{\mathbf{z}_q \in \mathbb{Z}_{\mathbf{x}_{ik},c_l}} \theta_q. \tag{9}$$

Constraints of the form (9) can easily be transformed to the form (5). Note that (3) requires that one row in E consists of ones only, and that the corresponding row in F is also a one.

We illustrate the reasoning with the following example.

Example 1 *Consider the case with two classes, $C \in \{c_1, c_2\}$, and a one-dimensional observation $\mathbf{X} \in \{\mathbf{x}_1, \mathbf{x}_2\}$. Define $\theta = (\theta_1, \theta_2, \theta_3, \theta_4)$ by*

$$p(\mathbf{X} = \mathbf{x}_1, C = c_1 | \mathbf{\Theta} = \theta, \mathbf{I}) = \theta_1, \; p(\mathbf{X} = \mathbf{x}_1, C = c_2 | \mathbf{\Theta} = \theta, \mathbf{I}) = \theta_2,$$

$$p(\mathbf{X} = \mathbf{x}_2, C = c_1 | \mathbf{\Theta} = \theta, \mathbf{I}) = \theta_3, \; p(\mathbf{X} = \mathbf{x}_2, C = c_2 | \mathbf{\Theta} = \theta, \mathbf{I}) = \theta_4.$$

Assume that we have the background knowledge that $p(\mathbf{X} = \mathbf{x}_k, C = c_1 | \mathbf{I}_\mathcal{E}) = p(\mathbf{X} = \mathbf{x}_k, C = c_2 | \mathbf{I}_\mathcal{E})$, $k = 1, 2$ is given. Expressed in terms of the parameters this means that $\theta_1 = \rho_{12}\theta_2$ and $\theta_3 = \rho_{12}\theta_4$. With $\rho_{12} = 1$, the matrices in (5) becomes

$$E = \begin{bmatrix} 0 & 0 & -1 & 1 \\ 1 & -1 & 0 & 0 \\ 1 & 1 & 1 & 1 \end{bmatrix}, \quad F = \begin{bmatrix} 0 \\ 0 \\ 1 \end{bmatrix}. \tag{10}$$

4. Inference Under Constraints

In this section we derive expressions for computing the probability distribution of $\mathbf{Z}$ given both data and constraints of the type (5). We conclude the section by presenting a method for performing the computations systematically by variable substitution.

4.1. Computing the Probability Distribution of $\mathbf{Z}$ under constraints

To compute the probability of $\mathbf{Z}$ given data and constraints, begin with marginalizing over the set Δ of parameters that fulfill (3). This gives

$$p(\mathbf{Z} = \mathbf{z}_q | \mathcal{D}, \mathbf{I}_\mathcal{E}) = \int_\Delta p(\mathbf{Z} = \mathbf{z}_q | \mathbf{\Theta} = \theta, \mathcal{D}, \mathbf{I}_\mathcal{E}) f(\theta | \mathcal{D}, \mathbf{I}_\mathcal{E}) d\theta. \tag{11}$$

For the first factor under the integral (11) we note that when the parameters $\mathbf{\Theta}$ are known, then $\mathbf{Z}$ is independent of $\mathcal{D}$ (for details, see [10]). We have $p(\mathbf{Z} = \mathbf{z}_q | \mathbf{\Theta} = \theta, \mathcal{D}, \mathbf{I}_\mathcal{E}) = p(\mathbf{Z} = \mathbf{z}_q | \mathbf{\Theta} = \theta, \mathbf{I}_\mathcal{E})$, which is given by (3). To determine the second factor in the integral (11), apply Bayes' theorem to obtain

$$f(\theta | \mathcal{D}, \mathbf{I}_\mathcal{E}) = \frac{p(\mathcal{D} | \mathbf{\Theta} = \theta, \mathbf{I}_\mathcal{E}) f(\theta | \mathbf{I}_\mathcal{E})}{\int_\Delta p(\mathcal{D} | \mathbf{\Theta} = \theta, \mathbf{I}_\mathcal{E}) f(\theta | \mathbf{I}_\mathcal{E}) d\mathbf{\Theta}}. \tag{12}$$

The factor $p(\mathcal{D} | \mathbf{\Theta} = \theta, \mathbf{I}_\mathcal{E})$ in (12) is computed by using (3) and the assumption that samples in training data are independent. This gives

$$p(\mathcal{D} | \mathbf{\Theta} = \theta, \mathbf{I}_\mathcal{E}) = \prod_{i=1}^{N} p(d_i | \mathbf{\Theta} = \theta, \mathbf{I}_\mathcal{E}) = \theta_1^{n_1} \ldots \theta_M^{n_M}, \tag{13}$$

where n_q is the number of samples in training data where $\mathbf{Z} = \mathbf{z}_q$ and $\sum_{q=1}^{M} n_q = N$.

To determine the factor $f(\theta|\mathbf{I}_\mathcal{E})$ in (12), we need to investigate the background knowledge $\mathbf{I}_\mathcal{E}$. It consists of two parts, $\mathbf{I}_\mathcal{E} = \{\mathbf{I}, \text{``}E\theta = F\text{''}\}$. The first part, $\mathbf{I}$, includes basic background knowledge, stating that the probability is parameterized by parameters θ according to (3), that θ is Dirichlet distributed, and knowledge about the prior probabilities for the classes. The second part is the statement that the parameters θ satisfies (5) as well as the values of E and F.

For continuous variables u, v we have that $f(u, v|U = V) = \rho_0 f(u, v)\delta(u - v)$, where f is the appropriate density function, ρ_0 is a normalization constant which guarantees that the density integrates to one, and δ is the Dirac delta distribution. Thus we have $f(\theta|\mathbf{I}_\mathcal{E}) = f(\theta|E\mathbf{\Theta} = F, \mathbf{I}) = \rho_0 f(\theta|\mathbf{I})\delta(E\theta - F)$, where $f(\theta|\mathbf{I})$ is Dirichlet distributed. By using (3), (12), and (13), Equation (11) now becomes

$$p(\mathbf{Z} = \mathbf{z}_q|\mathcal{D}, \mathbf{I}_\mathcal{E}) = \frac{\int_\Delta \theta_1^{n_1+\alpha_1-1} \ldots \theta_q^{n_q+\alpha_q} \ldots \theta_M^{n_M+\alpha_M-1}\delta(E\theta - F)d\theta}{\int_\Delta \theta_1^{n_1+\alpha_1-1} \ldots \theta_q^{n_q+\alpha_q-1} \ldots \theta_M^{n_M+\alpha_M-1}\delta(E\theta - F)d\theta}. \quad (14)$$

Equation (14) gives an expression for the probability that we search. We now present a systematic way of solving the integrals by using variable substitution.

4.2. A Solution Method Based on Variable Substitution

To solve the integral (14) we change variables from $\mathbf{\Theta}$ to $\mathbf{\Phi} = (\mathbf{\Phi}_1, \ldots, \mathbf{\Phi}_M)$, such that each of the new variables $\mathbf{\Phi}_i$ appears *either* inside the delta function, or outside it. We can then integrate over the delta function separately. Let $\mathbf{\Phi}_{1:M-l}$ be the $M - l$ variables outside the delta function, and $\mathbf{\Phi}_{M-l+1:M}$ be the l variables inside it.

We begin with finding a suitable transformation for variables $\mathbf{\Phi}_{1:M-l}$. First, note that the matrix E has always full row rank, otherwise there are constraints with the same meaning and one of them can be discarded. Without loss of generality we can assume that first l columns of E forms a full rank matrix E_l[2]. We can the write

$$E\mathbf{\Theta} = F \iff \begin{bmatrix} E_l & E_{M-l} \end{bmatrix} \mathbf{\Theta} = F \iff \theta_{1:l} + E_l^{-1}E_{M-l}\mathbf{\Theta}_{l+1:M} = F_l^{-1}F. \quad (15)$$

Augmenting $\mathbf{\Theta}_{1:l}$ in (15) with $\mathbf{\Theta}_{l+1:M}$, and setting $\mathbf{\Phi}_{1:M-l} = \mathbf{\Theta}_{l+1:M}$ gives

$$\begin{bmatrix} \theta_{1:l} \\ \theta_{l+1:M} \end{bmatrix} = \underbrace{\begin{bmatrix} -E_l^{-1}E_{M-l} \\ I \end{bmatrix}}_{Q} \phi_{1:M-l} + \underbrace{\begin{bmatrix} E_l^{-1}F \\ 0 \end{bmatrix}}_{G} \quad (16)$$

To express $\mathbf{\Phi}_{1:M-l}$ in terms of $\mathbf{\Theta}$ we multiply (16) by the left inverse Q^{-L} of Q, which gives

$$\mathbf{\Theta} = Q\mathbf{\Phi}_{1:M-l} + G \iff \mathbf{\Phi}_{1:M-l} = Q^{-L}\mathbf{\Theta} - Q^{-L}G. \quad (17)$$

For the remaining variables $\phi_{m-l+1:m}$ that will appear inside the delta function we choose $\mathbf{\Phi}_{M-l+1:M} = E\mathbf{\Theta} - F$. From (17) we now obtain the complete variable transformation, which is given by

$$\phi = \underbrace{\begin{bmatrix} Q^{-L} \\ E \end{bmatrix}}_{A} \theta + \underbrace{\begin{bmatrix} -Q^{-L}G \\ -F \end{bmatrix}}_{B}.$$

---

[2]Otherwise we can always find a permutation matrix that converts E such that E_l has full rank.

We can now compute the integrals in (14) by changing to the variables $\mathbf{\Phi}$. Let $D_{i.}$ denote the ith row in matrix D. Then we have

$$\int_\Delta \theta_1^{k_1} \dots \theta_M^{k_M} \delta(E\theta - F)d\theta =$$

$$|A|^{-1} \int_{\Delta_{\phi_{1:M-l}}} (Q_{1.}\phi_{1:M-l} + G_{1.})^{k_1} \dots (Q_{M-l.}\phi_{1:M-l} + G_{M-l.})^{k_M} d\phi_{1:M-l}, \quad (18)$$

where $\Delta_{\phi_{1:M-l}}$ is the area of integration in terms of the variables ϕ, and $k_i = n_i + \alpha_i - 1$ or $k_i = n_i + \alpha_i$. To investigate the computations in detail, return to Example 1. For this case the integral (18) becomes

$$\int_0^{0.5} (0.5 - \phi_1)^{k_1} (0.5 - \phi_1)^{k_2} \phi_1^{k_3} \phi_1^{k_4} d\phi_1 = \frac{1}{2^{1+\sum_i k_i}} \frac{\Gamma(k_1 + k_2 + 1)\Gamma(k_3 + k_4 + 1)}{\Gamma(2 + \sum_i k_i)},$$

Although an analytical solution was easily found in our example, this is generally not the case. To the authors knowledge, there is no closed form solution to the integral in general. One possibility is to use Laplace approximation [7], where the integrand is approximated by an unnormalized Gaussian density function.

5. Conclusions

We have shown explicitly how Bayesian inference can be made from data and background knowledge in terms of constraints on the underlying probability distributions. The constraints mean that mean that variables may be dependent under some of their values but not for all, and we have discussed how they may arise in practical problems.

References

[1] Luc Devroye, Laszlo Györfi, and Gabor Lugosi. *A Probabilistic Theory of Pattern Recognition.* Springer, New York, 1996.

[2] Adom Giffin. Updating Probabilities: An Econometric Example. In *Lecture Notes in Economics and Mathematical Systems.* Springer-Verlag, 2007.

[3] Peter Grünwald. *The Minimum Description Length Principle.* MIT Press, 2007.

[4] David Heckerman, Dan Geiger, and David M. Chickering. Learning Bayesian Networks: The Combination of Knowledge and Statistical Data. *Machine Learning*, 20(3):197–243, 1995.

[5] Edwin. T. Jaynes. *Probability Theory - the Logic of Science.* Camebridge University Press, Cambridge, 2001.

[6] Petri Kontkanen, Petri Myllymaki, Tomi Silander, Henri Tirri, and Peter Grünwald. Comparing predictive inference methods for discrete domains. In *Proceedings of the Sixth International Workshop on Artificial Intelligence and Statistics, Ft. Lauderdale, Florida.*, pages 311–318, 1997.

[7] David J. C. MacKay. *Information Theory, Inference and Learning Algorithms.* Cambridge University Press, 2005.

[8] Radu Stefan Niculescu, Tom Mitchell, and R. Bharat Rao. Bayesian Network Learning with Parameter Constraints. *Journal of Machine Learning Research*, pages 1357–1383, 2006.

[9] Anna Pernestål. *A Bayesian Approach to Fault Isolation with Application To Diesel Engine Diagnosis.* Lic. Thesis, Royal Institute of Technology, Stockholm, Sweden, February 2007.

[10] Anna Pernestål and Mattias Nyberg. Bayesian Fault Isolation Based on Data and Prior Knowledge Applied to Engine Diagnosis. Submitted to *IEEE Transactions on Systems, Man, and Cybernetics, Part A*, 2008.

[11] Teemuu Roos, Hannes Wettig, Peter Grünwald, Petri Myllymäki, and Henry Tirri. On Discriminative Bayesian Network Classifiers and Logistic Regression. *Machine Learning*, pages 267–296, 2005.

[12] Devinder. S. Sivia. *Data Analysis: A Bayesian Tutorial.* Oxford University Press, 1996.

Tenth Scandinavian Conference on Artificial Intelligence
A. Holst et al. (Eds.)
IOS Press, 2008

Acting under Interference by other Agents with unknown Goals

NICOLAJ SØNDBERG-JEPPESEN and FINN VERNER JENSEN

Department of Computer Science, Aalborg University, Denmark

Abstract. We consider the situation where two agents try to solve each their own task in a common environment. A general framework for representing that kind of scenario is presented. The framework is used to model the analysis depth of the opponent agent and to determine an optimal policy under various assumptions on analysis depth of the opponent. The framework is applied on a strategic game, Ausgetrickst, and experiments are reported.

Keywords. Agents, Dynamic Influence Diagrams, Reasoning in Games

1. Introduction

Consider a partially observable environment where 2 agents try to solve each their task. The agents do not reveal their task to each other, and they do not communicate. To solve a task takes a number of changes to the environment and the agents take turns in performing such changes. An agent may plan how to solve her task. However, each time she performs a change, the other agent, in his effort to solve his task, may interfere with her plan, and the situation seen from the first agent's point of view may be worse than it was in the first place.

The classical solution to this kind of scenarios has been to search for Nash-equilibrium strategies [1]. However, in real-life strategic situations, Nash-equilibria may not be a proper solution. In case the agents do not act according to a Nash-equilibrium you will be better off deviating as well.

To solve this problem we will instead build models which make it possible to include assumptions about the other agents' model and depth of analysis. That is, if the agent is assumed to follow a simple strategy, then we shall be able to determine an optimal strategy based on this assumption.

In related work Carmel and Markovitch [2] propose the M^* algorithm which builds on assumptions about the opponents' models. M^* returns the optimal strategy when it is given the agent's analysis depth d, her own evaluation function f_d together with $f_{d-1}, f_{d-2}, \ldots f_0$, the evaluation functions she assumes to be used on each level. When $d = 0$, M^* simulates Min-Max using f_0 and $-f_0$ as evaluation functions of the agent and her opponent respectively, and when $d > 0$, M^* simulates the opponent with $d - 1$ and f_{d-1}. One disadvantage of this approach is that the agent is rarely certain about the opponent's evaluation function and the evaluation functions assumed to be used at each level. Also, M^* works only in deterministic environments.

We propose to use a different approach for solving this kind of problems which models the opponent's analysis depth and allows uncertainty in the opponent's evaluation functions by representing his possible tasks as a random variable. Also as modeling technique we will be using Dynamic Influence Diagrams. As an example of an environment we use the game Ausgetrickst[1].

2. Design of a General Framework

We consider the following scenario: n agents take actions in turn in a finite world W with states $w_1, \ldots, w_m$. An action a is an attempt of changing the state of W. The impact of a is a deterministic or probabilistic function of a and the current state of W. The state of W is always known by all agents. Each agent has an assignment, which is not known by the other agents. The assignment is fulfilled when certain states of W are achieved. (You may think of W as a board with pieces, which may be moved according to some rules – perhaps after a roll of dices). The crucial point is that other agents' decisions interfere with the agent's plans. In this paper we focus on scenarios with only two agents, $\mathcal{A}$ and $\mathcal{B}$. We assume $\mathcal{A}$ to be female and $\mathcal{B}$ to be male. We shall refer to the scenario as *covert interference*(CI)

First we shall follow the traditions of probabilistic graphical models to establish a graphical representation of CI.

2.1. Background

We shall use the classical paradigms from probabilistic graphical models (PGMs) [3, 4]. A graphical model is a directed acyclic graph with three types of nodes, *chance nodes* (circular nodes), *decision nodes* (rectangular nodes), and *utility nodes* (diamond shaped nodes). A directed link into chance node reflects (causal) impact, which may be of non-deterministic character; a link into a decision node represents information. That is, if C is a parent of the decision node D then the state of C is known by the decision maker when D is to be decided.

The quantitative part of a PGM consists of utility functions and conditional probabilities. For a utility node U with parents $pa(U)$ we specify the utility as a function of $pa(U)$. For a chance node C with parents $pa(C)$ we specify $P(C|pa(C))$, the conditional probability of C given $pa(C)$.

A *solution* to an influence diagram is an *optimal strategy*. A strategy consists of a set of *policies*, one for each decision node. A policy for a decision node is a function which, given the known past, provides a decision. A strategy is *optimal* if it maximizes the decision maker's expected utility.

There are standard algorithms for solving influence diagrams, and systems for specifying and solving influence diagrams are commercially available. We shall in this paper take these algorithms for granted.

The framework of influence diagrams has been extended in various ways. In particular, Koller and Milch (2003) introduced *multi-agent influence diagrams* (MAIDs) [5], where the various acting agents are given decision and utility nodes of particular colors (or shadings).

---

[1]Ausgetrickst is German and means something like "outsmarted".

2.2. Graphical representation of CI

We adapt the framework of MAIDs to CI. This is illustrated in Figure 1. In Figure 1 player $\mathcal{A}$'s nodes are lightly shaded, and $\mathcal{B}$'s nodes are darkly shaded.

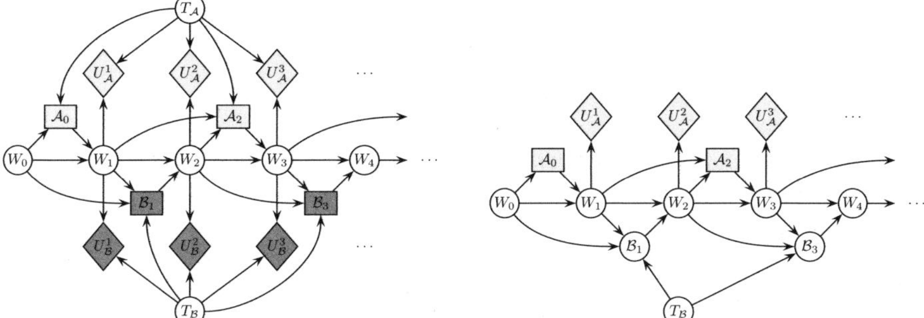

Figure 1. A graphical representation of CI.

Figure 2. Player $\mathcal{A}$ takes player $\mathcal{B}$'s next move into consideration.

The nodes $W_0, W_1, \ldots$ represent the world state, the chance nodes $T_{\mathcal{A}}$ and $T_{\mathcal{B}}$ represent the players' assignments, the nodes with $\mathcal{A}$-labels represent the moves by player $\mathcal{A}$. The links from a W-node and a T-node to a U-node indicate that the utility is a function of the world state and the assignment only. Each player has a utility for each move. The links from the $T_{\mathcal{A}}$-node to decision nodes represent that player $\mathcal{A}$ knows his assignment. The links from W-nodes to decision nodes represent that the state of the world is always known. The dots at the right of the graph indicate that there is no time limit specified.

The game starts in W_0, and $\mathcal{A}$ makes her first move knowing her assignment and the initial world state. For notational convenience we index $\mathcal{A}$'s decisions with even numbers and $\mathcal{B}$'s decisions with odd numbers. $\mathcal{A}$'s first move leads to a new state W_1, and player $\mathcal{B}$ now takes his first move knowing the initial state and the state after $\mathcal{A}$'s move. Note that in this model we assume that the two players' utilities are independent.

If there is a pre-specified finite time horizon for the game, the game can in principle be solved through dynamic programming similar to the methods for solving influence diagrams [6, 7]: compute iteratively a policy for each decision starting with the last decision (whether it be $\mathcal{A}$'s or $\mathcal{B}$'s).

2.3. The game seen in the eyes of $\mathcal{A}$

Solving CI as indicated above has several disadvantages. First of all, the game needs not be very complex before the solution is intractable. After some moves, the domains for the policies are way too large. Secondly, if there is no finite time horizon, this method does not work, and methods from POMDPs [8, 9] will face even larger complexity problems. Furthermore, in real-world situations this is not a proper model of players' behavior.

Instead we will incorporate how many steps ahead the players consider. Seen from the point of view of player $\mathcal{A}$, she has a model incorporating the moves of player $\mathcal{B}$, where she makes some assumptions on how many moves ahead he analyzes the situation. In other words, if $\mathcal{A}$ knows the policies of $\mathcal{B}$, the model in Figure 1 can be transformed to a graphical model, where $\mathcal{B}$'s decision nodes are replaced with chance nodes, and $P(W_{i+1}|\mathcal{B}, W_i)$ is the policy (see Figure 2). Note that the node $T_{\mathcal{B}}$ reflects that $\mathcal{B}$'s assignment is unknown to $\mathcal{A}$. The model shall include prior probabilities for $T_{\mathcal{B}}$. To obtain an estimate of $\mathcal{B}$'s policies, player $\mathcal{A}$ needs to come up with an assumption on his moves ahead analysis. If she assumes that he only analyzes one move ahead, the model in Figure 3 can be used to calculate $\mathcal{B}$'s policy.

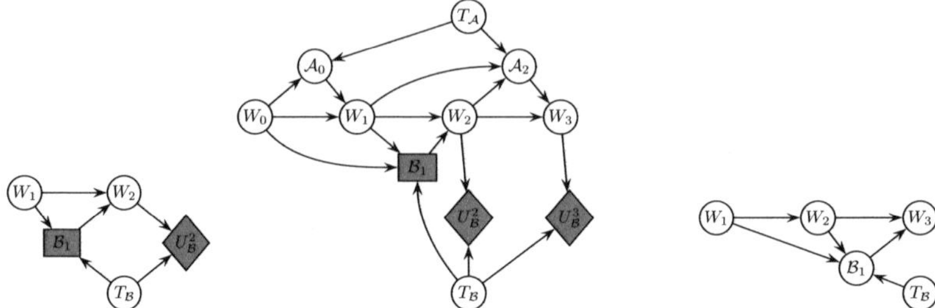

Figure 3. Player $\mathcal{B}$ takes player $\mathcal{A}$'s next move into consideration.

Figure 4. Player $\mathcal{B}$ takes player $\mathcal{A}$'s next move into consideration.

Figure 5. A Bayesian network for calculating $P(T_{\mathcal{B}}|w_1, w_2, w_3)$.

Under this assumption, $\mathcal{A}$ solves the influence diagram in Figure 3 and uses the policies as $P(W_{i+1}|\mathcal{B}, W_i)$ in the model in Figure 2.

If the resulting model is not solvable in practice, $\mathcal{A}$ must decide on an analysis horizon; for example three steps ahead, and then solve the resulting influence diagram. We call such a model an *LA-3* model. In general, a model with an n-step look-ahead is denoted an LA-n model.

Player $\mathcal{A}$ may have higher respect for player $\mathcal{B}$. The next model would be that player $\mathcal{B}$ takes player $\mathcal{A}$'s next move into consideration. This is illustrated in Figure 4. For this model, player $\mathcal{A}$ has to figure out what she believes that player $\mathcal{B}$ believes of her. We let $\mathcal{A}$ assume that $\mathcal{B}$ in an LA-2 model uses an LA-1 for determining $\mathcal{A}$'s policies. That is, he uses a model similar to the one in Figure 3.

In general, when player $\mathcal{A}$ uses an LA-n model he also has to decide on the lookahead m for $\mathcal{B}$. When calculating further down as above, we assume that the look-aheads go down with one. We call such model LA-(n, m) models. That is, in an LA-$(5, 3)$ model, $\mathcal{A}$ looks five steps ahead under the assumption that $\mathcal{B}$ looks three steps ahead. She assumes that $\mathcal{B}$ when looking three steps ahead assumes $\mathcal{A}$ to look two steps ahead under the assumption that $\mathcal{B}$ looks one step ahead.

2.4. Learning

The agents' private information is their assignments, but the impact of their actions is public knowledge. Whenever an agent performs an action, the other agent can use this knowledge to infer something on the assignment of the acting agent. We have that agent $\mathcal{B}$'s policy is a function of two world states and his assignment. With the policy represented as $P(\mathcal{B}_1|W_1, W_2, T_{\mathcal{B}})$, and with evidence "world state w_1, world state w_2, and world state w_3", the calculation can be taken care of in the Bayesian network in Figure 5. Actually, the formula is

$$P(T_{\mathcal{B}}|w_1, w_2, w_3) = \mu \sum_{\mathcal{B}_1} P(w_2|w_1, \mathcal{B}_1)P(\mathcal{B}_1|w_1, w_0, T_{\mathcal{B}})P(T_{\mathcal{B}}), \qquad (1)$$

where μ is a normalizing constant, and the calculation is in fact implicitly done by the calculation of optimal policies for influence diagrams.

3. Ausgetrickst

Ausgetrickst is played by 2 players, say agent $\mathcal{A}$ and agent $\mathcal{B}$. The board is a 3 by 3 grid on which the players play take turns moving with pieces. Each piece belongs to one of 3 suits (say ♠, ♣ and ◇) with 2 pieces belonging to each suit. The game also has a deck of cards (the *assignments*). An assignment is a pattern of 3 suits. The aim of the game is to move the pieces on the board such that the pieces in either a row or a column form the pattern on the assignment. When that is done the assignment is *solved*. We shall assume that the set of assignments is known by both players.

The players, $\mathcal{A}$ and $\mathcal{B}$ sit face to face with the board between them. The pieces are shuffled and placed on the board and each player draws a card without showing it to the opponent. The players take turns each time moving one piece to an unoccupied cell trying to solve each their assignment. The rules for moving are:

1. A piece may be moved to an adjacent empty cell either vertically, horizontally or diagonally.
2. A piece may be moved over one adjacent cell to a second cell in row if the adjacent cell is occupied and the second cell is free (called a *jump*).
3. A sequence of jumps is allowed.
4. It is not allowed to "undo" the opponents most recent move.

The players draw assignments from the card deck, solve them and keep them until the game has ended. We will deviate from the original Ausgetrickst game and assume that it is not a competition between agent $\mathcal{A}$ and agent $\mathcal{B}$. Rather we will assume that they are rewarded each time they solve an assignment and they do not get any extra reward for having collected more assignments than the opponent when the game ends. This way $\mathcal{A}$ can assume that her reward is independent of $\mathcal{B}$'s reward and vice versa.

3.1. Notation

The two players are denoted agent $\mathcal{A}$ and agent $\mathcal{B}$. We use lower-case letters when referring to states in discrete random variables and decision nodes, i.e. t_A and t_B refer to states in the random variable T_A and T_B respectively while w_i refers to a state in the random variable W_i. When we need to refer to any assignment we use the letter t and when we refer to any state (or board configuration) we use the letter w. We let w^t denote any board configuration satisfying t.

3.2. Representing CI with dynamic assignments

In Ausgetrickst a player is assigned a new assignment as soon as her current assignment is solved which is not the case with the models in Figure 2 through Figure 4. Therefore we replace the chance nodes T_A and T_B with the chance nodes, T_A^i and T_B^i for each time step W_i in the models of player $\mathcal{A}$ and $\mathcal{B}$. We also introduce a new chance node: *Solved?*, which informs whether an assignment is solved by a certain world state. Figure 6 shows how these nodes are connected. The links from each T_A^i and *Solved?* node to the next $T_{\mathcal{A}}^{i+1}$ indicates that if the player's assignment at $T_{\mathcal{A}}^{i}$ is solved, that assignment is no longer among the possible assignments at $T_{\mathcal{A}}^{i+1}$.

$\mathcal{A}$ must construct her model such that her initial assignment node $T_{\mathcal{A}}^{0}$ contains the nodes that she knows are either still in the assignment deck or currently in $\mathcal{B}$'s possession. $\mathcal{A}$ knows her own assignment, say t_0, so $P(T_{\mathcal{A}}^{0} = t_0) = 1$. In $T_{\mathcal{A}}^{1}$, she will let this probability distribution be unchanged, only if the assignment was not solved with $W_1 = w_1$. If, however, the assignment was solved with $W_1 = w_1$ the result in $T_{\mathcal{A}}^{1}$ is a uniform distribution among the possible assignments.

More specifically, in cases when $Solved = no$ she will let $P(T_{\mathcal{A}}^{i+1} = t_0 | t_{\mathcal{A}}^{i} = t_0, Solved? = no) = 1$ and for assignments t_1 where $t_1 \neq t_0$, $P(T_{\mathcal{A}}^{i+1} = t_1 | t_{\mathcal{A}}^{i} = t_0, Solved? = no) = 0$. If $Solved? = yes$, she will let $P(T_{\mathcal{A}}^{i+1} = t_0 | t_{\mathcal{A}}^{i} = t_0, Solved? = yes) = 0$ and she will let $P(T_{\mathcal{A}}^{i+1} = t | t_{\mathcal{A}}^{i} = t_0, Solved? = yes)$ be an even distribution over each assignment t where $t \neq t_0$.

Regarding $\mathcal{B}$'s assignment in $\mathcal{A}$'s model, $\mathcal{A}$ sets the initial probability distribution in $T_{\mathcal{B}}^{0}$ to her belief of $T_{\mathcal{B}}^{0}$ and the conditional probabilities in $T_{\mathcal{B}}^{1}$, $T_{\mathcal{B}}^{2}$ and $T_{\mathcal{B}}^{3}$ are similar to those for $T_{\mathcal{A}}^{1}$, $T_{\mathcal{A}}^{2}$ and $T_{\mathcal{A}}^{3}$.

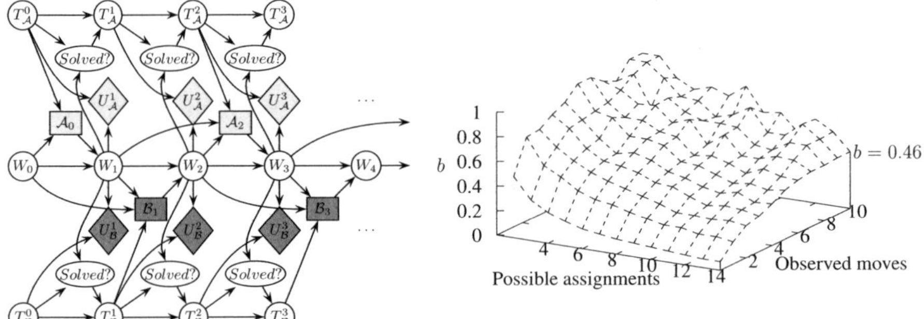

Figure 6. The Model where a new assignment is received when one is solved.

Figure 7. Agent $\mathcal{A}$'s average belief (b) of agent $\mathcal{B}$'s true assignment as a function of possible assignments and the number of moves by $\mathcal{B}$.

3.3. Specifying the Reward Functions

We will use a measure of distance as the reward for the players. In general, the closer the agent is to having solved her assignment the happier she will be. Let term c^w denotes the set of configurations achievable from w (i.e. w's children), and let w^t denotes the set of all board configurations satisfying t. Similarly, $D(w, w^t)$, denotes the length of the shortest path from w to any w' satisfying t. We will use $U(w_i, t_{\mathcal{A}}) = -D(w_i, w^{t_{\mathcal{A}}})$ as the reward function in utility node U_i.

4. Experimental results

We have evaluated our framework by letting agents $\mathcal{A}$ and $\mathcal{B}$ play Ausgetrickst. First we have analyzed the efficiency of Eq. (1) as a means for learning the opponent's assignment. Secondly we have performed experiments where models of different analysis depth are compared.

Table 1. Results of encounters between $\mathcal{A}$ and $\mathcal{B}$ playing with different analysis depths. The n-column represents the number of games played in each encounter. The t column shows the average time $\mathcal{A}$'s model has used on each move.

Experiment	n	$\mathcal{A}$ wins	$\mathcal{B}$ wins	draw	t
$\mathcal{A}$:LA-2 VS $\mathcal{B}$:LA-1	100	55	45	0	$2.8s$
$\mathcal{A}$:LA-3 VS $\mathcal{B}$:LA-2	100	67	32	1	$2m\ 15s$
$\mathcal{A}$:LA-(4,2) VS $\mathcal{B}$:LA-2	109	74	30	2	$2h\ 28m\ 0s$
$\mathcal{A}$:LA-(2,2) VS $\mathcal{B}$:LA-2	100	52	46	2	$2m\ 9s$
$\mathcal{A}$:LA-(4,1) VS $\mathcal{B}$:LA-2	101	54	41	5	$4m\ 16s$

4.1. Learning the opponent's assignment

To show how well Eq. (1) can be used for learning the opponent's assignment by observing his moves, we report the fraction of probability that agent $\mathcal{A}$ has assigned to agent $\mathcal{B}$'s true assignment. Let $b = P_\mathcal{A}(t_\mathcal{B})$, where agent $\mathcal{B}$ has assignment $t_\mathcal{B}$. We have let $\mathcal{A}$ and $\mathcal{B}$ play 600 games all starting with 15 assignments. Both agents play with an LA-2 model assuming the opponent plays with an LA-1 model.The results are plotted in Figure 7, which shows the average value of b as a function of the number of unobservable assignments ('Possible assignments') and the number of observed opponent's moves ('Observed moves'). There is a clear trend that for any number of unobservable assignments, b increases with the number of observed moves.

4.2. Comparison of different analysis depths

In another series of experiments we have let the players play Ausgetrickst with models with different analysis depths. In all the following experiments the total number of assignments in the game has been set to 6.

The results are in Table 1. In the first encounter, $\mathcal{A}$ plays with an LA-2 model, i.e. she is looking 2 steps ahead and she assumes, correctly, that $\mathcal{B}$ is looking 1 step ahead ($\mathcal{B}$ has an LA-1 model). As expected $\mathcal{A}$ seems to be winning slightly more than $\mathcal{B}$. In the second encounter both agents have slightly more advanced models. $\mathcal{A}$ plays with an LA-3 model, i.e. she is looking ahead 3 time steps while she correctly assumes that $\mathcal{B}$ is playing with an LA-2 model. $\mathcal{A}$ also wins in this case which was expected since she has the most advanced model and she has the correct assumption about $\mathcal{B}$'s analysis depth. In the third experiment $\mathcal{A}$ plays with an LA-(4,2) model, i.e. she is looking 4 steps ahead in her analysis while she still correctly assumes that $\mathcal{B}$ is playing with an LA-2 model. As expected $\mathcal{A}$ performs better in this case than in any other case. In the fourth and fifth encounter we see what happens if $\mathcal{A}$ does not analyze deeper than $\mathcal{B}$ or when $\mathcal{A}$ has a wrong assumption about $\mathcal{B}$'s analysis depth. When $\mathcal{A}$ plays with an LA-(2,2) model gainst $\mathcal{B}$ playing with an LA-2 model she wins only slightly more games than $\mathcal{B}$. Lastly, $\mathcal{A}$ plays with an LA-(4,1) model against $\mathcal{B}$ with an LA-2 model. In this last experiment $\mathcal{A}$ has a wrong assumption about $\mathcal{B}$'s model while she is looking 4 steps ahead. Also here $\mathcal{A}$ seems to be winning slightly more games than $\mathcal{B}$ which can be explained by her deeper analysis. Note that $\mathcal{B}$ in here (as well as in the previous encounters) also has a wrong assumption about $\mathcal{A}$'s model.

The t column of Table 1 shows the average time $\mathcal{A}$ used for her analysis in each move in the game. The time analysis was performed separately on a 900MHz SUN Fire v880R machine with 32 GB RAM. When she was playing with the LA-2 model she on average spent 2.8 seconds. The time usage increases heavily with the complexity of $\mathcal{A}$'s model. When she plays with the most advanced model in our experiments (LA-(4,2)) she spent 2 hours and 28 minutes on each move. A possibility for speeding up $\mathcal{A}$'s decision making could be to use particle filters. However, the major complexity problem for influence diagrams is that the relevant past for a policy will become intractably large and therefore the main problem is memory usage [3]. A more promising approach seems to be Limited Memory Influence Diagrams (LIMIDS) [10] which will be investigated in future work.

Acknowledgments.

We want to thank the staff in the Machine Intelligence Group at the Department of Computer Science at Aalborg University. In particular, we are grateful to Zeng Yifeng for his valuable comments.

References

[1] J. Nash. Equilibrium points in N-person games. In *Proceedings of the National Academy of Sciences of the United States of America*, volume 36, pages 48–49, 1950.

[2] David Carmel and Shaul Markovitch. Incorporating opponent models into adversary search. In *Proceedings of the Thirteenth National Conference on Artificial Intelligence*, pages 120–125, 1996.

[3] F. V. Jensen and T. D. Nielsen. *Bayesian Networks and Decision Graphs*. Springer, 2007.

[4] K. B. Korb and A. E. Nicholson. *Bayesian Artificial Intelligence*. Chapman & Hall / CRC, 2004.

[5] D. Koller and B. Milch. Multi-agent influence diagrams for representing and solving games. *Games and Economic Behavior*, 45(1):181–221, 2003.

[6] F. Jensen, F. V. Jensen, and S. L. Dittmer. From influence diagrams to junction trees. In R.L. Mantaras and D. Poole, editors, *Proceedings of the Tenth Conference on Uncertainty in Artificial Intelligence*, pages 367–374. Morgan Kaufmann, 1994.

[7] R. D. Shachter. Evaluating influence diagrams. *Operations Research*, 34(6):597–609, 1986.

[8] R. Bellman. A markovian decision process. *Journal of Mathematics and Mechanics*, 6, 1957.

[9] R. A. Howard. *Dynamic Programming and Markov Processes*. The MIT Press, 1960.

[10] S. L. Lauritzen and D. Nilsson. Representing and solving decision problems with limited information. *Management Science*, 47:1235–1251, September 2001.

Tenth Scandinavian Conference on Artificial Intelligence
A. Holst et al. (Eds.)
IOS Press, 2008

165

Sharing Moral Responsibility with Robots: A Pragmatic Approach

Gordana DODIG-CRNKOVIC[1] and Daniel PERSSON[2]

School of Innovation, Design and Engineering,
Mälardalen University, Västerås, Sweden

Abstract. Roboethics is a recently developed field of applied ethics which deals with the ethical aspects of technologies such as robots, ambient intelligence, direct neural interfaces and invasive nano-devices and intelligent soft bots. In this article we look specifically at the issue of (moral) responsibility in artificial intelligent systems. We argue for a pragmatic approach, where responsibility is seen as a social regulatory mechanism. We claim that having a system which takes care of certain tasks intelligently, learning from experience and making autonomous decisions gives us reasons to talk about a system (an artifact) as being "responsible" for a task. No doubt, technology is morally significant for humans, so the "responsibility for a task" with moral consequences could be seen as moral responsibility. Intelligent systems can be seen as parts of socio-technological systems with distributed responsibilities, where responsible (moral) agency is a matter of degree. Knowing that all possible abnormal conditions of a system operation can never be predicted, and no system can ever be tested for all possible situations of its use, the responsibility of a producer is to assure proper functioning of a system under reasonably foreseeable circumstances. Additional safety measures must however be in place in order to mitigate the consequences of an accident. The socio-technological system aimed at assuring a beneficial deployment of intelligent systems has several functional responsibility feedback loops which must function properly: the awareness and procedures for handling of risks and responsibilities on the side of designers, producers, implementers and maintenance personnel as well as the understanding of society at large of the values and dangers of intelligent technology. The basic precondition for developing of this socio-technological control system is education of engineers in ethics and keeping alive the democratic debate on the preferences about future society.

Keywords. Intelligent agents, Moral responsibility, Safety critical systems

Introduction

Engineering can be seen as a long-term, large-scale social experiment since the design, production and employment of engineered artifacts can be expected to have long-range effects [1]. Especially interesting consequences might be anticipated if the engineered artifacts are intelligent, adaptive and autonomous. Recently, Roboethics, a field of

---

[1] gordana.dodig-crnkovic@mdh.se
[2] dpn04001@student.mdh.se

applied ethics, has developed with many interesting, novel insights.[3] Topics addressed within Roboethics include the use of robots, ubiquitous sensing systems and ambient intelligence, direct neural interfaces and invasive nano-devices, intelligent soft bots, robots aimed at warfare, and similar, which actualize ethical issues of responsibility, liability, accountability, control, privacy, self, (human) rights, and similar [2].

This article deals specifically with the issue of (moral) responsibility in artificial intelligent systems. We argue that this should be handled by adopting a pragmatic approach, where responsibility is seen as a social regulatory mechanism.

1. Moral Responsibility and Intelligent Systems

Moral responsibility is understood as consisting of two parts: causal responsibility and intention. Traditionally only humans are considered to be capable of the mental state of intention. This mental state can be seen as the origin of an act that, depending on the effects it causes, can imply moral responsibility [3][4].

A common argument against ascribing moral responsibility to artificial intelligent systems is that they are not considered to have the capacity for mental states like intention [3][4]. Another argument maintains that it is pointless to assign praise or blame to an agent of this type when it has no meaning to the agent [5].

Both these arguments stem from a view in which agents are seen primarily as isolated entities. Dennett and Strawson suggest that we should understand moral responsibility not as individual duty, but as *a role defined by externalist pragmatic norms of a group* [6][7]. In this functionalist view moral responsibility can best be seen as a social regulatory mechanism which aims at enhancing actions considered to be good, and simultaneously minimizing what is considered to be bad.

We argue that to address the question of ascribing moral responsibility to intelligent systems we must adopt the functionalist view and see them as parts of larger socio-technological systems with distributed responsibilities, where responsibility of a moral agent is a matter of degree. From such a standpoint ascribing responsibility to an intelligent system has primarily a regulatory role. Delegating a task to a machine is also delegating responsibility for the safe and successful completion of that task to the machine [8]. A machine that takes care of certain tasks intelligently, learning from experience and making autonomous decisions gives us good reasons to talk about a machine as being "responsible" for a task in the same manner that we talk about a machine being "intelligent". No doubt, technology is morally significant for humans, so the "responsibility" for a task with moral consequences could be seen as moral responsibility. Moral responsibility as a regulative mechanism shall not only locate the blame but more importantly assure future appropriate behavior of the system. *Consequential responsibility,* which presupposes *moral autonomy,* will however be distributed through the system.

---

[3] See, e.g. http://www.roboethics.org, http://roboethics.stanford.edu/, or *International Review of Information Ethics* Vol. 6, IRIE, 2006, that was dedicated to Ethics of Robotics, http://www.i-r-i-e.net/archive.htm

2. Risks and Distribution of Responsibility in Intelligent Technology

Based on the experiences with safety critical systems such as nuclear power, aerospace and transportation systems one can say that the socio-technological structure which supports their beneficial functioning is a system of safety barriers preventing and mitigating malfunction. The most important part is to assure safe functioning under normal conditions, which is complemented by the supposed abnormal/accidental condition scenarios. There must be several levels of organizational and physical barriers in order to cope with different levels of severity of malfunctions [9].

In every design process there are uncertainties that are the result of our limited resources. All new products are tested under certain conditions in a given context. This implies that an engineered product may, sooner or later, in its application be used under conditions for which it has never been tested. Even in such situations we expect the product to function safely. Handling risk and uncertainty in the production of a safety critical technical system is done on several levels. Producers must take into account everything from technical issues, through issues of management and organization, to larger issues on the level of societal impact [10]. Risk assessment is a standard way of dealing with risks in the design and production of safety critical systems [11], also relevant for intelligent systems.

Any technology subject to uncertainty and with a potentially high impact on human society is expected to be handled cautiously, and intelligent systems surely fall into this category. Thus, preventing harm and having the burden of proof of harmlessness is something that producers of intelligent systems are responsible for. (Precautionary Principle[4])

A precondition for this socio-technological control system is an engineer informed about the ethical aspects of engineering, where education in professional ethics for engineers is a fundamental factor [12].

3. Conclusion

According to the classical approach, free will is essential for an agent to be assigned moral responsibility. Pragmatic approaches on the other hand focus on social, organizational and role-assignment aspects of responsibility. We argue that moral responsibility in intelligent systems is best viewed as a regulatory mechanism, and follow essentially a pragmatic (instrumental, functionalist) line of thought. Intelligent systems can be seen as parts of socio-technological systems with distributed responsibilities, where responsible (moral) agency is a matter of degree. We claim that for all practical purposes, the question of responsibility in safety critical intelligent systems may be addressed in the same way as the safety in traditional safety critical systems, such as nuclear industry and transports.

Long-term, wide range consequences of the deployment of intelligent systems in human societies must be discussed on a democratic basis as the intelligent systems have a potential of radically transforming the future of humanity. Education in professional ethics for engineers is a fundamental factor for building a socio-technological system of responsibility.

---

[4] http://ec.europa.eu/dgs/health_consumer/library/pub/pub07_en.pdf

References

[1]   Martin, M.W., Schinzinger, R., *Ethics in Engineering*, McGraw-Hill, 1996.

[2]   Dodig-Crnkovic G., Professional Ethics in Computing and Intelligent Systems, *Proceedings of the Ninth Scandinavian Conference on Artificial Intelligence* (SCAI 2006), Espoo, Finland, October 25-27, 2006.

[3]   Johnson D. G., Computer systems: Moral entities but not moral agents, *Ethics and Information Technology*, Vol. 8, Springer, 2006, pp. 195-204.

[4]   Johnson D. G. and Miller K. W., A dialogue on responsibility, moral agency, and IT systems, *Proceedings of the 2006 ACM symposium on Applied computing table of content*, Dijon, France, 2006, pp. 272 – 276.

[5]   Floridi L. and Sanders J. W., On the morality of artificial agents, *Minds and Machines*, Vol. 14, Kluwer Academic Publishers, 2004, pp. 349-379.

[6]   Dennett, D. C., Mechanism and Responsibility, in *Essays on Freedom of Action*, T. Honderich (ed), Routledge & Keegan Paul, Boston, 1973.

[7]   Strawson P. F., Freedom and Resentment, in *Freedom and Resentment and Other Essays*, Methuen, 1974.

[8]   Johnson D. G. and Powers T. M., Computer systems and responsibility: A normative look at technological complexity, *Ethics and Information Technology*, Vol. 7, Springer, 2005, pp. 99-107.

[9]   Dodig-Crnkovic G., ABB Atom's Criticality Safety Handbook, ICNC'99 Sixth International Conference on Nuclear Criticality Safety, Versailles, France, (1999) , Available: http://www.idt.mdh.se/personal/gdc/work/csh.pdf

[10] Huff, C., Unintentional Power in the Design of Computing Systems, in T. W. Bynum and S. Rogerson, eds., *Computer Ethics and Professional Responsibility*, Blackwell Publishing, Kundli, India, 2004, pp. 98-106.

[11] Stamatelatos M., Probabilistic Risk Assessment: What Is It And Why Is It Worth Performing It?, NASA Office of Safety and Mission Assurance, 2000, Available: http://www.hq.nasa.gov/office/codeq/qnews/pra.pdf

[12] Dodig-Crnkovic G., On the Importance of Teaching Professional Ethics to Computer Science Students, Computing and Philosophy Conference, E-CAP 2004, Pavia, Italy, in L. Magnani, ed., *Computing and Philosophy*, Associated International Academic Publishers, 2005.

Tenth Scandinavian Conference on Artificial Intelligence
A. Holst et al. (Eds.)
IOS Press, 2008

Foundation for program understanding

Erkki Laitila
erkki.laitila@swmaster.fi
Jyväskylä University & SwMaster Oy, Sääksmäentie 14, 40520 JKL, Finland

Abstract. This paper presents a symbolic framework for program understanding. The framework makes use of three approaches, each of which has the following conceptual spaces: syntax, semantics, simulation, and pragmatics. The paper starts by focusing on grammars and then progresses via semantics and the automaton theory to program proving, which goal is typical for maintainers. The captured argumentative information helps them to create new logic-based knowledge, in which abstract program concepts are used to connect lower-level representations. A tool, JavaMaster, is used for simulating Java and for proving the results.

Keywords: Reverse engineering, Program comprehension, Source code analysis, Maintenance. Semiotics, Artificial Intelligence, Theory Building.

Introduction

Until now there has been no consensus about what is human thinking. Several of the cognitive theories and architectures that are known [7], have been subjected to strong criticisms. In real life descriptions, problems such as symbol grounding and the Chinese room-metaphor [5] raise their ugly heads.

In this paper we focus on the formal aspects of the world around us, an approach that enables us to solve the problem of symbol grounding. Computer software research is a natural and promising area for the application of AI technologies. This paper deals with Java code understanding, which is extended into a framework for maintenance.

Programming languages have developed from a machine language via assembler, byte-code and higher level notations into a more general direction. The problem is that there is no gradually deepening language enabling an effective dependency analysis, which is the most laborious phase to follow on in program understanding. Thus programming and the design process are still challenging phases. The problems surface during maintenance; it is not safe to change code without mastering its dependencies [16]. To tackle this, there is an approach known as program comprehension (PC), which forms part of reverse engineering [4].

In this paper we present three standpoints for PC. First, with the help of a small example, we describe the propositional nature of language (Section 1) for evaluating one single proposition. Then we extend the scope for the whole Java language, which uses an atomistic model (Section 2) consisting of propositional terms. Finally, we describe a tool, JavaMaster, to illustrate symbolic analysis in order to explain how the tool can help the maintainers in exploring and validating program flows.

Each standpoint is illustrated by four phases based, roughly, on syntax, semantics, pragmatics, and running (e.g., simulation). Section 5 deals with related work and conclusions.

1. Example about a language and its propositional structure

In Figure 1 there is a simple clause *if (OldFriend) print (Hello)*, which could be Java code or normal English after some minor changes. It is a widely a held view that every sentence in a language can be interpreted as an assertion [14] and, further, as a proposition that is either true or not. This view leads to propositional calculus.

In the figure, Point 1 deals with syntax, i.e., the rules constraining the expressions in the language. Semantics can be considered as a model with its elements and links. In Point 2 the elements are shown arranged in a tree. Below, in the depiction of that hierarchy, an empty matrix describing the links is shown. However, these connections can be expressed more efficiently as Prolog predicates, as we do in this paper.

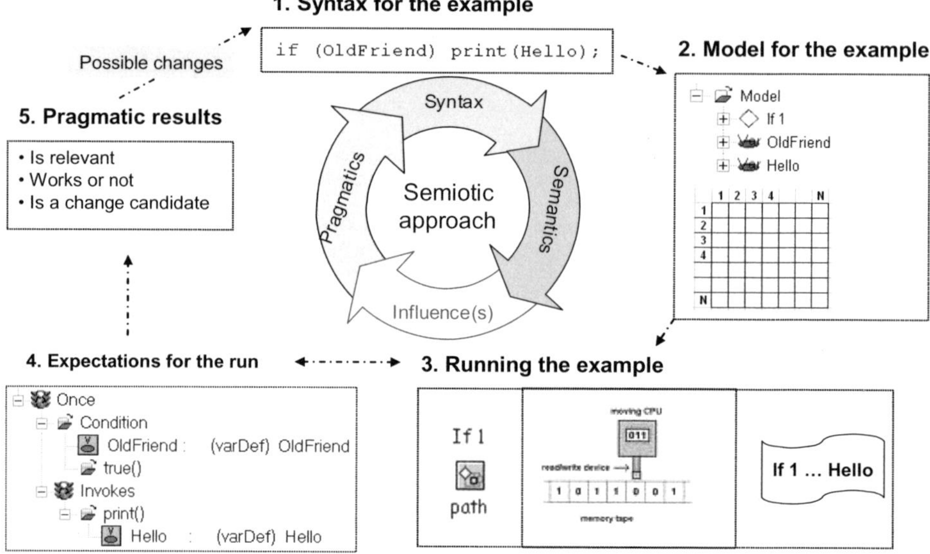

Figure 1.   Practical example: evaluating a proposition.

Point 3 shows how the example is run. From the part of the user it requires thinking to evaluate whether a proposition is true or not. From the part of the computer, on the other hand, it requires computations of the kind that can be done with the automaton. It is not widely known that the Turing machine [15] is a complete formalism to express any sequential computation sequence, and thus it is important to mention it here. In our example an *if*-structure is evaluated by solving its condition, which here points to an old friend (OldFriend). If the condition turns out to be true, then the inner block is initiated by the greeting ("Hello"). The thinking process is saved to an output tape.

In the output tape the expectations placed on execution can be presented as a logical structure, which is a function of the elements occurring earlier. In Point 4 the *once* command defines the condition as a precondition and the *hello* output (*invokes*) the invocation to be tested. The results, in Point 5, are a set of arguments with three levels [11]. Deduction is used to decide whether the proposition is relevant and correct. Categories for generalization can interactively be derived by induction. By using abduction the user can modify existing expressions and create new features.

2. Four-phase understanding process for Java

In Java the code consists of statements, which can be interpreted as propositions, because every statement can either be performed by branching to its specific program flow or it can be interrupted by an exception. The elements for a simulation in range Start .. Target build chain Y, if we assume that the program has been split into small elements f:　$Y = y(Start) = Start$　$\bullet f1 \bullet f2 \bullet .. \bullet Target.$
　　This equation uses a mathematical notation, called chopping[13].

Figure 2 depicts a Java understanding process. In Point 1 the grammar of a language is described. Each separate type of formal language T_X defines a queue (syntax), which consists of reserved words and sub-types $T_X(I)$ in the correct order. For each type we create a predicate, later referred to as a computation, abbreviated to cmp_X.

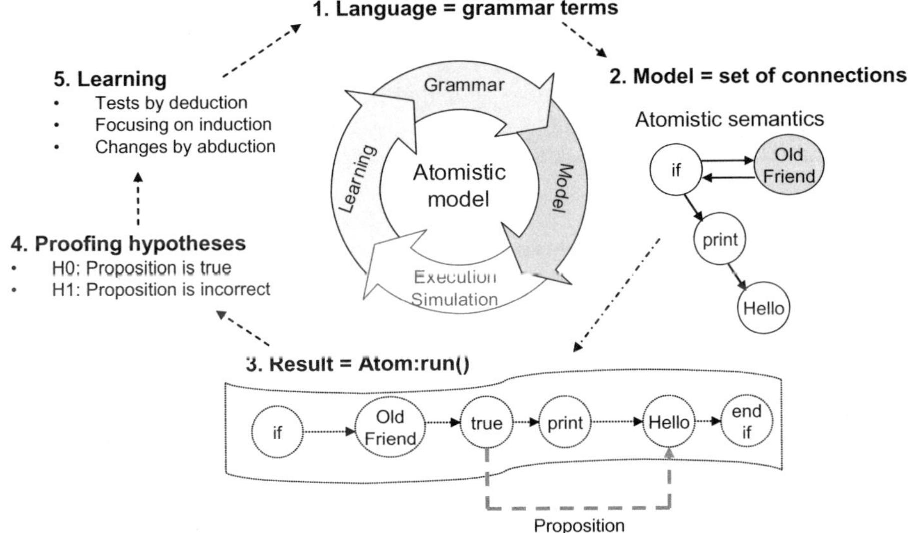

Figure 2.　　　Java understanding process.

Point 2 refers to semantics of code model, which is needed for analysis. Current practices consist of static and dynamic analyses, whereas symbolic analysis [9] is the approach of this paper. It is based on atomistic semantics to combine grammar atoms.
　　Static analysis [3] is a way to derive, for each key symbol S_I, a group of out-going relations $S_I(i)$ so that each term T_X in the grammar is substituted by key symbol S_I. Symbol S_I should have the same relations to its sub-terms $S_I(i)$ as T_X has to its terms $T_X(i)$. Static analysis is not sufficient for analyzing object-oriented code, because current situation in execution greatly influences the behavior [18].
　　Dynamic analysis [3] means running the code for obtaining relevant results. It is needed, because object-oriented programs contain context-sensitive features due to object instantiations $d(S_I \to S_I(J), S_I(J+1), ..)$. They can be detected in the output trace. In practice, dynamic analysis is an expensive process, because it requires a complete code with its environment, but it only can process a few selected use cases at a time.

Symbolic analysis is a method [9], which eliminates many drawbacks of static and dynamic analysis. In it running the code is replaced by simulation, where for each S_I for its computation type C there is a state automaton, A_C. It is essential that an atomistic model, M, is created so that there is, for each symbol, an atomistic structure, i.e., an atom (Point 2 in Figure 2).

For example, for the *print(Hello)* command two atoms are created: one for *print* and the other for *Hello*. The structures are connected as a predicate. Thus clause *if(A, B)* creates an *iff*-atom with predicate links to atom A and to each statement of atom B.

Each atom has a simulation method *run*, which implements the corresponding automaton, $A_C{}^1$. In addition to the atoms captured from the code there are dynamic elements, atoms that we call side effects. For example, for a condition clause *if (OldFriend) then Something* a side effect is created as a result of running *OldFriend*. Furthermore, for each clause due to *Something*, an individual atom is saved.

The side effects are of the form $sideEff_I(Arguments)$. Because they are linked to static elements in the model, it is possible to express the results of a symbolic analysis as predicates connecting code elements and side effects. This makes it possible to prove that correct elements have been run in a correct order, which enables proving the selected hypotheses for the propositions. For that purpose there is a formalism called temporal logic [12]. It describes higher order logic, *what should happen*, whereas the original language illustrates first order logic, *what really happened*.

3. Reverse engineering tool JavaMaster

The purpose of reverse engineering is most often to get feedback from the current system for forward development. JavaMaster tool is programmed in Visual Prolog [17] and can be used to load Java 1.5 applications and make focused symbolic analyses for them. This approach works best in code familiarization, in planning changes and in troubleshooting. The tool contains four technology spaces: GrammarWare, ModelWare, SimulationWare, and KnowledgeWare (Figure 3).

GrammarWare. The code is read by a loader (Point 1). For abstracting code we developed *Symbolic,* a symbolic language. In it Java structures are encoded as structures that all have the same base *clause*. Each *clause* can be further divided into substructures such as *def, set, get, ref, loop, path* (condition), *op* (operation) and *const*, which are optimized for different types of analyses. Because each Symbolic term can only contain *clause*s, implementing analysis software with them is straightforward. Furthermore, this principle corresponds to atomistic human thinking [2].

ModelWare. On loading, a model is created by a model weaver. An atomistic model (Point 2) can be drawn as a state diagram in which atoms are shown as nodes and predicates are links connecting the invoked atoms.

SimulationWare. The purpose of simulation is to capture the behavior model of the code. This is useful in describing critical low-level dependencies. For simulation, there is the formalism of Turing machine, an automaton to sequentially simulate any program or any computer [15]. We extended it to contain the Symbolic language by creating a symbolic abstract machine (SAM), which can simulate code atom by atom. In Figure 3 the output tape produced by SAM is presented as Point 3.

---

[1] Atomistic semantics deals with relations between atoms calling other atoms [9].

KnowledgeWare. With the help of the tool the user can select an abstract or concrete *ProgramConcept* to be studied. A *ProgramConcept* is a selection made by the user for chunking new information. The intention is to ground it step by step [1] to the code and to the atoms by studying the structures with the help of *ProgramContexts*. A *ProgramContext* is a typical use of the selected program element, which include initializating a database, starting a server, or any invocation logic. The user localizes the *ProgramConcept* to the atoms of the code (Point 3, input). In Point 4 there is a user interface of the theorem prover for demonstrating how a hypothesis can be defined and verified. Because each atom can be invoked in many places, different *ProgramContexts* must be dealt with. The user simulates the relevant *ProgramContexts* and builds a mental representation for the *ProgramConcept*. The feedback resulting from matching the current knowledge and new representations makes it possible to use new information as corrections and modifications for the next installation.

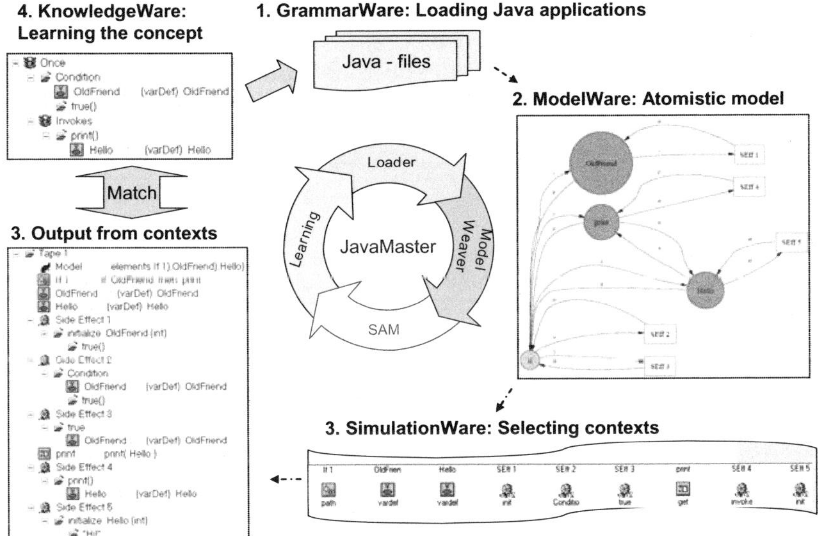

Figure 3.　　　Feedback loop created by the JavaMaster tool.

4. Summarizing the approaches and technology spaces

We have gradually introduced a logic-based approach for PC. Section 1 deals with one proposition, Section 2 with whole of Java. Finally, in Section 3 the tool, JavaMaster, demonstrates the symbolic power for code analysis, which enables supporting both the top-down and bottom-up approach and further, building situation models for code [16].

One essential problem considering PC relates to symbol grounding [5], due to prevalence of vague concepts and holism of thoughts in this area. By using the atomistic model derived from grammar terms we have succeeded in formalizing the code inspection and simulation and the most typical verification related efforts. We have proved that the atomistic model is a complete framework for source code simulation [9]. Our hybrid atomistic construction seamlessly combining logic and objects is useful in problem solving and modeling cases of software engineering when the concepts are formal and the accuracy of propositions is sufficient for decisions.

5. Conclusions and future work

In computer science, theories are mostly studied by using a deepening strategy to solve specific research questions. This is not sufficient for solving practical problems. For example, in software engineering, ModelWare is a separated space from GrammarWare [8] and simulation [9]. Due to this the current level of reverse engineering is not adequate to fulfill practical challenges faced by software production.

In this article we described how symbolic analysis can combine the functions of static and dynamic analyses for creating a symbolic result set as a solution. Symbolic analysis consists of grammar, modeling, simulation and automata theory as well as a constructive way to derive information for maintenance by using deduction and proving critical sequences. The work has been evaluated with the JavaMaster tool. The thinking principle presented here forms a novel approach in the develelopment of the research field and should attract wide interest in future for this reason.

References

[1] Aamodt, A., and Nygård, M. (1995). Different roles and mutual dependencies of data, information, and knowledge - an AI perspective on their integration, *Data and Knowledge Engineering*, North-Holland Elsevier, **16**, 191-222.

[2] Anderson, J. R. (2004). Human Symbol Manipulation Within an Integrated Cognitive Architecture, *Cognitive Science, Cognitive Science Society, Inc* **29**, 313–341.

[3] Binkley., D. (2007). Source Code Analysis: A Road Map. Future of Software Engineering, ICSE 2007.

[4] Chikofsky, E. J., and Cross, J. H. (1992). Reverse Engineering and Design Recovery: A Taxonomy. (editor Robert S. Arnold), *Software Reengineering*, IEEE Computer Society Press 54–58.

[5] Harnad, Stevan (1990). The symbol grounding problem. *Physica D, 42,* 335–346.

[6] Hoare, C. A. R. (1969). An axiomatic basis for computer programming. *Communications of the ACM* **2**(10), 576–585.

[7] Hofkirchner, W. (1999) Cognitive Sciences In the Perspective of a Unified Theory of Information. *43rd Annual Conference of ISSS, In Allen, J. K., Hall, M. L. W., Wilby, J. (Eds.), 1999.*

[8] Klint, P., Lämmel, R., and Verhoef, C. (2005). Towards an Engineering Discipline for Grammarware, url= http://www.cs.vu.nl/grammarware/agenda (10.1.2008).

[9] Laitila, E. (2008). Symbolic Analysis and Atomistic Model as a Basis for a Program Comprehension Methodology. PhD-thesis, Jyväskylä University, April 2008.

[10] Müller, H. A., Jahnke, J. H., Smith, D. B., Storey, M.-A. D., Tilley, S. R., and Wong:, K. (2000). Reverse engineering: a roadmap. ICSE 2000.

[11] Peirce, C. S. (1958). Collected Writings (8 Vols.). Harvard University Press, Cambridge, MA.

[12] Pnueli, A. (1977). The temporal logic of programs, In Proceedings of the 18th Annual Symposium on the Foundations of Computer Science, New York, 46–57.

[13] Reps, T., and Rosay., G. (1995). Precise interprocedural chopping. SIGSOFT 95.

[14] Tarski, A. (1983). The concept of truth in formalized languages, in J. Corcoran (ed.), Logic, semantics, metamathematics, Hackett Publishing Co, 152–278.

[15] Turing, A. (1936). On Computable Numbers with an Application to the Entscheidungsproblem. Proc. London Math Soc, **2**:42, 230-265.

[16] Vans, A. M., von Mayrhauser, A., and Somlo, G. (1999). Program understanding behavior during corrective maintenance of large-scale software. *Human-Computer Studies (1999)* 51, 31.

[17] VisualProlog (2007). The Visual Prolog Development-tool. url=www.visual-prolog-org (10.1.2008).

[18] Wilde, N., and Huitt, R. (1992). Maintenance Support for Object-Oriented Programs. *IEEE Transactions on Software Engineering* **1** SE-18, 1038–1044.

Tenth Scandinavian Conference on Artificial Intelligence
A. Holst et al. (Eds.)
IOS Press, 2008

Looking for Planning Problems Solvable in Polynomial Time via Investigation of Structures of Action Dependencies [1]

Lukáš CHRPA [a] and Roman BARTÁK [a]

[a] *Department of Theoretical Computer Science and Mathematical Logic, Faculty of Mathematics and Physics, Charles University in Prague, Czech Republic*

Abstract. There are a lot of planning techniques for solving planning problems and many of them solve the planning problems by 'brute force' even though some problems (or parts of them) are easy. An easy planning problem typically has a plan with a specific structure. The structure described in this paper is based on action dependencies that appear in plans. We are looking for such constraints that are in the plan structures that provide algorithms running in polynomial time.

Keywords. Planning Problems, Polynomial Complexity, Plan Analysis, Action Dependencies

1. Introduction

Planning is an important area of AI. Many planners translate planning problems into other formalisms like SAT or CSP and then use particular solvers to solve them. For further improvement the planners often use heuristics guiding the search for plans [1].

Despite the promising techniques and heuristics, plans are still being found by 'brute force' which means that the planners have to walk through a huge state space. It is true that complexity results showed that planning, even if we focus only on the classical planning in set-theoretic or ground representation, is a hard problem. On the other hand if we take a look at the planning problems more deeply we can see that many of them are not so hard and some of them can be solved in polynomial time. In [6,7] it is proved that some of well known planning problems from International Planning Competition [8] can be solved in polynomial time. However, the analysis of the planning problems individually does not seem to be much contributive. A better approach for investigating the complexity of planning problems can be based on plans analysis. In [10] it is presented a structure called Causal Graph which describes dependencies between state variables. In [5,9] it is studied the complexity of planning problems with respect to structures of their Causal Graphs.

---

[1]The research is supported by the Czech Science Foundation under the contracts no. 201/08/0509 and 201/05/H014 and by the Grant Agency of Charles University (GAUK) under the contract no. 326/2006/A-INF/MFF.

This paper investigates the structure of action dependencies based on ideas described in [2,3]. The main contribution of this paper rests in looking for such plan structures that provide us algorithms running in polynomial time.

This paper is organized as follows. The next section introduces basic notions from the planning theory. Then, we provide the theoretical background of the problem of action dependencies in plans. After that, we investigate the structures of action dependencies to find conditions providing a possibility of solving a given planning problem in polynomial time. Finally, we give a summary and plans for future research.

2. Preliminaries

Traditionally, AI planning deals with the problem of finding a sequence of actions transforming the world from some initial state to a desired state. State s is a set of predicates that are true in s. Action a is a 3-tuple $(p(a), e^-(a), e^+(a))$ where $p(a)$ is a set of predicates representing precondition of action a, $e^-(a)$ is a set of negative effects of action a and $e^+(a)$ is a set of positive effects of action a and $e^-(a) \cap e^+(a) = \emptyset$. Action a can be performed on the state s if $p(a) \subseteq s$ and when action a is performed on state s, new state s' is obtained where $s' = (s \setminus e^-(a)) \cup e^+(a)$. A planning domain is represented by a set of states and a set of actions. A planning problem is represented by the planning domain, an initial state and a set of goal predicates. A plan is an ordered sequence of actions which leads from the initial state to any goal state containing all of the goal predicates. For deeper insight in this area, see [4].

3. Action Dependencies in Plans

We know that every action needs some predicates to be true before its performance. These predicates are provided by other actions (or by the initial state) that are performed before. If we have a plan solving a planning problem, we can find out which actions are providing predicates to other actions that need them. The idea rests in describing of these dependencies which can be helpful for further plan analysis. In the following paragraphs we define basic notions that describe action dependencies in plans.

Definition 1.1: Let $S =< a_1, \ldots, a_n >$ be an ordered sequence of actions. Action a_j is *straightly dependent on the effect of action* a_i (denoted as $a_i \rightarrow_S a_j$) if and only if $i < j$, $(e^+(a_i) \cap p(a_j)) \neq \emptyset$ and there does not exist any $k_1, \ldots, k_l$ such that $i < k_1, \ldots, k_l < j$ and $(e^+(a_i) \cap p(a_j)) \subseteq \bigcup_{t=1}^{l} e^+(a_{k_t})$.
Let $E(a_i, a_j)$ be a set of predicates defined in the following way:

- $E(a_i, a_j) = (e^+(a_i) \cap p(a_j)) \setminus \bigcup_{t=i+1}^{j-1} e^+(a_t)$ iff $a_i \rightarrow_S a_j$
- $E(a_i, a_j) = \emptyset$ otherwise

Action a_j is *dependent on the effect of action* a_i if and only if $a_i \rightarrow_S^* a_j$ where $\rightarrow_S^*$ is a transitive closure of the relation $\rightarrow_S$.

Meaning of the relation of straight dependency on the effect of action (hereinafter $\rightarrow$ only) is such that if $a_i \rightarrow a_j$ is satisfied then the particular predicate (or predicates) needed for action a_j is provided by action a_i which is the last action providing this predicate (or predicates) before action a_j. It is also clear that an action may be in the relation $\rightarrow$ with more than one action.

We also need another relation which can help to detect which actions can be swapped without loss of validity of the plan.

Definition 1.2: Let $< S = a_1, \ldots, a_n >$ be an ordered sequence of actions. Actions a_i and a_j (without loss of generality we assume that $i < j$) are *independent on the effects* (denoted as $a_i \leftrightarrow_S a_j$) if and only if $a_i \rightarrow^*_S a_j$ is not satisfied, $p(a_i) \cap e^-(a_j) = \emptyset$ and $e^+(a_j) \cap e^-(a_i) = \emptyset$.

It can be proved that adjacent actions being in relation $\leftrightarrow$ can be performed in any order (or paralely) without loss of plan validity. The full proof can be found in [3].

4. Investigation of Plan Structures

As we mentioned in the introduction that some planning problems can be solved in polynomial time [6,7]. In planning we can apply algorithms based on forward search, backward search or combination of both. However, these algorithms have a high complexity in general. The complexity can be reduced (to polynomial) on such problems, where the plans have a specific structure.

The following theorem says that if a plan structure with respect to relation $\rightarrow$ looks like a path, there exists a polynomial algorithm which solves the particular problem.

Theorem 2.1: Let $\pi =< a_1, \ldots, a_n >$ be a plan solving planning problem $P = (\Sigma, s_0, g)$, $a_0 = (\emptyset, \emptyset, s_0)$ and $a_{n+1} = (g, \emptyset, \emptyset)$. If $a_i \rightarrow_\pi a_{i+1}$ for $0 \leq i \leq n$ and not $a_k \rightarrow_\pi a_l$ for every $k \neq l - 1$ then there exist an algorithm which solves the planning problem P in $O(m^2 \log(m))$ steps where m is the number of actions defined in Σ.

Proof: We can apply the following algorithm:

1. Let A be a set of all actions defined in Σ. Let $Q = \{s_0\}$ be a queue. Let $D = \emptyset$ be a set of visited states.
2. If $A \neq \emptyset$ and $Q \neq \emptyset$ then pick first element s from Q, otherwise fail.
3. If $g \subseteq s$ then succeed.
4. For each $a \in A$ test whether $p(a) \subseteq s$ and $e^+(a) \notin D$. If satisfied then $A := A \setminus a$, $D := D \cup e^+(a)$ and put $e^+(a)$ to the end of Q.
5. Continue with step 2.

The algorithm decides whether there exists a plan solving planning problem P satisfying the conditions from the assumption. It can be easily modified to return a plan (it only decides plan's existence), but for this proof it is not necessary. We can easily see that the algorithm always terminates, because the loop can be performed at most $m + 1$-times (will be explained in the second part of the proof). Steps 1-3 and 5 are corresponding with the well known algorithm for forward planning (using breath-first search). Step 4 differs from the forward planning algorithm in two cases. At first, we set action's positive effects as the result of action's performance. It can be done thanks to the assumption which says that only the subsequent action can use the effects of the current action. At second, we use actions at most once. It is clear that when some action is performed a second time we obtain the same state as in the first time (due to the first case). Now it is clear that the algorithm is correct.

In the second part of the proof we focus on the complexity of the algorithm. At first, we prove that the loop (steps 2-5) can be performed at most $m+1$ times. In the beginning (step 1) Q contains one element. In step 4 we see that when an element is pushed into Q, an element is removed from A. We know that $|A| = m$. At second, we can see that step 4 is performed for each element from A which can be done at most m times. At third, we have to test (at step 4) whether a state was already visited or not which can be done at $O(\log(m))$ steps when we keep the set D sorted. To keep the set D sorted we must take care when adding new elements. In this case, we are adding the same element as we looking for before which means that we know where the element should be placed. Finally, we can put all these results together, thereby we get that the algorithm can be run in $O(m^2 \log(m))$ steps. $\qquad\square$

The following theorem says that if actions in a plan are all in relation $\nleftrightarrow$, there exists a polynomial algorithm which solves the particular problem.

Theorem 2.2: Let $\pi = <a_1, \ldots, a_n>$ be a plan solving planning problem $P = (\Sigma, s_0, g)$. If $a_i \nleftrightarrow_\pi a_j$ for each $i < j$, then there exist an algorithm which solves the planning problem P in $O(m^2)$ steps where m is the number of actions defined in Σ.

Proof: We can apply the following algorithm:

1. Let A be a set of such actions that $p(a) \subseteq s_0$, $e^+(a) \cap g \neq \emptyset$ and $e^-(a) \cap g = \emptyset$.
2. Compute graph $G = (V, E)$, where $V = A$ and $(a_i, a_j) \in E$ iff a_i is not in relation $\nleftrightarrow$ with a_j (here, relation $\nleftrightarrow$ is not still connected to an existing sequence of actions and we must secure its validity in any plan we find).
3. Let PE be a multi-set such that $PE = \bigcup_{a \in A} e^+(a)$.
4. If $g \nsubseteq PE \cup (s_0 \cap g)$ the fail.
5. If G is a discrete graph then succeed.
6. Pick $a \in A$ such that $g \subseteq (PE \setminus (e^+(a)) \cup (s_0 \cap g)$ and with the highest degree in G. If there is no such an action then fail, otherwise set $A := A \setminus \{a\}, PE := PE \setminus e^+(a)$ and remove a from G.
7. Continue with step 5.

The algorithm decides whether there exists a plan solving planning problem P satisfying the conditions from the assumption. It is clear that we need such actions that are in relation $\nleftrightarrow$ which means all actions can be performed in any order. We can see that the algorithm always terminates, because the loop can be performed at most $O(m)$-times (will be explained in the second part of the proof). In step 1 we choose only actions that can be performed on the initial state and that provide at least one predicate required in the goal state. In step 2 we build a graph representing a violation of relation $\nleftrightarrow$ (required in the assumption) between actions. Despite relation $\nleftrightarrow$ is not yet connected to an existing plan we simply check all required conditions (see definition 1.2) including the violation of relation $\rightarrow$ which can be expressed as an empty intersection of positive effects of the first action and precondition of the second action. In step 3 we create a multi-set representing all predicates that will be added after performing of all actions (we can store predicates in these multi-sets more than once). If the condition in step 4 is not satisfied, it is clear that we cannot find a solution (we know that no predicate from $s_0 \cap g$ cannot be removed, because for every action a $e^-(a) \cap g = \emptyset$ holds. If the condition in step 5 is satisfied then we have a solution (all actions in A) because there does not exist any pair of actions violating relation $\leftrightarrow$. Otherwise, we must continue removing of actions violation relation $\leftrightarrow$ (we prefer such an action that violates the relation with the most actions) which is done in step 6, but we cannot break the condition $g \subseteq (PE \setminus (e^+(a)) \cup (s_0 \cap g)$ (similar to the condition in step 4). When the action is removed from A, we update graph G and multi-set PE and continue the loop (step 5). If no action can be removed, it is clear that we cannot find a solution. Now, it is clear that the algorithm is correct.

In the second part of the proof we focus on the complexity of the algorithm. It is clear that step 1 and step 3 run at most in $O(m)$ steps. It is also clear that step 2 runs at most in $O(m^2)$ steps. The loop between step 5 and 6 runs at most in $O(m)$ steps, because we have at most m actions and in each step we remove one (or exit, when we found a solution or no action can be removed). Step 6 runs at most in $O(m)$ steps, because we have at most m actions and each action can be tested at most once. Now, it is clear that the loop runs at most in $O(m^2)$ steps. Finally, when we put these results together, we see that the algorithm can run in $O(m^2)$ steps. $\qquad\square$

We can extend this idea to more complex plans. We decompose these plans to layers, where each layer contains actions performable in any order. In the following lines we show how whole plans can be decomposed to such layers.

Definition 2.3: Let $\pi = < a_1, \ldots, a_n >$ be a plan solving planning problem $P = (\Sigma, s_0, g)$, $a_0 = (\emptyset, \emptyset, s_0)$ and $a_{n+1} = (g, \emptyset, \emptyset)$. Let $level_\pi : A \to N_0$ be a function such that:

1. $level_\pi(a_0) = 0$
2. For each $j < i$, where a_j not in relation $\leftrightarrow_\pi$ with a_i $level_\pi(a_j) < level_\pi(a_i)$ holds.
3. For each action a $level_\pi(a)$ is as small as possible.

Definition 2.4: Let $\pi = < a_1, \ldots, a_n >$ be a plan solving planning problem $P = (\Sigma, s_0, g)$, $a_0 = (\emptyset, \emptyset, s_0)$ and $a_{n+1} = (g, \emptyset, \emptyset)$. Let a sequence of actions with the same value of $level$ function be a *layer*. Let sl_k be an *after-layer state* defined as $sl_k = \bigcup E(a_i, a_j)$, where $level_\pi(a_i) \leq k$ and $level_\pi(a_j) > k$.

Now we know how to decompose a plan into layers with respect to function $level$. The next theorem shows the advantage of such a decomposition.

Theorem 2.5: Let $P = (\Sigma, s_0, g)$ be a planning problem. If there exists any plan solving P which can be decomposed to at most polynomial number of layers and if we are able to compute all after-layer states in polynomial time then P can be solved in polynomial time.

Proof: From the assumption we know that we can compute all after-layer states $(sl_0, \ldots sl_k)$ in polynomial time. Then we apply the algorithm listed in the proof of theorem 2.2 on planning problems $P_1, \ldots P_k$, where $P_i = \{\Sigma, sl_{i-1}, sl_i\}$. As we proved in theorem 2.2, all planning problems $P_1, \ldots P_k$ can be solved in polynomial time. From the assumption we also know that we have at most a polynomial number of these plan-

ning problems which means that planning problem P can be solved in polynomial time.
$\square$

5. Conclusions

Despite promising planning techniques and heuristics, the existing planners are still using 'brute force' methods to solve planning problems even though some problems (or parts of them) are easy to solve. In this paper, we proposed a method for plans analysis via action dependencies. In terms of this method we are looking for some characteristics that can be used for designing fast algorithms that can run usually in polynomial time.

We showed that when a structure of a given planning problem matches the given criteria then a plan can be found in polynomial time. Despite the presented theorems illustrate very specific problems, they can be applied to more realistic planning problems because many of the problems contain subproblems matching these criteria. When we are able to decompose a planning problem into a polynomial number of layers and find all after-layer states (definition 2.4) then we can solve the problem in polynomial time (as it is said in theorem 2.5). For instance, PSR domain from IPC 4 is very interesting, because every solution of a problem from this domain can be easily decomposed into the layers (the number of the layers is bounded by constant). Each layer has a specfic characteristics which can be applied on computing of after-layer states.

On the other hand, we have to obtain more knowledge about planning domains and planning problems defined on these domains, especially about decompositions of the problems. We believe that the combination of the planning problems decomposition and the methods for polynomial solving of the 'specific' planning problems should lead to more improved planning methods by which we can solve more complex problems significantly faster.

References

[1]   Bonet, B., and Geffner, H. 1999. Planning as heuristic search: New results. In *Proceedings of ECP*, 360–372.

[2]   Chrpa, L. 2007. Using of a graph of action dependencies for plans optimization. In *Proceedings of IMCSIT/AAIA*, volume 2, 213–223.

[3]   Chrpa, L., and Bartak, R. 2008. Towards Getting Domain Knowledge: Plans Analysis through Investigation of Actions Dependencies In *Proceedings of FLAIRS*, To appear.

[4]   Ghallab, M.; Nau, D.; and Traverso, P. 2004. *Automated planning, theory and practice.* Morgan Kaufmann Publishers.

[5]   Gimenez, O., and Jonsson, A. 2007. On the hardeness of planning problems with simple causal graphs. In *Proceedings of ICAPS*, 152–159.

[6]   Helmert, M. 2003. Complexity results for standard benchmark domains in planning. *Artificial Intelligence*, 143(2):219–262.

[7]   Helmert, M. 2006. New complexity results for classical planning benchmarks. In *Proceedings of ICAPS*, 52–61.

[8]   International Planinng Competition http://ipc.icaps-conference.org

[9]   Katz, M., and Domshlak, C. 2007. Structural patterns of tracable sequentialy-optimal planning. In *Proceedings of ICAPS*, 200–207.

[10]   Knoblock, C. 1994. Automatically generated abstractions for planning. *Artificial Intelligence* 68(2):243–302.

Tenth Scandinavian Conference on Artificial Intelligence
A. Holst et al. (Eds.)
IOS Press, 2008

Reducing temporal delays in a real time train management system

Per KREUGER, Malin FORSGREN, Martin ARONSSON
Swedish Institute of Computer Science (SICS)

Abstract We report results on a combined scheduling and resource allocation problem in transportation. The problem occurs in a real time management system for vehicles when it is disturbed by introducing unplanned service tasks and temporal delays of the transportation and service tasks. A method to solve the the problem using a constraint programming model is described in some detail. Preliminary test runs of the solver on problem sets generated by a simulator taking statistic models of the wear of the vehicle components into account are also reported.

Keywords. Routing and scheduling, rail transportation, dynamic re-planning, delay minimisation

1. Introduction

This report describes the result of a study of a vehicle routing and scheduling problem in rail transportation. The problem occurs where we have a planned vehicle circulation that is disturbed, either in terms of the introduction of unplanned vehicle service tasks or in terms of temporal delays of planned service and transportation tasks. The latter would include delays that are consequences of vehicle malfunctions, also requiring service.

Although generating optimal vehicle routes for a fixed schedule is regularly used in transportation [10], combining such problems with scheduling [3,7] and/or rescheduling are much more difficult in practice, although a significant body of work on this type of problem does exist, e.g. [9,13,14]. An example of a successful practical application of such a model is reported in [2] and the model described here is an adaption of similar ideas to the case of dynamic re-planning.

In earlier work [6], re-planning methods based on local search were used to dynamically re-plan the routes of the individual vehicles so that circuits were maintained but supplied by several vehicles over time with the objective to eliminate breaches of service requirement deadlines. Reducing temporal transportation task delays in such a schedule can be done by shortening dwell times in the current routes of the individual vehicles. However, doing so in a straightforward way does not exploit options posed by rerouting the vehicles.

We will describe a method to solve such problems based on constraint programming scheduling [1,4,11] techniques. We will also report the results of running an implementation of the method on problems generated by a complex simulator of the dynamics of a running transportation system. This simulator maintains the position and state of each vehicle in a system that evolves with time. Each vehicle is represented by statistical models of several of its sub-components, e.g. doors, compressors, brakes etc. The model is used to generate vehicle service requirements with associated deadlines. A software module in the simulator schedules service tasks and re-plans the routes of the individual vehicles to eliminate breaches of service requirement deadlines. Such deadlines are typically expressed in terms of e.g. number of door openings, actual run times of compressors etc. These accumulators are more strongly correlated with the number of kilometers travelled than with time, and in general also dependent on the route travelled and transportation the task performed.

In order to obtain a more realistic simulation and evaluate methods to solve this kind of problem, we introduced temporal transportation task delays into the system. The problems studied in the empirical section of this report were generated in this way. The solutions generated by our solver were read back into the graphical interface simulator and verified by manual inspection. The simulator can also be restarted using the generated solution as a starting point and used to reduce any remaining breaches with respect to the service requirement deadlines.

Note that the solver described here does not take service requirement deadlines into account in any other way than trying to reduce any temporal delays of the planned and dynamically introduced service task and ensuring that they are in fact performed on the correct vehicle. Comparing alternative schedules with respect to some other measure than time would be a much more more difficult problem to solve to optimality with exhaustive search of the kind studied here. Instead we envision a hybrid system where the vehicle service demands are handled by local search of the kind currently built into the simulator and transportation task delays by complete methods by the kind described herein.

Integrating two such systems into a decision support tool would constitute a major further development but also has the potential to improve the management of transportation systems of this kind most significantly. The currently implemented systems together constitute a crude first attempt to implement a hybrid of this kind.

2. Further background on the considered case

The particular case we consider in the simulator emulates the dynamic management of a medium sized real train system in Mälardalen with 1060 scheduled transports performed repeatedly by 11 vehicles. The original turnaround plan supplied by the operator may have been modified by the simulator in order to route the vehicles to a single service site on demand. However, each vehicle is associated with a current sequence of transports and service tasks for the coming week. We will call such a sequence of transportation and service tasks the *(task) chain* of the vehicle.

We presume that we have sufficient information about the state of the train system to be able to reliably estimate the current delay of start and end times of each transport and service task. In the simulator such data is currently produced by manually entering delays for individual arrivals and projecting the delays forward in the current task chains of the involved vehicles. In a more realistic setting information of this kind would not be completely reliable and would also ideally include information on future expected delays caused by e.g. performance reductions due to some types of vehicle malfunctions. Such complications has not been considered in the work reported here.

To take projected future delays into account would be straightforward in our current model. How the search behaviour of our current solver implementation would be affected by e.g. opportunities to reduce delays by routing vehicles through transports where a performance reduction matters less, has however not yet been addressed.

To reroute, based on statistical estimates of future delays, would naturally be a much more difficult task but also a very interesting one, as a future research direction.

The state description exported from the simulator includes the original schedule and current delays as well as the task chain of each vehicle. Our solver relaxes the schedule and the chains in an interval from the "now" of the simulator to a future time that can be set as a parameter but currently defaults to *six hours* from "now". The start and end times of tasks in this interval are relaxed to a time window ranging from the originally scheduled time to either the currently projected delayed time or the original planned time plus a fixed offset, whichever is larger. The fixed offset is a parameter to the solver and has been set to *six hours* for the experiments. In addition all tasks with delayed start times that occur after the relaxed interval are relaxed to time windows ranging between the originally planed time for the task and the currently projected delay of its start time.

The task chains are also relaxed so that the successor of each task in a chain is relaxed to range over the entire set of tasks. Service tasks scheduled during the relaxed interval may also be delayed temporally but the vehicle involved is guarantied to be routed through the task. The maximum delay of a service task is a separate parameter.

Before and during search, the domains of both the time and successor variables are reduced by constraint propagation. Delays are reduced by routing vehicles through new task chains so as to minimise the overall delay. The chains after the relaxed interval are maintained which guaranties that the schedule is repeatable unless the relaxed interval includes the last task in some initial task chain, which is unlikely since the initial chains are based on the unfolded turn-around plan for a week from "now" and delays are not expected to propagate over several days.

The solver produces a new schedule and a set of task chains that can be read back into the simulator as an improved plan.

3. Problem model

The solver is realised as a combined (re-)scheduling and resource allocation problem where the start and end times of each transport and service task in the relaxed interval are (discrete) decision variables. In addition, the vehicle used to perform a task and its successor are also decision variables. Each vehicle is regarded as a unique resource that can be allocated to at most one task at any given time. There are also constraints that relate the chain variables with time and vehicle variables.

3.1. Problem parameters

t The number of tasks in the problem
v The number of vehicles in the problem
s_i^0, e_i^0 originally planned start and end times of task i
sd_i^0, ed_i^0 projected delay of the start and end of task i
v_i^0 index of original planned vehicle for task i
n_i^0 the originally planned successor of task i in the task chain of vehicle v_i[1]

---

[1] or the vehicle index v_i itself, if i is the last task in the original chain of v_i

l_i^o, l_i^d origin and destination location of task i
db_i bound on the maximum delay of task i in the revised plan[2]
nw, re The current time and end of the relaxed interval

3.2. Decision variables

s_i, e_i the start and time of task i in the revised plan
sd_i, ed_i expected delay of the start and end of task i in the revised plan
d_i allocation time, i.e the task duration plus the vehicle turn time in a given task chain[3]
v_i the vehicle allocated to task i in the revised plan
n_i the successor of task i in the task chain of vehicle v_i [4]

3.3. Constraints

3.3.1. Bounds

Vehicle and successor variables

$0 \leq i < t$ task indices
$-v \leq v_i < 0 \ \forall i \, (0 \leq i < t)$ vehicle indices are negative

Time variables   Bounds for tasks in the relaxed interval are limited by the following inequalities

$$s_i^0 \leq s_i \leq \max \left(s_i^0 + db_i, s_i^0 + sd_i^0\right) \ \forall i \, (0 \leq i < t) \, nw \leq s_i^0 + sd_i^0 < re \ \text{task start times}$$
$$e_i^0 \leq e_i \leq \max \left(e_i^0 + db_i, e_i^0 + ed_i^0\right) \ \forall i \, (0 \leq i < t) \, nw \leq e_i^0 + ed_i^0 < re \ \text{task end times}$$

Furthermore, other delayed tasks in the future, i.e. after re are relaxed as follows

$$s_i^0 \leq s_i \leq s_i^0 + sd_i^0 \ \forall i \, (0 \leq i < t) \, re \leq s_i^0 + sd_i^0 \ \text{task start times}$$
$$e_i^0 \leq e_i \leq e_i^0 + ed_i^0 \ \forall i \, (0 \leq i < t) \, re \leq e_i^0 + ed_i^0 \ \text{task end times}$$

as a consequence, tasks that are not delayed keep their initially scheduled times.

3.3.2. Vehicle chain constraints

$v_i = v_{n_i} \ \forall i \, (0 \leq i < t)$ chains preserve vehicle
$\quad n_i < 0 \rightarrow v_i = n_i \ \forall i \, (0 < i \leq t)$ successor of last task in chain identifies vehicle
$\qquad$ (negative index)
$l_i^d \neq l_j^o \rightarrow n_i \neq j \ \forall ij \, (0 < i, j \leq t)$ start location of successor must be same as end location of predecessor

The above constraints are realised by reifying[5] the (in)equalities as boolean variables and boolean reasoning in the constraint solver.

---

[2]In practice, only two distinct values are used for these parameters, one for the transport tasks, and one for the service tasks.

[3]This is the length of the interval between the start s_i and the start of its successor s_{n_i} in the chain of v_i in the revised plan; the last task in a task chain will have a duration equal to that of the performed task only

[4]or the index of v_i itself whenever i is the last task in the chain of v_i in the revised plan

[5]i.e. encoding the truth of the constraint as a boolean variable

$(i \neq j \rightarrow n_i \neq n_j) \; \forall ij \, (-v < i, j \leq t)$ Distinct successors

Since there are as many distinct values in the domains of the variables as there are variables, this condition ensures that there will be exactly v distinct task chains. The condition is realised by the global constraint `all_distinct` [12].

3.3.3. Scheduling constraints

$e_i^0 - s_i^0 \leq e_i - s_i \leq d_i = s_{n_i} - s_i \; \forall ij \, (0 \leq i, j < t)$ Task duration
$(v_i = v_j) \rightarrow (s_i + d_i \leq s_j \lor s_j + d_j \leq s_i) \; \forall ij \, (0 \leq i, j \leq t)$ Non overlapping tasks
       on each single resource

Note that the duration between the start times of two consecutive tasks in a chain is used as task duration, not only the time taken by the task itself. This condition effectively prunes the successor variables by reasoning on non-overlap, once the vehicles has been allocated and is essential for the scalability of the approach. The actual scheduling constraint is realised as geometric constraint on t unit height rectangles with length d_i in the plane (`disjoint2`) [5].

3.4. Objective

$$\min \left(\sum_{0 < i < n} (ed_i) \right)$$

i.e. minimise the sum of all arrival time delays.

4. Search heuristic

The heuristics used to explore the search space generated by the relaxation of successor, vehicle and task start and end times can be described as follows:

1. Store the original solution (chains and projected times) and its objective value as the currently best solution
2. Constrain the objective to be strictly less than the best previously found solution

   (a) Find a feasible assignment of the successor variables n_i
   (b) Find the optimal assignment of the start and end variables of each task with respect to the total temporal delay

3. If any of the steps under 2 fails, the stored solution is optimal: If so, go to 4, else store the generated solution and the value of the objective for that solution as the currently best and go to 2
4. Terminate and report the stored solution and its associated objective value.

In practice some cases can be too difficult to solve to optimality. For such cases the above algorithm is augmented with a time-out mechanism that will terminate the computation and report the currently best solution after a fixed maximum duration. In the experiments reported below, the time-out was set to 3 minutes, which was, in all considered cases, sufficient to find an optimal solution.

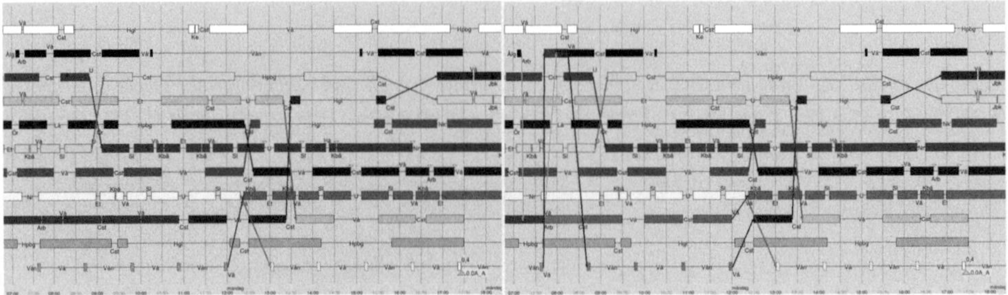

Figure 1. Schedule and vehicle allocation before and after application of the re-scheduler

5. Experimental results

The above constraint model was implemented as a constraint logic program implemented in SICStus Prolog [8] and applied to a series of problems generated by the simulator mentioned above. Each problem was relaxed as indicated above except the service tasks for which we maintained the vehicle allocation.

This resulted in a series of problems with between 50 and 70 relaxed tasks of which all could be solved to optimality within a few minutes. The solutions improved the objective (total temporal delay) with 10-20%. The solutions were also manually inspected by re-reading them into the simulator and displaying them in the graphical interface.

In a few cases increasing the relaxed interval to 12 hours improved the solutions marginally but for one particularly difficult case the solver took more time than the pre-configured time-out to produce even a first improved solution for this relaxation. It seems reasonable to assume that most realistic cases where temporal delays cannot be eliminated within 6 hours would have to be handled in some other way, probably by cancelling certain transport tasks.

Although these tests were far from systematic and exhaustive the implementation of the model and a relaxed period of 6 hours proved reasonably stable and improved almost all considered cases and many of them significantly.

6. Conclusion and perspective

We have implemented and run a preliminary set of tests on a method to reroute and reschedule a set of tasks in a disturbed real time transportation system. The method employs standard scheduling mechanisms available in most modern day constraint programming systems [8] but appear to capture a fair amount of the relevant aspects of the real problem and reliably return improved solutions for the stated problem. Testing at this point remains superficial but the solver model should be of general interest. The use of allocation time rather than task duration in the scheduling constraints introduced in section 3.3.3, in particular appears to improve the scalability of the solver significantly and allows the use of a fairly straightforward search heuristic.

Future work would include taking into account vehicle performance reductions, and through this more realistic overall delay situations. This would also make possible a more realistic assessment of the proposed method as a candidate for deployment in industry. As already mentioned a more systematic integration with methods for minimising breaches of maintenance task deadlines would also be highly desirable.

References

[1] K.R. Apt. *Principles of Constraint Programming*. Cambridge University Press, 2003.

[2] Martin Aronsson, Per Kreuger, and Jonatan Gjerdrum.   An efficient MIP model for locomotive scheduling with time windows.   In Riko Jacob and Matthias Müller-Hannemann, editors, *ATMOS 2006 - 6th Workshop on Algorithmic Methods and Models for Optimization of Railways*, number 06002 in Dagstuhl Seminar Proceedings, DagstUhl, Germany, 2006. Internationales Begegnungs- und Forschungszentrum fuer Informatik (IBFI), Schloss Dagstuhl, Germany. <http://drops.dagstuhl.de/opus/volltexte/2006/683> [date of citation: 2006-01-01].

[3] K.R. Baker. *Introduction to sequencing and scheduling*. Wiley & Sons, 1974.

[4] Philippe Baptiste, Claude Le Pape, and Wim Nuijten. *Constraint-Based Scheduling*. Kluwer Academic Publishers, Norwell, MA, USA, 2001.

[5] Nicolas Beldiceanu and Mats Carlsson.   Sweep as a generic pruning technique applied to the non-overlapping rectangles constraint. In *CP '01: Proceedings of the 7th International Conference on Principles and Practice of Constraint Programming*, pages 377–391, London, UK, 2001. Springer-Verlag.

[6] Markus Bohlin and Malin Forsgren.   Utvärdering av simulerat dynamiskt underhåll för spårbundna fordon. Technical report T2008:02, SICS, 2007.

[7] J. Carlier and E. Pinson.   An algorithm for solving the job-shop problem. *Management Science*, 35(2):164–176, 1989.

[8] Mats Carlsson et al. *SICStus Prolog Users Manual*. SICS, 1995. ISBN 91-630-3648-7. For latest version see `http://www.sics.se/isl/sicstus/docs/`.

[9] J. Desrosiers, Y. Dumas, M.M. Solomon, and F. Soumis. *Network Routing*, volume 8 of *Handbooks in Operations Research and Management Science*, chapter Time Constrained Routing and Scheduling, pages 35–139. North-Holland, 1995.

[10] J. Drott, E. Hasselberg, N. Kohl, and M. Kremer. A planning system for locomotive scheduling. Technical report, Swedish State Railways, Stab Tågplanering, Stockholm, Sweden, and Carmen Systems AB, Jul 1997.

[11] V. Gosselin.   Train scheduling using constraint programming techniques.   In *13th conference on AI, expert systems and natural language*, Avignon, 1993.

[12] J. C. Régin. A filtering algorithm for constraints of difference in CSP's. In *Proceedings of the twelfth national conference on artificial Intelligence AAAI-94*, 1994.

[13] M.M. Solomon.   Algorithms for the vehicle routing and scheduling problem with time window constraints. *Operations Research*, 35(2):254–265, March-April 1987.

[14] M.M. Solomon and J. Desrosiers. Time window constrained routing and scheduling problems. *Transportation Science*, 22(1):1–13, 1988.

3. Invited Talks

Tenth Scandinavian Conference on Artificial Intelligence
A. Holst et al. (Eds.)
IOS Press, 2008

The Many Faces of Biosurveillance

Kathleen A. McCORMICK, Ph.D., FACMI
Rockville, MD USA

Keywords. Biosurveillance, Visual Imaging, Detection, Vaccine Development, Monitoring and Surveillance, Response, Outreach, and Dissemination

Introduction

In 1918 forty million people died from a major influenza pandemic that swept the globe. There were no decision support systems, no geographic mapping systems, no robotics, no machine learning, no automated knowledge representations, natural language processing (NLP), or automated planning and scheduling systems, and many of the industrial computer applications were another 50 years coming. SARS swept the globe with all of these toolkits in place and time to discovery was shortened because of them. There is no question that in the future we will see another pandemic – we just do not know when it will occur, and how bad it will be.

For the next pandemic, technology innovations in biotechnology discovery, drugs and vaccines may be able to lower the impact. However, responding to a pandemic will demand the use of new technologies, international collaboration, and cooperation of the entire world community. The multiple groups of biosurveillance include the family, neighborhood, local community, large cities, states, countries, continents and the global community which will be affected. The toolkits needed include advanced virus and disease detection, enhanced surveillance and alert systems, decision support tools for emergency responders and clinicians, GIS mapping, NLP with Really Simple Syndication (RSS) feeds, automated planning and scheduling of essential personnel, broad communication links and outreach.

In addition to the pandemic threat, the environment in which the threat takes place is in a rapidly growing information society with advanced collaboration networks. There are now 898 billion personal computers (up from 131 million in 1990); 2.7 billion cell phones (up from 11.2 million in 1990); 209 countries connected to the Internet (up from 20 in 1990); 110 million internet sites (up from 9,300 in 1990); 395 million host computers connected to the Internet (up from 313,000 in 1990); and 532,897 Internet storage in terabytes (up from 0 in 1990) [1].

In 2007, the amount of digital information created, captured, and replicated was 2.25×10^{21} bits (or 281 exabytes or 281 billion gigabytes). That converts to about 45 gigabytes per person around the world [2]. This was about 3 million times the information in all the books ever written in 2006. Herein lies the challenge: managing the information for business and consumers, and finding knowledge nuggets in this vast sea of digitization -searching for unstructured information.

A country's first line of surveillance is the environment, and the second is the healthcare system. How many times does one see on television the pictures of the person initiating a threat on a surveillance camera? Detecting the symptoms come from national laboratories; but recognizing the symptoms come from the point of care in clinical healthcare. The flow of information oftentimes goes from individual clinicians to epidemiologic surveillance systems. The many faces of biosurveillance described in this paper include: 1) visual images, 2) advanced virus and disease detection, 3) antiviral and vaccine development, 4) monitoring and surveillance, and 5) response, outreach and dissemination of information.

1. The First Face of Surveillance – Visual Images

The explosion of digital information created, captured and replicated worldwide comes from camcorder clips, digital television signals, camera telephones, iPods, global positional systems, games, laptop PCs, PDAs, digital journals, and surveillance cameras. Add to this first use of digital, the social network growth from blogs and WIKIs; and the DVD movie storage industry. The Radio Frequency Identification (RFID) tags in the manufacturing industry such as drugs, trucks, and other packets; and the number of sensors in the retail/wholesale industry, coupled with environment screening of air, water, microbes; plus VoIP add to the volume of digital information. The energy industry is developing grid solutions to electrical distribution. In healthcare, the principal growth of digital is in radiographic images and surveillance for public health and adverse reactions in the electronic health record. The growth of digital images is occurring in the US, Europe, China, India and most major urban centers on the globe [2].

2. The Second Face of Surveillance – Advanced Virus and Disease Detection

The discoveries related to pathogens and global pandemic disease is no different than the discoveries leading to cancer, heart disease, and diabetes cures. The science is atomic, digital, and genetic, and the IT support is digital, biotechnology and nanotechnology innovations. We are on a path to translate the new discoveries at the bench to services at the bedside. We are on a path to build on knowledge and technology fusions that can enable that unravel the volume of webs and provide new products and/or services.

Research advances in the genetic structures of the virus have accelerated the maturation of DNA vaccines against influenza viruses. Working in this area of cell biology, the tools of computational biology involve all the robust computational biology, mathematical modeling, simulation, NLP reading of literature, robotics in chip technology, and grid platform technology to integrate multiple databases for accelerated discovery. The US collaborates with the World Health Organization (WHO) and other international partners in creating mechanisms to develop and deliver virus and disease detection toolkits in a coordinated manner around the world.

The searches for rapid diagnostic tests and sensors are in development, with the hope that these toolkits will shorten the time from the suspected diagnosis to the confirmation of diagnosis so that treatment can begin early. Rapid diagnostic and evaluation kits are used for screening and surveillance. The challenge involves capturing these data at the point-of-care in clinics and outpatient healthcare facilities, and distributing the results through local networks to national repositories and global alert laboratories. A recent study by Mackay et al., published in March in the Journal of Clinical Virology, indicated that the accuracy of detection of positive human viruses ranged from 35–98% and subtypes of viruses ranged from 32–87% [3]. Incorrect subtyping results included the reporting of avian influenza viruses as human strains and vice versa. Much work still needs to be done for rapid molecular detection in laboratories around the world. Most of this process can be totally automated with Laboratory Information Management Systems, computational biology, decision logic, and advanced algorithms.

3. The Third Face of Surveillance – Antiviral and Vaccine Development

The National Institute of Allergy and Infectious Diseases (NIAID, 2003) Biodefense Research Agenda for CDC Category A Agents (NIAID) describes the use of microorganisms as a cause of human disease, or of toxins derived from them, that harm people or elicit widespread fear or intimidation of a nation [4]. In this report the NIAID identified that these pathogens are just variants of general problems of emerging infectious diseases, the only difference is that one is caused by increased virulence and the other is a deliberate act of man rather than the consequence of natural evolution of pathogens. The development cycle of antiviral and vaccine development is another challenge of information technology and intelligence systems. A unique part of the strategy is in mining the data already deposited in national public repositories of genes and biomarkers, drug monitoring, detecting and surveillance of adverse drug events (ADE) and integration into the clinical record environment.

4. The Fourth Face of Surveillance – Monitoring and Surveillance

The preparedness of a local, state, country, or nations monitoring and surveillance involves the same set of computational and intelligence systems as for any naturally occurring, accidental, or terrorist-induced emergencies. Epidemic sequellae are now predicted using computer simulation models. The virtual social network system called EpiSims ingests demographic, daily activity, geography, and location and other elements to simulate pathogens entering a large urban population [5]. Through simulation and modeling systems, one is able to release any virtual pathogen and examine the resultant epidemic and test for the effects of intervention strategies. When these systems are integrated into the public health network, the resultant infection can be isolated and the length of delay of public health official response can shortened.

Another system called Models of Infectious Disease Agent Study (MIDAS) has been developed by the National Institute of General Medical Sciences (NIGMS) that modifies EpiSims to model naturally occurring diseases with global threat potential have released a study using MIDAS to evaluate the effectiveness of antiviral drugs for mass prophylaxis to contain and outbreak [6].

At the center of IT in biosurveillance is integration. In a previous paper by Snee and McCormick, the elements for an integrated public health system were described [7]. The Centers for Disease Control and Prevention in Atlanta develop a Public Health Information Network (PHIN) that set the standards and framework to unify data for early detection and efficient response. The National Health Information Network (NHIN) within DHHS has extended the biosurveillance standards with use case scenarios and recommended standards for linking data in emergency situations.

Preparing for a pandemic or any national disaster requires the utilization of medical information since the populations bring into those disasters their medical conditions and the results of chemical, biological, radiological, and nuclear explosives are disease, disability, and or death [8]. The IT requirements to support biosurveillance involve integration of agency data, integration of voice, images, geographic locators, and legal and clinical records. What Hurricane Katrina demonstrated in the US was that at a minimum the data required to make clinical decisions for continuity of care in evacuees with chronic health conditions needed to include allergies, current diagnosis, medication profiles, and laboratory results. With the movement of evacuees to 52 states in the country, additional IT resources required were intake registries, scheduling and staffing, tracking of computerized physician order entries, GIS systems, and the visual movement of evacuees.

In the 2002 report by the Agency for Healthcare Research and Quality, the tools for diagnostics and decision support for use by clinicians were described. They included the need for 1) detection and monitoring systems, 2) analytic systems, 3) information and knowledge management resources, 4) alerting and communication technologies, and 5) response systems [9]. Bravata et al. in 2004 described 217 existing IT computerized decision support tools that would be utilized when to responding in biosurveillance [10]. The group found that clinicians needed decision tools in diagnosis, management, prevention, and reporting to public health agencies. In real world examples, simulation and modeling described by Barrett in March 2005, may provide a way to virtually access the accuracy and effectiveness of decision support [5].

A review article of all the architectures, methodologies and tools that could be used at the local and regional levels to protection against bioevents was published by Kohane 2002 [11].

Kun and Bray described all the surveillance systems relevant to biosurveillance in 2002 and defined a matrix information infrastructure that links federal and state governments [12].

An example of international cooperation for monitoring and surveillance was as recent as late last year in 2007. For the first time a human suspected on having H5N1 arrived from Pakistan to New York. The person was quickly found negative of H5N1 and no risk to the community, however what the incident underscored was the need for international collaboration to detect and monitor the presence of the virus [13].

Special use of GIS mapping identifies where disease is occurring. Decision analytics rely on statistical models for predicting the presence/absence of disease. However, new forms of predictive algorithms need to be developed since the predictive power of the models lose much of their power when extrapolated outside the spatial range of their training data, which is usually a large metropolitan city, or a state or country. When the prevalence rates are low, logistic regression models to disease data are also problematic [14].

5. The Fifth Face of Surveillance – Response, Outreach and Dissemination of Information

According to the IDC, in the next 5 years 2 billion people will be on the Internet and 3 billion on mobile phones [2]. Therefore, the capability to respond, outreach, disseminate at the individual level is possible. This is raising regulatory and policy issues like personal security, privacy, manage and store the information. When is use with surveillance acceptable such as in a pandemic, and when is it an invasion of personal rights.

Inherent in these technologies are those that support surge capacity in hospitals and other healthcare facilities, staffing and scheduling systems. Two types of legitimate surveillance uses of information systems that are linked include the number of cases surging into healthcare environments due to a local or national disaster, the equipment available and the staffing shortages that could be activated throughout hospital groups and regional networks. In a pandemic, not only will the patient census reach unprecedented levels, but health providers will be ill, have to leave work to care for family members, or decline to serve for fear of contagion.

From the fair distribution of vaccines, and antiviral drugs, to the distribution of scarce staffing resources, to the distribution of ventilators, to the decisions a family needs to make during a pandemic, the use of decision support tools are required. Here are two specific examples:

1)　web based staffing and scheduling systems have been designed to allocate resources of healthcare providers, not only within a hospital, but across hospitals [15]. These systems include pre-qualified certification information and census of healthcare professionals. These decision aids when enlisted across hospital, treat the healthcare professional supply as a community resource rather than a particular site.
One system in the United States called BidShift was put into task this past winter with the seasonal influenza. The monitoring and surveillance of who is sick in the workforce is an often forgotten piece of outreach and dissemination.

2)　When there are more sick patients than there are ventilators to treat those in respiratory distress, the state of New York developed a task for allocation in a public health disaster [16]. Involved in the decision support systems are surge capacity, staffing ratios, ventilator availability, category of patients, histories of acute versus chronic diseases such as end stage renal disease, and level of function. The integration of the SOFA scoring system into hospital care record systems would be required for these decisions.

Communities of practice are an essential feature in a digital environment. That is why the blogs, WIKI communities are rising since they focus on one knowledge area in a particular domain. First responders, firemen, rescue personnel, healthcare professionals and providers, and public health agencies and laboratories are forming networks to communicate without going through the larger web of webs.

6. Concluding Challenges

The faces of surveillance occur in at least 5 dimensions [17]. When applied to large population health issues, digital information needs fusion of national and global systems. The science of the digital future is finding information in unstructured forms. This involves fusion of information from literature, images, and surveillance cameras. Integrated data can be searched, but current copyright protections do not cover digital reuse of data. Communities have to decide when data need to be preserved and what data need to be preserved indefinitely. The preservation of the data is a government and private sector discovery, yet no tools for long-term preservation and access of data exist [18]. Communities of practice are essential in the outreach and dissemination of digital data, but the balance of personal privacy and security and national interests have not been worked out. The life cycle of a pandemic requires digital management at each step of the process with common standards and ontologies [19]. For the artificial intelligence society the challenge is providing data in a timely and accessible format; providing users with tools for summarization, synthesis, analysis, and visualization of information for decision making; research focused on the creation of knowledge from digital data, including novel algorithms, data mining, and dimension reduction methodologies; create innovation technologies to address data confidentiality, privacy, and security; the development of advanced mobile and distributed information for emergency personnel; and to develop measures and management systems to evaluate human responses to data.

References

[1]   Council on Competitiveness. Five for the Future. Annual meeting report, October 26, 2007.
[2]   Ganz, JF, Chute, C, Manfrediz, Al, et al. The Diverse and Exploding Digital Universe: An Updated Forecast of the Worldwide Information Growth Through 2011. IDC. White Paper, March 2008.
[3]   Mackay, WG, vanLoon, AM, Niedrig, M et al. Molecular detection and typing of influenza viruses: Are we ready for an influenza pandemic? J Clin Virol.
[4]   NIAID Biodefense Research Agenda for CDC Category A Agents. Progress Report. August 2003. NHIN. www.hhs/nhin/healthit.gov.
[5]   Barrett, CL, Eubank, SG, and Smith, JP. If smallpox strikes Portland.... Sci Am, 292(3) 42-29, March 2005.
[6]   Longini, JM, Nizam, A, Xu, S, et al. Containing Pandemic Influenza at the Source. Science Express Reports online. August 3, 2005 (DOI 10.1126/science.1115717).
[7]   Snee, NL, McCormick, KA. The Case for Integrating Public Health Informatics Networks. IEEE Eng. Med. Biol. Mag. 23(1) 81-88, Jan-Feb. 2004.
[8]   McCormick, KA, Weiner, E, Devoll, JR. Biodefense and Public Health Response. In Press, IEEE 2008.
[9]   Bioterrorism Preparedness and Response: Use of Information Technologies and Decision Support Systems. Prepared by UCSF-Stanford Evidence-Based Practice Center. Evidence Report No. 59, June 2002.
[10] Bravata, DM, McDonald, KM, Szeto, H, Smith, WM, Rydzak, C, and Owens, DK. A conceptual framework for evaluating information technologies and decision support systems for bioterrorism preparedness and response. Med Decis Making. 24(2) 192-206, 2004.
[11] Kohane, IS. The contributions of biomedical informatics to the fight against bioterrorism. J Am Med Inform Assoc. 9(2) 116-199, March-April 2002.
[12] Kun, LG and Bray, DA. Information infrastructure tools for bioterrorism preparedness: Building dual- or multiple-use infrastructures ins the task at hand for state and local health departments. IEEE Eng Med Biol Mag 21(5) 69-85, September-October 2002.
[13] Leavitt, MO. USDHHS Pandemic Planning Update V. Washington, DC: HHS, March 17, 2008.
[14] Gilbert, M; Xiao, Z, Pfeiffer, DU, et al. Mapping H5N1 highly pathogenic avian influenza risk in Southeast Asia. Proceedings of the National Academy of Sciences of the USA, online 105:12, 4769-4774, March 25, 2008.
[15] Brown, EV. Shifting Priorities. Health Management Technology. http://www.healthmgttech.com October 2007.
[16] Powell, T, Crist, KC, Birkhead, GS. Allocation of Ventilators in a Public Health Disaster. Disaster Medicine and Public Health Preparedness 2(1) 20-26, 2008.
[17] Geer, C. Science in 5 Dimensions. NCO, NITRD, Washington, DC, February 17, 2008.
[18] Furlani, C, Romine, C, and Geer, C. Interagency Working Group on Digital Data, NITRD, Washington, DC: February 17, 2008.
[19] McCormick, KA. National efforts for Biosurveillance Standardization: Impact on the International Community. MEDINFO2007, Australia, Brisbane.

Probabilistic-Logic Models: Reasoning and Learning with Relational Structures

Manfred Jaeger

Institut for Datalogi, Aalborg Universitet,
Selma Lagerlöfs Vej 300, DK-9220 Aalborg Ø
`jaeger@cs.aau.dk`

Introduction

Over the last decade several strands of research in Artificial Intelligence and Machine Learning have come together in an emergent field sometimes called *probabilistic logic learning* or *statistical relational learning*. In this extended abstract the origins, development and some current challenges of this field are briefly sketched.

Probability and Logic in AI

Knowledge representation and reasoning under uncertainty is one of the long-standing challenges for AI. In most approaches to reasoning under uncertainty, the classical calculus of probabilities is used as the underlying framework for quantifying uncertainty. To implement probabilistic reasoning in a formal system, the first natural idea was to build on standard logics, and extend their syntax and semantics so as to obtain systems in which one could not only reason about the truth of falsity of a proposition, but more generally about the probability of a proposition being true. Propositional logic was extended in this way by Nilsson [11] (and, in fact, already 130 years earlier by Boole [2]); first-order logic by Halpern [5] and Bacchus [1].

Several problems emerged for using these *probabilistic logics* in practice: the computational complexity of probabilistic inference, the weak implications often obtained in these logics (i.e. a knowledge base *KB* would often not entail much more for a query proposition ϕ than that the probability of ϕ lies between 0 and 1), and the fact that the logic-based representation languages were not well suited to express knowledge about stochastic independence or causal relations, two important aspects of probabilistic reasoning.

As a result, *probabilistic graphical models*, notably *Bayesian Networks* [12,9], became the more successful paradigm for probabilistic reasoning in AI. Graphical models specify a unique distribution over the possible worlds (and hence over the propositions) for a fixed propositional vocabulary. The specification of graphical models relies heavily on knowledge of independence and/or causality, and inference in graphical models, while still intractable in the worst case, has proven to be feasible in many practical applications.

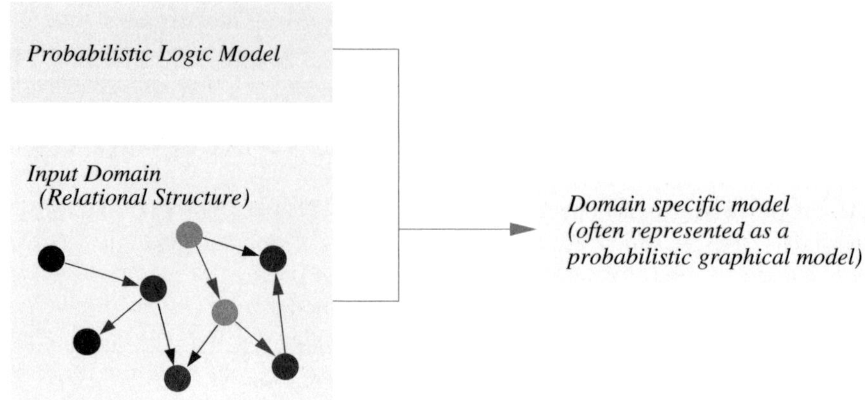

Figure 1. Probabilistic Logic Models

There is a price to pay for these advantages of graphical models over logic-based representations: first, graphical models require a high specification effort, and do not allow for a modular, incremental compilation of partial (probabilistic) knowledge. Second, a probabilistic graphical model is restricted to one particular domain represented by its propositional variables, and does not allow to express more high-level knowledge that generalizes over wide classes of domains. For example, a single graphical model could represent the probability distribution over the propositional variables *bloodtype(John,A)*, *bloodtype(John,B)*, *bloodtype(John,AB)*, *bloodtype(John,0)...*, *bloodtype(Mary,A)*, ..., *bloodtype(Mary,0),...bloodtype(Paul,0)*, representing the bloodtype in the domain *John*, *Mary*, *Paul*, where, say *Mary* and *Paul* are the parents of *John*. However, we can not represent a general model about the probabilities of bloodtypes and the laws of inheritance that could be applied to arbitrary pedigrees.

The second limitation of graphical models is addressed in frameworks for *knowledge based model construction* [3]. Here high-level representation languages using elements of first-order logic are used to specify general knowledge that for each concrete domain (consisting of a set of objects, and possibly some known structure, e.g. the kinship relations in a pedigree) defines a unique probability distribution over a domain-specific set of propositional variables. We call any such high-level model a *probabilistic-logic model*, Figure 1. Examples of formal languages for the specification of probabilistic-logic models are *Prism* [16], *relational Bayesian networks* [6], *Bayesian logic programs* [10], and *Markov logic networks* [15].

Learning from Structured Data

The classical data model in machine learning consists of a list of *examples* (or observations, data-items, ...), each of which consists of values for a certain set of attributes. However, in many modern applications of machine learning, the available data is not easily represented in this format: the world wide web in web mining, bio-molecular data in bioinformatics, social network data – data often comes in the form of labeled graphs, trees, time sequences, or, specifically, relational databases, rather than a plain attribute-value table. Specialized sub-fields of machine learning, notably *inductive logic programming* [13] and *graph mining* [4] have long considered such non-standard forms of data.

Probabilistic-logic models afford a unifying view of many different types of data and connect some of these traditional disciplines of machine learning: many non-standard forms of data can be seen as models over a finite domain of objects (web pages, atoms, ...) for a logical language containing relation symbols of various arities representing attributes and relations (links between web pages, bonds between atoms, ...) of objects. Structured data, thus, has the form of input domains for a probabilistic-logic model as depicted in Figure 1, and Probabilistic-logic models can be used as predictive models for structured data. For example, a probabilistic-logic model for a certain genetic trait over pedigree input domains can be used to predict whether a given person is affected by that trait. Moreover, predictive models with structured output fall within the scope of probabilistic-logic models: a probabilistic-logic model, for example, can also return a probability distribution over possible kinship structures, given an input domain specified only by a set of persons and some of their (genetic) attributes. Thus, the model could be used to predict the underlying pedigree structure from observed genetic data.

Relational Bayesian Networks

Relational Bayesian Networks [6,7] are a representation language for probabilistic-logic models that is based on the syntax of *probability formulas*. These formulas can be seen as probabilistic generalizations of predicate logic formulas: a predicate logic formula $\phi(x_1, \ldots, x_k)$, built via the syntactic constructors *atomic formulas*, *boolean connectives*, and *quantification*, defines for every tuple $c_1, \ldots, c_k$ of domain elements a truth value $\phi(c_1, \ldots, c_k) \in \{true, false\}$. A probability formula $F(x_1, \ldots, x_k)$, built via the syntactic constructors *atomic formulas*, *convex combinations*, and *combination functions* (which closely correspond to the three predicate logic constructors), defines for every tuple $c_1, \ldots, c_k$ of domain elements a probability value $F(c_1, \ldots, c_k) \in [0, 1]$.

A main strength of the Relational Bayesian Network language is the parsimony and recursive nature of its syntax, which enables theoretical analyses as well as algorithmic procedures to be performed by a straightforward induction over the construction of probability formulas. For example, the learning from data of parameter values in relational Bayesian networks is essentially performed by computing partial derivatives of probability formulas by induction over their syntactic form [8].

The *Primula* system (http://www.cs.aau.dk/~jaeger/Primula) is a publicly available implementation of relational Bayesian networks.

Challenges

From a Computer Science and AI perspective, one of the main benefits of developing and studying probabilistic-logic languages is to identify the common, abstract structure of probabilistic models for many domains, and to provide uniform inference and learning methods that are applicable over a wide spectrum of domains and application types. However, it is often unrealistic to expect that the generic algorithms implemented in a system like *Primula* can compete against highly engineered special purpose tools for concrete application tasks like protein structure prediction, or other core tasks in bioinformatics. Nevertheless, the flexibility and richness of probabilistic-logic modeling languages affords also for such applications new opportunities for developing and testing new types of predictive models. The potential of probabilistic-logic models in bioinformatics applications has been demonstrated in a major EU research project, which is documented in [14]. The more specific application for biological sequence analysis is the subject of an ongoing Danish national research project (http://lost.ruc.dk).

Many challenges also remain in the further theoretical and algorithmic development of probabilistic-logic modeling. With regard to inference problems, the focus, so far, has been on "fixed domain" inference problems: how to compute probabilities in models induced by one concrete input domain. However, one can also consider more general questions like: what are the bounds for the probability values of a certain proposition that are obtained when the model is instantiated over a range of input domains? Can inference results obtained for one domain be dynamically updated under incremental changes of the domain?

References

[1]   F. Bacchus. *Representing and Reasoning With Probabilistic Knowledge*. MIT Press, 1990.

[2]   G. Boole. *Investigations of Laws of Thought on which are Founded the Mathematical Theories of Logic and Probabilities*. London, 1854.

[3]   J. S. Breese, R. P. Goldman, and M. P. Wellman. Introduction to the special section on knowledge-based construction of probabilistic decision models. *IEEE Transactions on Systems, Man, and Cybernetics*, 24(11), 1994.

[4]   D. J. Cook and L. B. Holder, editors. *Mining Graph Data*. Wiley, 2007.

[5]   J.Y. Halpern. An analysis of first-order logics of probability. *Artificial Intelligence*, 46:311–350, 1990.

[6]   M. Jaeger. Relational bayesian networks. In Dan Geiger and Prakash Pundalik Shenoy, editors, *Proceedings of the 13th Conference of Uncertainty in Artificial Intelligence (UAI-13)*, pages 266–273, Providence, USA, 1997. Morgan Kaufmann.

[7]   M. Jaeger. Complex probabilistic modeling with recursive relational Bayesian networks. *Annals of Mathematics and Artificial Intelligence*, 32:179–220, 2001.

[8]   M. Jaeger. Parameter learning for relational Bayesian networks. In *Proceedings of the 24th International Conference on Machine Learning (ICML)*, 2007.

[9]   F.V. Jensen and T. D. Nielsen. *Bayesian Networks and Decision Graphs*. Springer, 2007.

[10] K. Kersting and L. De Raedt. Towards combining inductive logic programming and bayesian networks. In *Proceedings of the Eleventh International Conference on Inductive Logic Programming (ILP-2001)*, Springer Lecture Notes in AI 2157, 2001.

[11] N. Nilsson. Probabilistic logic. *Artificial Intelligence*, 28:71–88, 1986.

[12] J. Pearl. *Probabilistic Reasoning in Intelligent Systems : Networks of Plausible Inference*. The Morgan Kaufmann series in representation and reasoning. Morgan Kaufmann, San Mateo, CA, rev. 2nd pr. edition, 1988.

[13] L. De Raedt. *From Inductive Logic Programming to Multi-Relational Data Mining*. Springer, 2008.

[14] L. De Raedt, P. Frasconi, K. Kersting, and S.H. Muggleton, editors. *Probabilistic Inductive Logic Programming*, volume 4911 of *Lecture Notes in Artificial Intelligence*. Springer, 2008.

[15] M. Richardson and P. Domingos. Markov logic networks. *Machine Learning*, 62(1-2):107 – 136, 2006.

[16] T. Sato. A statistical learning method for logic programs with distribution semantics. In *Proceedings of the 12th International Conference on Logic Programming (ICLP'95)*, pages 715–729, 1995.

Tenth Scandinavian Conference on Artificial Intelligence
A. Holst et al. (Eds.)
IOS Press, 2008

201

CBR for Advice Giving
in a Data-Intensive Environment

Agnar AAMODT
Volve AS, Trondheim, Norway

Abstract. Reusing past experiences by reasoning from past cases poses particular problems when the input to case retrieval comes from large amounts of online data. Volve has developed a system in which data from oil well drilling logs are continuously monitored, interpreted, and used to check if previous incidents exist that may predict an unwanted event to happen unless preventive actions are taken. The system is currently being tested.

Keywords. case-based reasoning, decision support, online data analysis, oil-well drilling

Invited talk summary paper.

Introduction

Reusing past experience, i.e. being reminded of similar situations and making use of decision steps made earlier, has turned out to be an efficient way to handle new situations for human beings. Case-Based Reasoning (CBR) builds upon this principle in order to provide improved computer-assistance to people in their daily work. As CBR is becoming more utilized for experience capture and reuse in real-world industrial settings (e.g. [1]), methods for linking human experiences to the observed data related to those experiences are getting increased attention. Many industries, including the oil & gas industry, have access to large amounts of data and information, and advanced tools for displaying various types of information. As the amount of available data increases, the need for tools to extract, or filter out, the relevant information in a given situation increases correspondingly.

We are developing a system that will assist oil well personnel during drilling operations in improving the quality and efficiency of the drilling process. This development is part of a cooperation with the Norwegian oil company StatoilHydro, which has enhanced drilling performance as one if its prioritized areas.

The current version of the system helps to avoid "unwanted events", i.e. events that lead to a slower drilling progression than expected. A particular focus of the system is to help with problems of "poor hole cleaning", i.e. problems that lead to increased resistance for the drill string due to erroneous accumulation of material along the well wall.

Human experience from earlier poor hole cleaning incidents are gathered in a case base. The case base is linked to a model of general domain knowledge, in a manner somewhat similar to the method in the Creek system [2, 3]. In that system the assumption was that case features given as input to the system, i.e. the index terms characterizing a new situation, were entered as symbolic entities. The current system under development at Volve [4] is linked online to an ongoing drilling process, supervises the process by continuously collecting numerical and symbolic data from a large number of parameter readings, interprets these readings, retrieves one or more past cases that match the current state of the drilling process, and on that basis gives advice about how to proceed in order to avoid a possible unwanted event.

In the rest of this paper the steps from the reading of well data to the advices being given to a drilling professional are explained in more detail.

1. Data collection and interpretation

As part of their normal work oil well drilling engineers and other operational personnel both offshore and in support centers onshore have at their disposal a large set of sensor measurements and other drilling parameters. The main portion of these data are continuous data streams from the drilling operation. Tools for keeping track of data from these drilling logs help the personnel to perform graphical comparisons through time- or depth-indexed graphs. This kind of software can be quite powerful visualization tools, but they have limited capabilities in giving the user advices based on interpretation and analyzes of the data.

Volve's software extends the screen information to ensure better decisions. One extension is by giving explicit high-level well status information based on the interpretation of the data. This is done by identifying and displaying particular "interpreted events" attached to the data logs, as the drilling process proceeds. These events are high level interpretations that characterize the status of the well. This is illustrated in the left part of Figure 1. The two leftmost columns are example data logs displaying parameter values (of block position and drill string torque, in this example) vs. time. The horizontal line below the log graphs indicate the current hole depth. The third column shows a sequence of the events interpreted by the software based on the streams of log data. The events below the horizontal line are events predicted by the system (stippled boxes refer to future entities). The middle and right parts of the figure illustrate the system modules responsible for the two main types of decision support functionalities:

- Prediction of unwanted events on a short time scale
- Predication of unwanted event on a longer time scale, with advice on preventive actions.

The Data Interpretation module 'listens' to the set of continuous data streams – typically 20-30 different logs. It has a set of methods, partly based on physical models, and partly on pattern analysis, that will suggest possible unwanted events directly from the data. This can only be done reliably in a short-time perspective – i.e. in the order of a few minutes. In the figure a Partly Stuck event has been predicted in this way. Typically, the user would be given an alarm or other kind of warning in a situation like this.

The Data Interpretation module also has a second role, in addition to short-term prediction: It interprets numerical log data into symbolic features such as qualitative parameter values, trends, interpreted activities, interesting events, etc. for the purpose of identifying useful features for the retrieval of relevant past cases. The cases, in turn, enable more long-term prediction of the well condition.

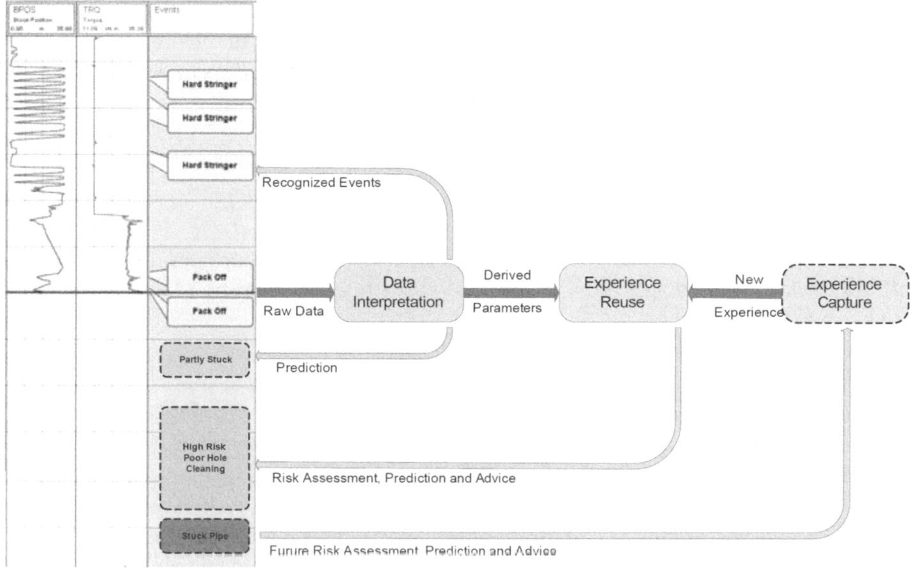

Figure 1. Excerpt from Volve system screen annotated with responsible method modules.

2. Case matching and reuse

The case base captures the human experiences related to previous unwanted events as a set of past cases. The case base is the primary knowledge source for the Experience Reuse module (see Figure 1). Initially, the cases are described manually, based on the analysis of written drilling reports and other textual sources, manually interpreted data logs, and if needed combined with interviews of drilling personnel who were involved in the past incidents. As the system is being used, methods for automated learning of new cases, and automated case base maintenance policies, will take over. This is illustrated by the Experience Reuse module to the right in Figure 1.

The Experience Reuse module attempts to find a matching case (or set of matching cases), with a degree of match above a certain threshold. The case or cases are then used to make predictions of possible unwanted events on a longer time scale. These predictions are based on what happened in the past case(s) retrieved. The user may want to inspect more cases than immediately displayed by the system, by moving down the similarity threshold ladder. On the basis of an identified past case that is sufficiently similar to the current situation, actions are suggested to the operators that should be taken to avoid the predicted event.

A case in this system is a rich source of knowledge. It contains structured data in the form of parameter hierarchies, it contains numerical, symbolic, and textual data.

The textual data is so far only human interpretable. A part of the case, corresponding to parameter values and context information available up to the point of time when the case was captured, is used as index features in the case matching. The rest of the case is used for advice giving after a satisfactory match has been found.

The similarity assessment method assumes that both numerical and symbolic parameters will be used in the matching. A particular challenge is posed by the fact that a realistic case matching process cannot be based on state descriptions in a single snapshot of time only, but needs to take sequence information into account as well.

After the system has predicted possible hazards, and the drilling operator has made the appropriate preventive actions and evaluated the result, the system should learn from its advice giving effort – whether the system's advice turned out successful or not. Learning as part of the normal run-time operation is a characteristic of case-based reasoning, compared to other machine learning methods. Each problem solving experience, i.e. each prediction of a possible unwanted event made by the computer, is a powerful source for learning. The system's learning from its own experience should at least ensure that a mistake once made is never repeated.

3. Status and Conclusion

Referring to figure 1, the Data Interpretation and Experience Reuse modules have been developed and are now undergoing testing. Testing is done partly by controlled tests on previous data logs, partly by coupling the system to ongoing drilling operations on platforms in the North Sea. The Experience Capture Module will be finalized at a later stage, when the other two modules are ready for field deployment and new cases will start to come into the system.

The tests made so far are very promising. Strong and active user support from StatoilHydro, combined with a highly iterative system development process, have ensured that requested adaptations in system functionality and user interface have been implemented as part of the normal development process.

As for CBR as a method for computerized advice giving and decision support in this type of environment, the need for methods that can deal with continuous streams of online data will be increasingly called for. Data abstraction methods need to be coupled with complex similarity assessment methods that go far beyond the traditional "feature vector" methods. This problem has been recognized and addressed in the CBR community (e.g. [5]). In the work described here some contributions have also been made in this direction, although the main contribution lies in demonstrating the usefulness of our combined data interpretation and case-based reasoning approach in a highly data-intensive, and reactive industrial setting.

Acknowledgements

The work reported here has been partly funded by StatoilHydro and the Research Council of Norway under contract no. 169463/S300, the RTDA project. Many people from StatoilHydro and Volve have contributed to the results presented, in particular the project officer at StatoilHydro, Erik Nyrnes, Volve's CEO Jone Rasmussen, the Volve development leaders Pål Skalle and Frode Sørmo, and Tore Brede, Christian

Schjølberg, Martin Stige, Odd Erik Gundersen, and Morten Vinter in the Volve development team.

References

[1]   Erik Olsen, Peter Funk, Ning Xiong. Fault diagnosis in industry using sensor readings and case-based reasoning. *Journal of Intelligent & Fuzzy Systems*, Vol. 15, ISSN 1064-1, p10, IOS Press, December, 2004.

[2]   Agnar Aamodt. Knowledge-intensive case-based reasoning in Creek. In Peter Funk, Pedro A. Gonzalez Calero (eds.), *Advances in case-based reasoning*. Lecture Notes in Artificial Intelligence, LNAI 3155, Springer, 2004. pgs. 1-15. ISBN0302-9743.

[3]   Aminul Islam, Pål Skalle. Improved efficiency and knowledge-based support of oil well drilling through case-based reasoning. In Proceedings of Intelligent Energy 2008. Society of Petroleum Engineers. SPE 111849.

[4]   Volve AS company web page: http://www.volve.no

[5]   Francisco J. Martín and Enric Plaza (2004), Ceaseless Case-Based Reasoning. In P.A. Gonzalez and P. Funk (Eds.) *Advances in Case-Based Reasoning*. Lecture Notes in Artificial Intelligence LNAI 3155, Springer, 2004. pgs. 287-301. ISBN0302-9743.

Tenth Scandinavian Conference on Artificial Intelligence
A. Holst et al. (Eds.)
IOS Press, 2008

Modeling Habituation in the Cnidarian Hydra

Malin AKTIUS [a,1], Mats NORDAHL [b] and Tom ZIEMKE [a]

[a] *University of Skövde*
School of Humanities and Informatics
SE-541 28 Skövde, Sweden
[b] *Department of Applied Information Technology*
Göteborg University and Chalmers University of Technology
SE-417 56 Göteborg, Sweden

Abstract. In the design of behavior-based control architectures for robots it is common to use biology as inspiration, and often the observed functionalities of insect behaviors are used as templates. While several robot behaviors have been successfully implemented using this approach, relatively little has been done when it comes to building models of animal behavior using quantitative empirical data. The work reported here uses a system identification approach to model constituent behaviors of a simple biological organism, the hydra. This paper reports on the evolutionary optimization of a behavior module that is based on the hydra's response to mechanical stimuli, which shows habituation. Two model representation schemes were investigated: a recurrent neural network, and a model based on cascaded leaky integrators. Both models were structurally and parametrically optimized by means of an evolutionary algorithm, and it was found that the leaky integrator model performed better on unseen data.

Keywords. data-driven modeling, habituation, evolutionary optimization, recurrent neural networks, leaky integrator model, behavior-based control, hydra.

Introduction

Ethological studies show that even rather simple animals are capable of quite complex overall behavior, provided that they operate in their natural environment. Examples can be found in [1], where the behaviors of several unicellular and lower multicellular organisms have been studied. The behavior of organisms that are referred to by man as simple, is still intelligent and complex enough to allow them to survive and reproduce in their natural, yet unstructured, habitats. In lower organisms, behavior and behavior selection occur not as a result of reasoning or trial-and-error behavior in the individual animal, but rather as a result of trial-and-error on an evolutionary time-scale. Through the course of evolution, these organisms have acquired skills that make them capable of functioning successfully, i.e. survive long enough to reproduce, in their natural environ-

---

[1] Corresponding author: Malin Aktius, University of Skövde, School of Humanities and Informatics, SE-541 28 Skövde, Sweden. E-mail: malin.aktius@his.se.

ment. Using a minimal amount of memory and "reasoning" in their adaptive behavior, simple biological organisms make good models for behavior-based robotic brains.

Several examples of animal behavior, on a functional level, have been successfully modeled and implemented in robots [2]. Making use of quantitative data from real animals in the modeling process may help generate deeper understanding of behavioral properties and thus give insights as to, for example, what might be suitable representation schemes for behavioral models.

As part of a behavior-based model of the overall behavior of the cnidarian [2] hydra, developed in [3] and summarized in [4], this work uses quantitative data from a habituating response shown by the hydra to derive a model of this behavior.

Following this introduction, this paper is structured as follows. Section 1 introduces the biological model organism, the hydra, and its behaviors. Section 2 describes the models and methods used in this work, by presenting the considered model representation schemes and optimization algorithm. Section 3 presents and discusses the results obtained, and Section 4 provides a summary of the work along with concluding remarks.

1. Background: the Hydra and its Behaviors

The hydra[3], shown in Figure 1, belongs to the phylum Cnidaria, the first evolved animals (that still exist) to possess nerve cells and sense organs. It lives in fresh-water ponds, lakes, and streams, where it is most often found attached to some vegetation by the base of its tubular body[4]. Its body is around 15mm tall, and it feeds on small aquatic invertebrates.

The distinct movement patterns of the hydra, resulting from alternating activity of its motor cells, consist of: (1) contraction and expansion of body and tentacles; (2) digestion; and (3) locomotion [5]. Locomotion is accomplished either by gliding (by means of cilia on the foot), or by somersaulting. It should be noted that most of the behavior in the hydra, characteristic for lower animals, is not specific but general. Thus, the animal reacts in a way that is usually beneficial, rather than to the specific situation [1].

1.1. Behavior Repertoire

The behavior of the hydra is often described, in the literature, in terms of responses to specific stimuli. This way of studying and describing behaviors lends itself well to the behavior-based modeling approach [7,8], where the overall behavior is generated from the combination of a set of constituent behaviors. The following behaviors have been identified in the hydra [9]: (1) spontaneous actions; (2) response to mechanical stimuli; (3) response to light stimuli; and (4) feeding. Behaviors (1), (2), and (3) evoke either contraction or locomotion of the animal, whereas feeding is constituted by a series of actions. The behaviors of the hydra are described in more detailed in [3]. This paper focuses on behavior (2) - response to mechanical stimuli, such as shaking or physical contact, which shows habituation to repeated stimuli.

---

[2]Cnidarians are small marine animals. They are radially symmetric and possess stinging organells. Their movements are coordinated by a nerve net that spreads throughout their bodies. Examples of cnidarians include jellyfish and sea anemones.

[3]Genus *Hydra*, class Hydrozoa, phylum Cnidaria.

[4]Henceforth, the base of hydra's body will be referred to as its foot.

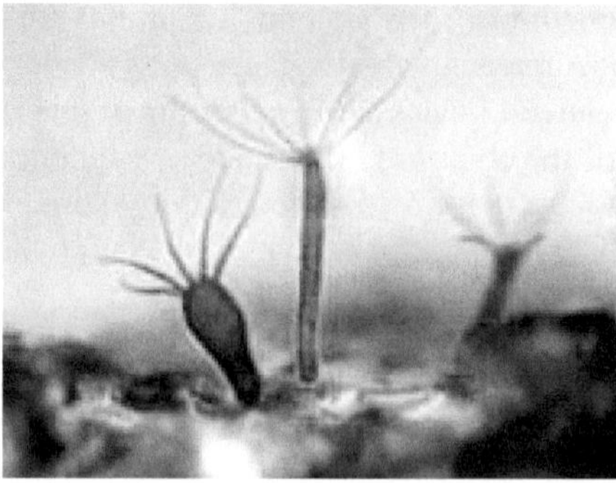

Figure 1. Three hydras. Image courtesy of BioMedia Associates [6].

1.2. Behavior Coordination

As described in the literature, feeding inhibits response to light and mechanical stimuli. In addition, response to light inhibits response to mechanical stimuli, thus forming a priority-based relation of the behaviors of the hydra [10,11]. The interrelation of hydra's behaviors is further described and modeled in [3,4].

2. Models and Methods

A data set for system identification of the hydra's response to mechanical stimuli was obtained in the following way. Experiments on the animal, documented in [12], resulted in data showing the response to repeated stimulus presentations, each lasting for 2 s, at 16 s inter-stimulus intervals (ISIs). The results from this experiment were used as training data to model the habituation property of this behavior. The decrease in response strength due to habituation is not permanent, but subject to recovery in the absence of any stimuli. However, no information concerning the recovery properties was found in the literature, and the recovery time was here taken, arbitrarily, to be 10000 s. This generates a training data set with inputs consisting of stimuli with intensity $M_c = 1$ lasting for 2s, presented every 16 s for 3 hours, followed by an absence of the stimuli for 10000 s, and then repeated presentation every 16 s for 4300 s. The outputs of the training data set were reconstructed from [12], and are shown in Figure 3 (solid lines).

In the system identification process, two different model representation schemes were investigated: (1) a recurrent neural network (RNN); and (2) a habituation model based on leaky integrators. Both models were optimized, parametrically and structurally, by means of an evolutionary algorithm (EA). The fitness measure was, in both cases, taken as $f = 1/e$, where e is the root mean squared error (RMSE) over the data set during periods of stimulus presentation[5]:

$$e = \frac{1}{N} \sqrt{\sum_{i=1}^{N} (o(i) - y(i))^2}, \tag{1}$$

---

[5]Note that no contribution to the RMSE occurs during the recovery period.

where $o(i)$ represents the $i{:}th$ measured response, and $y(i)$ the corresponding response from the model. On the occurrence of a stimulus the output from the habituation unit, the response strength, s, is related to the probability of a stimulus evoking a response [12]. To ensure a valid range of the response probability, p_{B2}, the following conversion was carried out:

$$p_{B2} = \begin{cases} s, 0 \le s \le 1, \\ 0, \quad s < 0, \\ 1, \quad s > 1. \end{cases} \tag{2}$$

Activation of the behavior occurs if the stimulus is present and $p_{B2} > X$, where X is a random variable drawn from the uniform distribution, $X \sim U(0, 1)$.

Validation of the results from the system identification process is twofold. First, the model performance on the training data set is considered. Secondly, its generalization capabilities are investigated by subjecting the model to unseen data. A known property of habituation is that weak or infrequent stimuli cause faster habituation than strong or frequent stimuli [13]. For this purpose, two validation data sets were created, with double and half the stimuli frequency compared to the training data set (ISI = 8 s and ISI = 32 s, respectively).

2.1. Evolutionary Optimization of a Recurrent Neural Network Model

As a first experiment it was tested whether an RNN, parametrically and structurally optimized by means of an EA to fit the described data set, could represent the habituation to mechanical stimuli. A continuous-time RNN was used. After applying Euler's method for numerical integration of the network equations, the dynamics of neuron i in the network is governed by the following equation:

$$y_i(t+\Delta t) = y_i(t) + \frac{\Delta t}{\tau_i} \left[-y_i(t) + \sigma \left(b_i + \sum_{j=1}^{n} w_{ij} y_j(t) + \sum_{j=1}^{m} w_{ij}^I I_j(t) \right) \right], \tag{3}$$

where b is the bias term, τ the time constant, I the input signal(s), and w and w^I are the synaptic weights from other neurons and input signals, respectively. The integration time step, Δt, was set to 0.2 s. The simulation time step (time between two consecutive input signals) is 2 s, which gives 10 integration steps between data points used in the calculation of Eq. 1. The RNN was evolved using an EA with the following properties: explicit encoding, elitism, no crossover, tournament selection, and structural as well as parametrical mutations. After an investigation of various mutation operators, six different operators were used, as described below.

m_1 - *Creep mutation:* The value of the gene is updated according to
   $w^{new} = w^{old}(1 - 2rc + c)$, where $r \sim U[0, 1]$ and c is the *creep rate*. Since this mutation may generate values outside the allowed range, the gene was scaled into its proper interval using $w \to w^{max}$ if $w > w^{max}$, and $w \to w^{min}$ if $w < w^{min}$.

m_2 - *Full-range mutation:* The gene is given a new, random value within the allowed parameter interval.

m_3 - *Add connection mutation:* A connection between two units (either between two neurons, or between an input signal and a neuron) with a randomly chosen synaptic weight (within the allowed range), is added.

m_4 - *Remove connection mutation:* Removal of a connection between two units.

m_5 - *Add neuron mutation:* One neuron is added to the RNN (at a randomly chosen location). To avoid a macromutation, i.e. a mutation that alters the performance of the resulting individual in a significant way, the neuron is added with all weights set to zero (and with randomly selected bias and time constant). Thus, only the *possibility* of new connections is established as a result of this mutation operator.

m_6 - *Remove neuron mutation:* Removal of one randomly chosen neuron and all its incoming and outgoing connections.

The EA properties used in this experiment are summarized in Table 1. The mutation operators are grouped into parametric mutations (m_1 and m_2), connection mutations (m_3 and m_4), and neuron mutations (m_5 and m_6).

Table 1. EA properties and settings for evolutionary optimization of an RNN-based habituation unit. For all three mutation cases, if a mutation occurs, one of its two mutation operators is selected. For example, if a connection mutation occurs, there is a 50% chance of a connection being added (m_3), and a 50% chance of a connection being removed (m_4).

Population size	50
Initial RNN size	2
Crossover	Not used
Tournament size	5
p_{tour}	0.65
$p_{mut1,2}$	0.10
$p_{mut3,4}$	0.15
$p_{mut5,6}$	0.10
Creep rate, c	2
Range, weights and biases	$[-5, 5]$
Range, time constants [s]	$[10, 2000]$

2.2. Evolutionary Optimization of a Leaky Integrator Model

As a second experiment, a proposed model of habituation dynamics was investigated, namely cascaded leaky integrators. This model has been suggested, for example, in [13] and is illustrated in Figure 2. With the stimulus input as Y_1, the equations for unit j in a cascade of n integrators become

$$V_j(k + 1) = a_j V_j(k) + b_j Y_j(k), \tag{4}$$

$$Y_{j+1}(k) = \begin{cases} Y_j(k) - V_j(k), & Y_{j+1}(k) > T_j \\ 0, & \text{otherwise.} \end{cases} \tag{5}$$

Here all thresholds, T_j, were set to 0. The response strength, s, is taken as the output from the last (*N:th*) unit, Y_{N+1}, on the occurrence of a stimulus, as proposed in [13]. An EA was used to evolve the size (N) and parameters $\{a_1, a_2, ...a_N, b_1, b_2, ...b_N\}$ of a habituation model on this form to fit the data previously described. For the EA, chromosomal real number encoding was used, with genes taking values in $[0, 1]$. Two-point crossover[6] and tournament selection was used, as well as two mutation operators, m_1 and m_2. Carrying out parametrical mutations, m_1 assigns a new (random) value to a gene. Mutation operator m_2 adds or removes, with equal probability, two genes (corresponding to one integrator unit), to an indidivual. The EA properties are shown in Table 2.

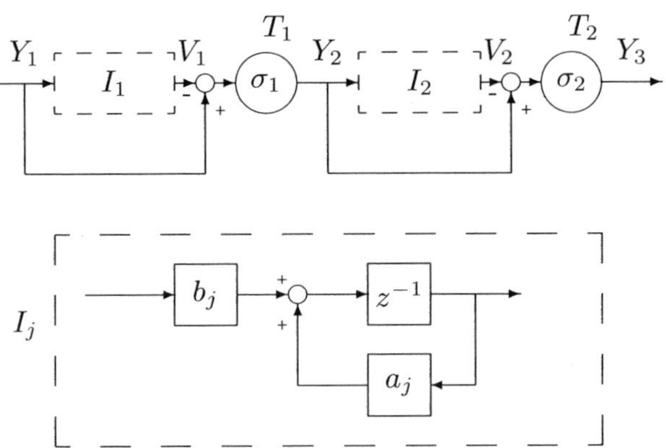

Figure 2. Habituation model based on leaky integrators. The top panel shows two cascaded units in compact form. Here, σ_j is a threshold unit with parameter T_j. The bottom panel shows the contents of each integration unit, I_j.

Table 2. EA properties used for optimization of a cascaded leaky integrators habituation model.

Population size	100
Initial model size	5 units
Tournament size	10
p_{cross}	0.5
p_{tour}	0.70
p_{mut1}	0.10
p_{mut2}	0.05
Parameter range (a,b)	$[0, 1]$

3. Results and Discussion

3.1. Evolving an RNN to Represent Habituation

The structure of the best evolved network was a three-neuron network. The evolved network parameters are shown in Eq. 6.

---

[6]Since each integrator unit is represented by two genes, a valid individual consists of an even number of genes. To avoid generating individuals with odd number of genes, the crossover points were restricted to every two genes.

$$w = \begin{pmatrix} 0.63 & -5.00 & 5.00 \\ -0.39 & 3.17 & -5.00 \\ 2.30 & -5.00 & 3.51 \end{pmatrix}, \qquad w^I = \begin{pmatrix} 0.51 & 0.00 & 3.71 \end{pmatrix},$$

$$b = \begin{pmatrix} -0.75 & -1.17 & -3.72 \end{pmatrix}, \qquad \tau = \begin{pmatrix} 1107.21 & 95.50 & 509.15 \end{pmatrix}. \tag{6}$$

As can be seen in Eq. 6, all connections but one input signal connection were established, making the RNN nearly fully connected. The evolved RNN performs adequately on the test data, as can be seen in Figure 3 (top). However, its generalization ability to other ISIs and stimulus intensities is poor, an example of which is also shown in Figure 3 (dashed line for ISI of 16 time-steps).

3.2. Evolving a Habituation Model Based on Leaky Integrators

Evolutionary optimization of the leaky integrator habituation model resulted in a 10 unit model, with parameter values as shown in Eq. 7.

$$a = \begin{pmatrix} 0.001 & 0.001 & 0.001 & 0.001 & 0.001 & 0.001 & 0.002 & 0.001 & 0.998 & 0.003 \end{pmatrix}$$

$$b = \begin{pmatrix} 0.124 & 0.010 & 0.105 & 0.012 & 0.711 & 0.204 & 0.107 & 0.549 & 0.004 & 0.010 \end{pmatrix} \tag{7}$$

The performance of the obtained model is shown in Figure 3 (bottom). In addition to representing the training data, this model also generalizes to show habituation properties when tested on unseen data. Thus, infrequent stimuli (ISI = 16 time-steps) generate habituation sooner than frequent ones (ISI = 4 time-steps). As can be seen in Figure 3, the recovery property is preserved for both validation cases.

4. Summary and Conclusion

This paper has reported on two cases of evolutionary optimization of a model of habituation. While both the RNN model and the cascaded leaky integrator model were able to represent the training data, only the latter model performed well on unseen data. In system identification [14], the terms *white box, grey box,* and *black box* models are used to classify models based on transparency. The RNN model can be considered a black box model, where the dynamics behind the input-output mapping is largely unknown. The leaky integrator model, however, can be considered a grey box model since its dynamics, while not derived from first principles, is still known to be of the same type as habituation dynamics. An RNN is a universal approximator [15] and it is therefore clear that it is, in principle, capable of representing the habituation dynamics in question here. However, the available training data does not contain enough information to constrain the network, during training, to the habituation dynamics. On the other hand, it was shown that a suggested model of habituation based on cascaded leaky integrators could be optimized by means of an EA to match very well the shown habituation dynamics in a real animal while at the same time generalizing well to known habituation properties.

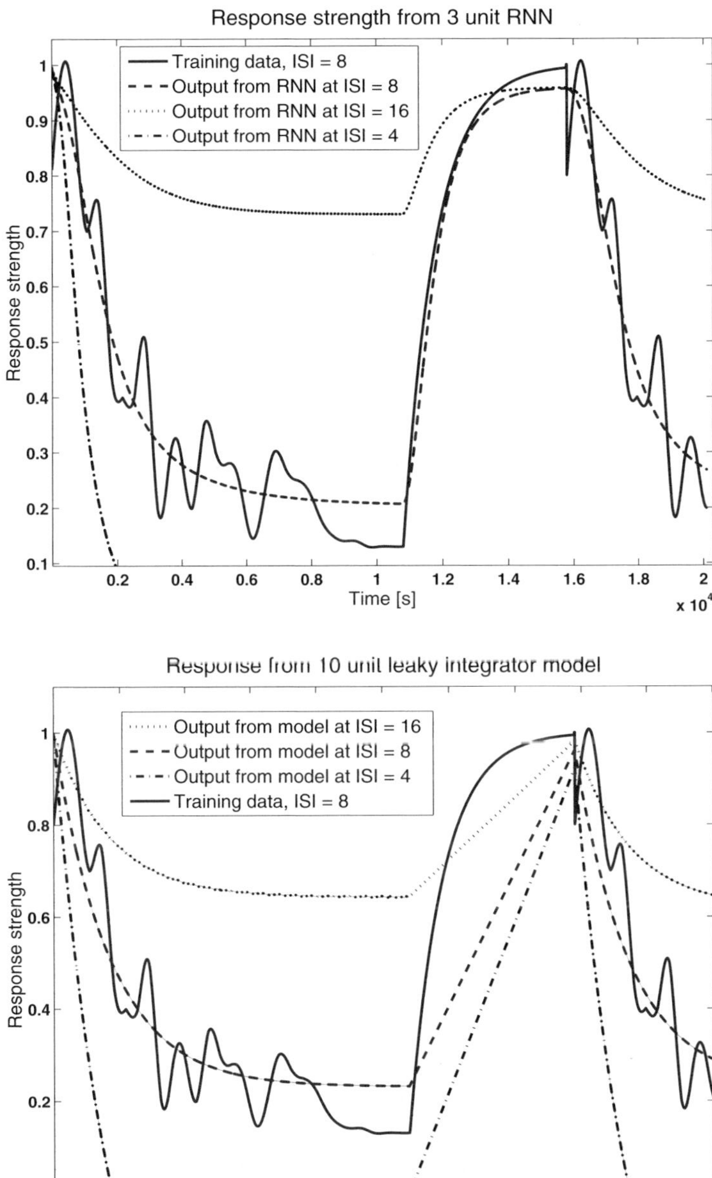

Figure 3. Decrease in response strength, s, as a result of the habituation effect. Output generated by the best evolved RNN model (top), and best leaky integrator model (bottom). ISIs are presented here in time-step units (1 time-step equals 2s). While the RNN performs well on training data (ISI = 8), note that the recovery from habituation is not adequate for stimuli of ISI = 16, whereas the leaky integrator model is able to generalize also to this situation.

Acknowledgements

The first and third author are supported by a European Commission grant to the FP6 project *"Integrating Cognition, Emotion and Autonomy"* (ICEA, IST-027819-IP, www.iceaproject.eu) as part of the European *Cognitive Systems* initiative. The experimental work was carried out while the first author was at Chalmers University of Technology [3].

References

[1]   H.S. Jennings. *Behavior of the Lower Organisms.* Indiana University Press, Bloomington, 1962.

[2]   B. Webb. Can robots make good models of biological behavior? *Behavioral and Brain Sciences,* 24:1033–1050, 2001.

[3]   M. Aktius. Modeling hydra behavior using methods founded in behavior-based robotics. Master's thesis, Chalmers University of Technology, Department of Applied Mechanics, Göteborg, Sweden, 2007. Report No. 2007:17.

[4]   M. Aktius, M. Nordahl, and T. Ziemke. A behavior-based model of the hydra, phylum cnidaria. In Fernando Almeida e Costa, Luis Mateus Rocha, Ernesto Costa, Inman Harvey, and António Coutinho, editors, *Advances in Artificial Life, 9th European Conference, ECAL 2007, Lisbon, Portugal, September 10-14, 2007, Proceedings,* volume 4648 of *Lecture Notes in Computer Science,* pages 1024–1033. Springer, September 2007.

[5]   C. Taddei-Ferretti and C. Musio. The neural net of Hydra and the modulation of its periodic activity. In José Mira and Juan Vincente Sánchez-Andrés, editors, *Foundations and Tools for Neural Modeling, IWANN '99,* volume 1606 of *Lecture Notes in Computer Science,* pages 123–137. Springer, 1999.

[6]   Biomedia associates. http://www.ebiomedia.com, Oct. 13th 2006.

[7]   R.A. Brooks. A robust layered control system for a mobile robot. *IEEE Journal of Robotics and Automation,* RA-2(1):14–23, 1986.

[8]   J.H. Connell. A colony architecture for an artificial creature. Technical Report 1151, MIT Artificial Intelligence Laboratory, June 1989.

[9]   H.M. Lenhoff and W.F. Loomis, editors. *The Biology of Hydra and Some Other Coelenterates.* University of Miami Press, Miami, FL, 1961.

[10] H.M. Lenhoff. Behavior, hormones, and Hydra. *Science,* 161:434–442, 1968.

[11] N.B. Rushforth, I.T. Krohn, and L.K. Brown. Behavior in Hydra: Inhibition of the contraction responses of Hydra Pirardi. *Science,* 145:602–604, 1964.

[12] N.B. Rushforth, A. Burnett, and R. Maynard. Behavior in Hydra: Contraction responses of Hydra Pirardi to mechanical and light stimulation. *Science,* 139:760–761, 1963.

[13] J.E.R. Staddon. *Adaptive Dynamics.* MIT Press, Cambridge, MA, 2001.

[14] L. Ljung. *System Identification: Theory for the User.* Prentice Hall, Inc, Upper Saddle River, N.J, 2nd edition, 1999.

[15] S. Haykin. *Neural Networks: A Comprehensive Foundation.* Prentice Hall, Upper Saddle River, NJ, 2nd edition, 1999.

Tenth Scandinavian Conference on Artificial Intelligence
A. Holst et al. (Eds.)
IOS Press, 2008

Subject Index

Tenth Scandinavian Conference on Artificial Intelligence
A. Holst et al. (Eds.)
IOS Press, 2008
© *2008 The authors and IOS Press. All rights reserved.*

Author Index